Leicester-Nottingham Studies in Ancient Society

Volume 2

CITY AND COUNTRY
IN THE
ANCIENT WORLD

CITY AND COUNTRY IN THE ANCIENT WORLD

Edited by

JOHN RICH

and

ANDREW WALLACE-HADRILL

London and New York

First published 1991
First published in paperback 1992
by Routledge
11 New Fetter Lane, London EC4P 4EE

Simultaneously published in the USA and Canada
by Routledge, a division of Routledge, Chapman and Hall, Inc.
29 West 35th Street, New York, NY 10001

Set in the University of Reading in the Department of Classics and the
Department of Typography and Graphic Communication.

Printed in Great Britain by T.J. Press (Padstow) Ltd, Padstow, Cornwall.

British Library Cataloguing in Publication Data available

Library of Congress Cataloging in Publication Data available

ISBN 0-415-08223-4

CONTENTS

PREFACE

This volume, like its predecessor *Patronage in Ancient Society*, is the result of a series of seminars jointly organised by the Classics Departments of Leicester and Nottingham Universities. 'The Ancient City' was chosen as the theme of the seminar series, which ran over two academic years, between 1986 and 1988. In addition to the seminars, which meet in both centres, two conferences were held at Nottingham, on 'City and Country in the Ancient World' (1987) and 'The City in Late Antiquity' (1988). These conferences promoted a lively exchange, particularly between archaeologists and ancient historians, and it was felt that each of them would make a good core for a volume of papers.

The present volume contains substantially revised versions of a selection of papers from the 1987 conference, together with others from the seminars that cohered with the theme. The first five papers are concerned with archaic and classical Greece, the last six with the Roman world. There is no attempt at complete chronological or geographical coverage. Approaches differ considerably, some more archaeological, some more text-based, some more concerned with problems of methodology and some with model-building. But all represent attempts to come to a better understanding of the town-country nexus that characterises 'the ancient city' and that lies at the heart of Greco-Roman civilisation.

The editors are grateful to many who have assisted in the production of this book, and in particular the following: the Society for the Promotion of Roman Studies which gave a generous grant towards the costs of the seminar series; to Jan Hamilton of the Classics Department at Nottingham for help with sub-editing; to Jo Wallace-Hadrill for translating Mireille Corbier's chapter from French; to Adrienne Edwards of the Classics Department at Nottingham for assistance with the administration of the conferences and seminars and to Sybil Lowery and Pella Beaven of the Classics Department at Reading for skill and patience in rising to the challenges of computer-typesetting.

JWR
AW-H

INTRODUCTION

Andrew Wallace-Hadrill

The towns are so many electric transformers. They increase
tension, accelerate the rhythm of exchange, and ceaselessly stir
up men's lives.

Braudel (1973)

If towns have a quickening effect on human life, they have no less
power to stir up academic discourse. Urban history is a fashionable
and flourishing subject; and when a Centre for Urban History was
established at Leicester University in 1985, with the express purpose
of focusing the common interests of specialists in different
disciplines, it seemed to the ancient historians of Leicester and
Nottingham a good opportunity to take 'the ancient city' as the theme
for their research seminar. Not that the theme, stretching back to
classics like Fustel de Coulanges (1866), Weber (1921) and Glotz
(1928), could be seen as a new one. But though old, it has become
the centre of lively current debate, and not only among ancient
historians, notably as the subject of one of Finley's most provocative
and polemical papers, but among archaeologists, who in dialogue
with historians have in the last decade made fundamental
contributions to the debate.

At once, a problem of definition obtrudes. What does it mean, in
the context of Greco-Roman antiquity, to call your theme 'the city'?
The urban historian of any period, whether or not they accept Marx's
claim that the whole economic history of society is summed up in
the movement of the antithesis of town and country, must have
difficulty in discussing the urban without simultaneously discussing
the rural; and as Abrams stressed in introducing the Past and Present
Society volume on *Towns in Societies*, approaches that insist that
'the town is a town' run into major conceptual difficulties; the current
tendency is to undo the separation of town and country and re-unite
the town with its non-urban environment (Abrams and Wrigley 1978,
1ff.). For the ancient historian, the separation is even more difficult:

even on a linguistic level, the same Greek word, *polis*, means both urban centre and the type of state characterised by the domination of an urban centre, leading, as Aristotle appreciated, to considerable confusion in discussion (see Morris below). It is persistently unclear, in authors from Aristotle to Finley, whether at any one moment talk of 'the city' is intended to contrast with or to embrace the countryside; use of 'the town' or in Greek *astu* is only a partial solution, since the object of discussion is not so often the physical urban environment as the system of power and social relations that focuses on but is not the same as the urban centre.

Town and country were antithetical for the ancients too. An image of the separation is the Avezzano relief, found near the Latin town of Alba Fucens (depicted on the cover of this volume), which juxtaposes the close-packed houses of the town, insulated within their wall, and the open countryside and its scatter of villas. Yet even the juxtaposition implies a relationship, represented by the roads which via town gate link town and country. The relationship is more visible if we picture the tentacles spread out by the Roman town into its hinterland in the form of aqueducts: symbolically siphoning off, as Corbier puts it (below), the resources of the land into the urban centre, to feed the public baths where the imported water acts as a focus of sociability, and as a symbol of the 'washed' and civilised way of life that rejects the stench of the countryman. Implicit in the aqueduct is a dynamic of power, flowing between country and town; and if we wish to represent that dynamic as exploitative, we may extend our picture to the sewers to which the water eventually flows, used memorably by Victor Hugo as an image of the wasteful consumption of the city:

> When the Roman countryside was ruined by the Roman sewer,
> Rome exhausted Italy, and when she had poured Italy through
> her drains she disposed of Sicily, then Sardinia, then Africa.The
> Roman sewer engulfed the world, sapping town and country
> alike. *Urbi et orbi* or the Eternal City, the bottomless drain.
> Hugo, Les Misérables, part V, i.

Not all the contributors to this volume would accept Hugo's bleak vision of the negative effects of the city; but all, in various ways, are concerned with city and country as a relationship, and one which was problematical yet of crucial importance in shaping the societies of antiquity. Interest in this relationship has blossomed recently: and this owes as much to developments in archaeological method as to debate on a theoretical level.

Archaeology's most important contribution to the study of the city has been the paradoxical one of shifting its attention away from the city and its monumental structures and towards the countryside. The rise of the new method of 'field survey' (discussed below by Snodgrass and Millett, but drawn on by most others) has many strands: the excitement of a new approach, the desire to assemble data systematically and 'scientifically' rather than haphazardly and anecdotally, and to give equal weight to the traces of the inconspicuous and unprestigious as to the monumental and grand; intellectual disillusionment with the descriptive and non-analytical character of much traditional excavation; but also (factors particularly potent in Mediterranean archaeology) the new possibilities and threats to the survival of evidence posed by new agricultural trends like deep-ploughing, the expense of excavation and the increasing difficulty in extracting permission to dig from local authorities, and the ease and attractions of taking groups of students to walk the Mediterranean terrain in lines abreast. From the pioneering days of the 1960s, of Ward-Perkins' British School survey in South Etruria and the Minnesota survey in Messenia, intensive field survey has grown to become the commonest Anglo-Saxon archaeological activity in the Mediterranean, with all the glamour of a 'new archaeology' (Snodgrass 1987, 99ff.). Contributors to this volume draw on surveys in Euboea and Boeotia (Snodgrass), Sparta and Megalopolis (Cavanagh), Samnium and Balboura in Lycia (Patterson), South Etruria (Potter), Tarragona (Millett) and make reference to many more.

The new archaeological approach has made possible a new level of dialogue with historians (not that the two disciplines have ever operated in complete isolation from each other). For the historian concerned with the city, town plans and monumental layouts have had a limited interest (though Perring's study of spatial organisation suggests that new approaches in this direction too are needed), whereas social, economic, political and cultural relationships between town and country go to the heart of their subject. Snodgrass shows how new archaeological evidence touches on almost every aspect of the questions previously posed about the Greek city by a non-archaeological historian. But in the younger generation of scholars, archaeologist and historian are hard to disentangle, as is suggested by the papers of his own pupils Morris and Osborne, or on the Roman side by Patterson.

Many common themes, shared concerns and related methods and approaches run through the papers in this volume, on both the Greek and Roman sides. In picking out only a couple of the major overarching themes, I want to illustrate both the extent to which the volume marks progress in moving towards new understanding and towards some measure of consensus at least about the questions worth posing about the ancient city, and also the extent to which it throws up difficulties of method, disagreement, and implicitly the need for further research.

One conspicuous theme is the rise of the polis, and the impact of city-formation on the territory as a whole. Here we may observe that the new archaeological approach has produced a swing-around in interpretation. The Greeks accounted for city-formation as the result of the bringing together of previously dispersed households and small clusters of households, *synoikismos*. Not unreasonably, archaeologists used to look for traces of this unification in the urban centres: the walled settlement of Old Smyrna was the prime example of the rise of the polis. The Aegean has now produced a handful of such early fortified sites: yet these did not give rise to poleis in the Archaic and Classical periods, and Snodgrass argues that it is not their fortification but their abandonment that marks the advent of the polis. Both Snodgrass and Morris see the crucial element of polis-formation not in an urban nucleus, but in changed social relationships, particularly the development of citizenship, reflected in the extension of access to burial rites, and the growth of common cults that unified the polis, not just at its centre, but also as markers at the edge of its territory. Morris in particular distinguishes urbanisation from state-formation, and arguing for the slowness of the process of urbanisation, sets the dividing line between 'city' and 'non-city' as late as the end of the sixth century.

If the archaeologist is less insistent on discovering an urban nucleus to the polis, he is more insistent on exposing the hierarchy of settlements that surround the centre. Cavanagh points to the difficulties arising from the use of the term *synoikismos*: if we look for a physical relocation rather than an act of political unification, the polis disappoints us, for what is found is an extension and elaboration of rural settlements, not the converse. Just as Cavanagh posits a hierarchy of settlements in the territory of Sparta, a city with a notoriously underdeveloped urban centre, so Osborne has argued that the strength of the polis of Athens, despite its relatively high degree of urbanisation, lay in its success in incorporating its rural demes (villages and even towns in our terms) into its political structures.

Perhaps the most striking illustration of the thesis that a strong network of rural settlements should be seen as supporting, not antithetical to, the polis, is in the innovative experiment of Rihll and Wilson (the latter a geographer concerned with contemporary problems of urban and regional planning) in using geographical theory to elaborate a mathematical model of exchanges between settlements. By plotting the known distribution of sites (of whatever size or importance) in Central Greece in the protogeometric period, despite making the counterfactual assumption that all started as sites of equal importance, and that the terrain was isomorphic (i.e. ignoring mountain barriers), the computer simulation of the patterns of exchange between the sites predicts that certain sites will emerge as 'terminals', i.e. as centres of hierarchical clusters; moreover, given the right conditions in the variables of ease of communication and benefit of centralisation, the model is remarkably successful in predicting the 'correct' terminals, i.e. those where urban centres did in fact evolve. Whether or not this gives us an insight into *why* the polis evolved (i.e. was the growth of the unified state determined by the geographical distribution of sites in the preceding period?), it illustrates very clearly how the corollary of a strong urban centre is not an empty countryside, but one with a dense network of intercommunicating settlements for which it provides the common focus.

Similar patterns are detected in the Roman world, though not uniformly. Millett shows how both in Britain and Spain a relatively powerful urban centre generates a penumbra of villas and settlements, becoming denser with proximity to the town; and he comments on the density of the settlement pattern of the Roman landscape in general, rising in Spain at some periods as high as one site per square kilometre. Potter too finds dense settlement in South Etruria in the late republican and early imperial period; but stresses that the pattern varies widely across Italy. Patterson offers an example of what may be seen as a contrary pattern in Samnium: the impact of Roman control on a non-urbanised mountainous area was concentration of resources, with central encouragement, in urban sites, leading to the evolution of a local elite that competed for power by the expenditure of resources in the urban centre, and to its own eventual assimilation into the Roman elite. The centralisation of resources was founded on the creation of fewer, larger landholdings; hence the growth of urbanisation seems here to be linked to a drop in number of rural sites. He provisionally posits a similar pattern in the interior of Asia Minor.

The pattern of contraction of the number of rural sites under the impact of Roman rule seems to emerge from a number of surveys in the eastern Mediterranean, and as the studies of Sue Alcock (1989 a and b) indicate, has important implications for our understanding of the impact of Roman imperialism. But whether the penumbra of settlements around the city grew denser or rarer, it is agreed that the city must be seen in the context of that penumbra. Corbier's analysis of the taxation system of the Roman empire illustrates why this must be so. The empire is seen as a chequerboard of cities, each with its own set of dependent communities; just as the power and wealth of the individual landlord depended on his ability to extract rents and profits from his tenants and workforce, so the power and wealth of each city depended on the extraction of taxes, rents and dues from its own network of villages and settlements, while Rome herself depended on the extraction of taxes from the provinces and their component cities. Epigraphy, through the wide range of local inscriptions that cast light on the relations between cities and their territories, here reinforces the sort of picture emerging from survey archaeology.

Intensive field survey has thus made enormous strides towards filling out the blanks in our mental maps of Greek and Roman cities, and towards repopulating the countryside. It is important to add, by way of caution, that the new approach is not without methodological difficulties, and cannot be expected to give us a complete and infallible picture of the settlement patterns of antiquity. Such problems are not always fully exposed in the presentation of the results of surveys, which, particularly when represented as a series of dots on maps, have a seductively cut and dried appearance. Hence the importance of Martin Millett's analysis of the problems of survey data. Survey depends heavily on the discovery of surface finds of 'diagnostic' pottery, i.e. pottery that is susceptible of dating. Not all pottery is equally datable; not all pottery survives in the ploughed ground equally well; not all pottery implies habitation. Identification of inhabited settlements at any given period depends on the supply and survival of pottery diagnostic for that period; yet it emerges that the volume of supply of such pottery fluctuates considerably from period to period. In the Tarragona survey the richest sites produce over 63 sherds per hectare for the Iberic period; but the comparable figure for the Republican period is 26 sherds or more, for the early Empire 6 or more, for the late Empire 1 or more. The gradient of decline is very steep, and at the very least figures need to be scaled to allow for fluctuation in supply. One might add that parallel excavation of the associated urban sites would be a valuable control. Field survey is a supplement, not an alternative, to traditional stratigraphic excavation. We may expect to see further development of sophistication and caution in the interpretation of the results of field survey over the next decade.

The most significant area of disagreement, however, lies at a different level. All agree that the ancient city needs to be seen in the context of its relations with the countryside; but over the nature of those relations there is deep disagreement, which emerges explicitly in several chapters, but implicitly underlies virtually all. In its most direct form, the question can be posed as one of economic balance: did the ancient city make significant return for the resources of the land it consumed? Was it more than Victor Hugo's Roman sewer, a bottomless drain? But as formulated by Max Weber, and reformulated, stridently yet powerfully, by Moses Finley, the question cuts to the heart of the study of ancient society. How did the economic relationship of town and country in the ancient city differ from that of other periods, notably the late medieval, and, assuming that, whatever the variations from city to city, from period to period, a historically distinctive relationship can be isolated, how did that contribute to the distinctive character of ancient society as a whole?

The Weber/Finley answer to these questions is partly summed up in the concept of the 'consumer city'. Yet it points to much more than the economic imbalance of a city draining and exploiting its territory, a criticism which can be made of capital cities at many historical periods (Hugo, after all, was comparing the Roman sewer to that of nineteenth-century Paris). Starting from the ambiguity of polis as city and as state, as town-not-country and yet town-and-country, it underlines the importance of the participation of the rural, from the large landowner to the peasant, in the operation of both state and town, and the consequences of that in preventing the emergence of a distinctively urban economy and society.

These are complex issues, and a range of positions on them is possible, as here emerges in various chapters. Finley's insistence that the question of the relationship of town and country matters was in itself a seminal contribution, and a stimulus to archaeological work, acknowledged for instance by Snodgrass and Morris. Some form of the model of the 'consumer city' may be implied by Corbier's account of the social imbalances generated by the flow of taxation from country to city; though that still leaves room for Hopkins' argument that the net effect of taxation was to stimulate the economy (1980; Hopkins' view of the consumer city in his important paper of 1978 is carefully nuanced). A strong version of the consumer-city model emerges in Perring's argument that the Roman city, at least in Britain, became increasingly exclusive, to the point that trade was ultimately driven out of the towns by the influx of the landowning class, leading to their eventual collapse.

Two papers in this volume directly question the Finley model. For both Osborne and myself, the model creates real difficulties in interpreting the relationship of the landowning elite to the town. That the relationship of town and country had fundamental implications for the structure of power in ancient societies and for the definition of the elite is an assumption shared by many of the contributors, for instance by Patterson in his account of urban construction and estate-extension by the Samnite and Lycian elites, by Corbier in her suggestions of the exploitation of the taxation system by the powerful, by Perring in his picture of a move from inclusivity to exclusivity in the spatial organisation of the Roman town. To this extent we all accept some version of the Finley model, or at least the importance of the problems it raises. But it is another matter to accept that for the elites of the Greek and Roman city the countryside was the only significant place of production, and the town essentially a place of consumption. Osborne suggests that the needs of the town for consumption are balanced as a driving force by the needs of the landowner to raise cash to meet political and social demands; hence by implication the countryside needs the cash-generating capacity of the urban economy as much as the town needs the food-generating capacity of the country. I suggest that the political and social imperatives that brought the Roman elite to reside in towns brought an intimate and positive contact between the big landowner and the world of trade. But both arguments seek to qualify, not to discard,

Finley's position.

In the end, we are left with the ambiguities about the definition of 'the city' with which we started. Defending Weber's model of the 'consumer city' (i.e. city in the sense of urban centre), Finley states, 'It still remains true, and needing an explanation, that the peasant was an integral element in the ancient city, but not in the medieval' (1981, 17). Was the peasant an integral element in the city as state, or in the city as urban centre? The answer is probably both. Citizenship gave him access to the citizen-state; but the concentration of political and cultural, and surely also economic, activity in the urban centre regularly drew him there. If the town was where the surplus of the countryside was consumed, the peasantry could join with the big landowners in consuming it there, in the festivals, rituals, games and entertainments that offered communion to the community of the ancient city.

We have still a considerable way to come in grappling with this paradox. Field survey and other new archaeological approaches should cast further light on town/country relations; though it might be hoped that a greater integration between new and traditional approaches could be achieved, and that survey of the landscape could be coordinated with excavation of the urban centres. Historians too have major problems to resolve. What does 'the ancient city' mean? Is 'it' a phenomenon about which useful generalisations can be made? Was it indeed different in essence from 'the medieval city', and if so, was it different in the sort of way which Weber suggested? How helpful is Weber's characterisation of the medieval city as the 'producer city'? Or should we allow greater significance to variations, from period to period, from region to region, and construct a more differentiated typology, if we are to construct typologies at all? These remain open questions; and before any satisfactory answers can be given to them, it will be necessary for ancient historians to enter into the same level of dialogue with their medievalist and early modernist colleagues as they have already achieved with archaeologists.

Bibliography

Abrams, P. and Wrigley, E.A. (eds.) (1978), *Towns in Societies, Essays in Economic History and Historical Sociology*, Cambridge.

Alcock, S. (1989a), 'Roman imperialism in the Greek landscape', *Journal of Roman Archaeology* 2, 5-54.

Alcock, S. (1989b), `Archaeology and imperialism: Roman expansion and the Greek city', *Journal of Mediterranean Archaeology* 2/1, 87-135.

Braudel, F. (1973), 'Towns' in *Capitalism and Material Life 1400-1800*, 373-440. London.

Finley, M.I. (1981), 'The ancient city: from Fustel de Coulanges to Max Weber and beyond', in *Economy and Society in Ancient Greece*, ed. B.D. Shaw and R.P. Saller, 3-23. London.

Fustel de Coulanges, N.D. (1866), *La Cité antique*, Paris. Translated by W. Small, 1873; reprint, Johns Hopkins University Press 1980.

Glotz, G. (1928), *La Cité grecque*, Paris. *The Greek City and its Institutions* (trans. N. Mallinson, 1929). London.

Hopkins, K. (1978), 'Economic growth and towns in Classical antiquity', in Abrams and Wrigley (1978), 35-77.

Hopkins, K. (1980), 'Taxes and trades in the Roman Empire (200 BC - AD 400)', *Journal of Roman Studies* 70, 101-25.

Snodgrass, A.M. (1987), *An Archaeology of Greece, the Present State and Future Scope of a Discipline*. Sather Classical lectures, vol. 53. Berkeley.

Weber, Max (1921), 'Die Stadt', *Archiv für Sozialwissenschaft und Sozialpolitik* 47, 621-772, translated by D. Martindale and G. Neuwirth as *The City* (Glencoe, Ill. 1958).

∞ 1 ∞

Archaeology and the study of the Greek city

A.M. Snodgrass

For well over a hundred years, people studied the Greek city as an entity without making more than negligible use of archaeological evidence. As late as 1969, in the translated second edition of Victor Ehrenberg's *Der griechische Staat*,[1] the reader has to search very hard indeed to find even a veiled recourse to archaeology. The historians of the polis saw themselves as dealing essentially with an abstraction; they avoided tawdry physical detail, much as they tended to eschew the whole diachronic approach; and both exclusions rendered archaeology superfluous. The archaeologists showed little sign of minding this: they carried on studying their temples, statues and pots, innocent not of *all* historical considerations - from the 1930s to the 1950s was, after all, the golden age of the 'political' interpretation of pottery-distributions - but certainly innocent of any concern with historical *entities* like the city-state.

Today, all that appears to have changed. Some books on aspects of the polis are being written by historians who make constant reference to archaeological findings; others are even written by archaeologists. What factors have brought about such a change? An important contributory factor has been the minor wave of new archaeological discoveries, relating especially to the era of the rise of the polis. But

[1] Ehrenberg (1969).

what generated this wave? The answer lies partially in an initiative on the part of historians: which brings us to a second and more fundamental factor. There has been a change of attitude, on the part of historians and archaeologists alike. The former are now no longer content to give, like Aristotle in the *Politics*, a more or less theoretical reconstruction of the advent of the polis, set in some indefinite early period: they feel an obligation to offer some kind of account of the date, causation and means whereby the entity that they are concerned with came into being. To do so, they must venture back into periods where the written sources on their own are manifestly inadequate. So they have called in the archaeologists, who in turn have been surprised to find that they are already sitting on a substantial body of existing evidence that is relevant to the problem, as well as responding to the call for new excavation to fill in the blank areas on the map of early Greece. The fact that so much of the evidence was long since available, however, must mean that it is this change of attitude that has been the decisive factor. In a nutshell, explanation has taken over from analysis and description as the prime aim, in both disciplines. I hope that, to most readers, these will be welcome developments.

These considerations all relate to one large area of the study of the polis, that of its origins and rise: this is indeed a topic where archaeology plays a major role, which is why it will feature prominently in this paper. But there is a second such topic in polis studies, which has likewise benefited from new archaeological work, and from a parallel change of attitude. It is the whole question of the physical basis on which the Greek city rested: the territorial sector and the rural economy. Here, the seeds of the change of attitude may be detected very much longer ago; but they were sown outside the boundaries of Classical scholarship (I have the name of Max Weber especially in mind) and, perhaps for that reason, they took an extraordinarily long time to germinate; indeed, but for the stubborn advocacy of Moses Finley, I rather doubt whether even now they would have burgeoned into the flourishing growth which they present today in ancient historical studies. In the archaeological field, they fell on even stonier ground, and I believe that the change of direction in archaeological studies has other causes. In passing, both sides alike should pay tribute to a third group, the epigraphists: with many of the relevant topics, from topography in general to the constitutional arrangements as they affected territories, to territorial boundaries, to agricultural slavery, it was they who were often first in the field.

The opening up of this second field of enquiry (or so I am suggesting) has come about through a fortunate coincidence of interests between recent historical and archaeological research. The historians, as soon as they became conscious of the need to examine the agricultural basis of the city, found that the evidence from the ancient written sources was seriously defective, and began to look round for alternative kinds of documentation. The archaeologists, having for so long followed the historians in their concentration on the urban sector of polis life, were in no position to assist. But help was at hand, and from an unexpected source. Archaeological colleagues in northern America were beginning to supplement, or even replace, excavation as the traditional medium of fieldwork with the new technique of area survey. Here was a technique which, unlike excavation, was designed to generate information on a regional scale, and with a rural bias. Methods which had been applied to the indigenous cultures of North America, by people who often had little interest in urbanised cultures and none at all in the Classical city, were found to be eminently applicable, first to pre-Roman or Etruscan Italy, then to the period of Roman rule in Italy and beyond, and finally to the world of the Greek city. A survey could provide a picture of the pattern of settlement over the whole territory of a medium-sized polis, or over parts of those of several poleis, and would also have an application in the more extended landscape of the average *ethnos* - exactly what the historians needed.

As a result of all these developments the study of the polis, at least when conducted at the generalised level, has become more and more deeply involved with the use of archaeological evidence. If we return to our first topic, that of the origins and growth of the city, we may begin our search for applications, actual or potential, of such evidence. In his opening chapter, Ehrenberg (1969) divided his treatment of this subject into five sub-headings: 'Land and Sea', 'Tribe and Town', 'The Gods', 'Nobles and non-nobles', and 'Forms of State'. Except for the last category, where the enquiry is essentially historical in nature and is conducted through backward projections from later documentation, I believe that archaeology can contribute in each of these spheres. It can offer not only the classes of evidence, referred to above, which are specific to the case of the Greek city, but also a body of recent work that is directed towards a general theory of state formation, based on anthropological research but later given an

Figure 1a: Extent of the regional Late Geometric pottery styles

archaeological application.[1] Although such work has been mainly applied to non-historical cultures, some of its findings are relevant to the case of ancient Greece: notably, the idea of an 'Early State Module' that is essentially small in scale,[2]though hardly as small as the typical Greek polis. Indeed, a case could be made for treating even the polis, at its stage of formation, as a non-historical instance, since it is almost entirely lacking in contemporary documentation. This is generally true of early states: the discovery of writing seldom precedes

[1]   See, e.g., Cohen and Service (eds.) (1978); Claessen and Skalnik (eds.) (1978); Cherry (1978 and 1984); Renfrew and Cherry (eds.) (1985).

[2]   See Renfrew (1975), who finds c. 1,500 sq.km to be a frequent modular size, and c. 40 km a mean distance between the central places of neighbouring modules. Both figures are far too high for the average Greek polis, notwithstanding the calculation of C.Doxiadis, cited by Renfrew at 14-16.

Figure 1b: Extent of the polis system (shaded)

state-formation by a long enough interval to generate coherent documents by the time of the political change.

A good starting-point for the discussion is the primary importance that Aristotle attached to 'community of place' - perhaps the earliest clear acknowledgment that the abstraction of the polis had an inseparable physical embodiment. Community of place incorporates both the *astu*, the central place, whose function was transformed when the state came into being, and the territory, which henceforth consisted of the sum of the landholdings of all members of the community. These are changes which can be expected to have manifestations in the archaeological record. What we must guard against is any expectation that these manifestations will be *uniform* in every case. The physical impact of polis-formation would vary according to the different prior conditions in the region where the particular polis arose. We know little enough about these prior conditions in any part of the Greek world, but what we do know can at least be expressed in archaeological terms. Thus there is the interesting fact, whose significance was spotted by Ehrenberg and has recently been enlarged upon by Nicolas Coldstream,[1] that the area of the Greek world where the Geometric style in pottery had reached its most advanced development (fig.1a), and the area where the polis was to prevail (fig.1b), roughly coincide. The priority of the archaeological phenomenon will stand unless we push back the rise of the polis to an improbably early date, nearer 900 than 800 BC. How much weight we attach to this coincidence will depend on our assessment of the importance of Geometric pottery: but we may at least recall the arguments advanced by Martin Robertson for thinking that, at this early period, painted pottery in general held a primacy among the visual arts which it never recovered later.[2] It may be that artistic sophistication was a foretaste of political progressiveness.

How then, precisely, might political transformation be reflected in the physical aspect of city or territory? We may begin with the *astu* itself, and assume that the circumstances were not those relatively simple ones where a physical *synoikismos* took place, with part of the population moving to a newly established urban nucleus, nor those even simpler ones of the colonisation of a new locality. In other words, we assume that there *was* a pre-existing settlement, whose status was now transformed through its becoming the centre of a polis. How will this show? It is possible that some kind of concentration will have occurred at the site, with new functions and perhaps new inhabitants being transferred to it, and that this will show itself in a nucleation of buildings - possible, but by no means to be counted on. That a 'nucleus' could continue to take the form of a cluster of separate villages, long after the transition to polis status, is proved not only by Thucydides' well-known reference to fifth-century Sparta (1.10.1), but by the findings of survey archaeology elsewhere in the Greek homeland. That an *agora* would now be a necessary feature is no guarantee of its archaeological traceability. An acropolis would in many cases have been in existence long since, and archaeology has contributed here by showing how often it was the very same that had once served as a Mycenaean citadel. Administrative

---

[1]   Ehrenberg (1969), 19; Coldstream (1983).

[2]   Robertson (1951), especially 152-4.

Figure 2: Fortified settlements of the ninth and eighth centuries BC in the Aegean

buildings, as is shown by the example of several cities, could at first be dispensed with. Sanctuaries are another matter, but they will be treated presently under the heading of religion. What we are looking for above all are the physical traces of *communal* activity, in the service of the polity as a whole.

Such traces have often been sought in the form of *fortification*. Here we must be more specific: the fortification must have clearly been designed to surround the whole inhabited nucleus, and not just a citadel; and that nucleus must be of an adequate size to represent a plausible *astu* for the territory and population in question, rather than being merely an isolated local stronghold. The second criterion is the one that invites most debate. We have, for example, a whole series of excavated sites in the Cyclades and other Aegean islands, where a fortification wall surrounds a nucleated settlement: the earliest of these begin in the ninth century BC, if not the tenth (fig.2). Perhaps the largest and most impressive of them is Zagora on Andros,[1] which may serve as an exemplar. It has a protecting wall (among the earliest dated structures on the site), areas of housing that show clear signs of planning, a probable contemporary temple, and plenty of open space for the siting of a hypothetical *agora*. Was Zagora then the centre of an early polis embracing the island of Andros? Given the low population figures estimated for Greece as a whole, and the islands in particular, in the earlier Iron Age, it is not impossible that the size of Zagora, at any rate, was commensurate with that function. But if this was an early experiment, it was a short-lived one for Zagora, like so many of this group of fortified island sites, was suddenly and permanently abandoned around 700 BC. Many of the other sites in this group fail to match up to Zagora in one or more respects, principally those of size and of the location of the fortification. Thus, Emborio on Chios[2] was a sizeable village, but its fortified area was confined to a narrow hilltop with only one structure of recognisable domestic function within, plausibly identified as the chieftain's hall; much the same could be said of Koukounaries on Paros,[3] where the fortified area is also a small hilltop citadel, while other nucleated sites in its vicinity are relatively small; Agios Andreas on Siphnos,[4] and Kavousi[5] and Vrokastro[6] in eastern Crete, look more like tactically sited hilltop refuge sites than the centres of populated territories; Vathy Limenari is an almost inaccessible fortified headland on a small islet (Donoussa), and would be much more reasonably interpreted as a pirate stronghold than as an abortive polis-venture;[7] and so on. The mere fact that these fortifications are mainly confined to island sites, at a time when mainland and offshore-island settlements (even those concentrated in the same epoch,like Lefkandi in Euboea[8] and Nichoria

---

[1] Cambitoglou *et al*. (1971); Cambitoglou (1981).

[2] Boardman (1967).

[3] See especially Schilardi (1983), with mention of other Parian sites at 180-82 and nn.39-42.

[4] Philippaki (1970).

[5] See most recently Gesell *et al*. (1983) and (1985).

[6] Hall (1914).

[7] Zaphiropoulou (1967-71).

[8] Popham *et al*. (1979-80).

in Messenia[1]) were unfortified, suggests that some special geographical factor, rather than a ubiquitous political change, is responsible for the walls. The long delay in building city-walls round even the most famous mainland poleis, or even, as at Sparta, their permanent absence, is a matter of record.

Instead, I think that we should concentrate our gaze on the other almost invariable feature of these fortified island sites: their lasting abandonment, usually in the years around 700 BC. It is, I think, this negative feature which gives the strongest hint of political change. What concerted process, if not state-formation, would lead to the roughly simultaneous desertion of a range of sites which for the previous century or two had been not merely occupied, but in some instances places of real local prominence (Zagora, Emborio and on the off-shore island of Euboea, Lefkandi)? Was it not that their siting, and the original purposes that had prompted it, became suddenly obsolete with the advent of a new system? That their inward-looking, security-conscious orientation formed no part of a wider community which itself promised security through communal action? If such proves to be the case, then archaeology, virtually unaided, has provided the first secure indication of the date and nature of the earliest historical state-formation in the islands of the Aegean.

By that date, the colonising process had already begun to testify to the advent of the polis in rather different circumstances; and earlier still, there had been the 'pre-colonial' phenomenon of the Ionian Migration. It has been suggested that Zagora itself may represent a relatively late and half-hearted contribution to this latter process; while today we have, in the evidence of the large Protogeometric cemetery at Torone in the Chalkidike,[2] a considerably earlier and entirely unexpected manifestation of the same migratory spirit. Several of the sites, both of the Migration and of the later colonies, also show fortification as an early feature. I refrain from introducing yet again the site of Old Smyrna into this analysis, pending the radical reinvestigation by Turkish archaeologists of the dates of its first two fortification circuits; but there is another early wall reported at Iasos in Karia,[3] and in due course the early colonies often demanded

---

[1] McDonald *et al.* (1983).

[2] For preliminary reports, see Catling (1983), 42-4 and (1986), 59-61.

[3] Levi (1961-2).

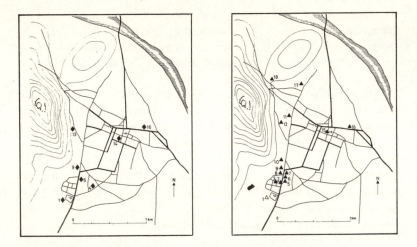

Figure 3: Early settlement traces from the city of Argos:
Protogeometric Period (left) and Geometric Period (right)

walls. We have seen enough to appreciate, however, that local
conditions often determined the construction of a fortification. City
walls, as the mainland shows, were not at first a necessary condition
of polis-formation; and our other instances are enough to cast grave
doubt on any belief that they were a sufficient condition either.

Now that the colonial sites have been introduced to the discussion,
we may note that they are the first to manifest another sign of that
communal action that we have been looking for: the planned layout
of an urban centre, with an *agora*, blocks of housing, and even
individual plots provided for; Megara Hyblaia in eastern Sicily[1] has
become a classic instance. From an historical point of view, however,
such a discovery has limited significance, since it had never been
doubted that the early colonies embodied the polis principle.
Historically, much the most interesting question is whether this
feature of the first colonies in itself presupposes the prevalence of the
same principle in the homeland communities that sent the colonies
out. I note in passing that the recent work of Irad Malkin[2] makes
some use of archaeological evidence to answer this question firmly in

[1] Vallet *et al.* (1976).
[2] Malkin (1971).

the negative, and instead pursues the idea of the colonising experience as a 'trigger' for the relevant political developments at home.

Comparable physical evidence is, predictably, much harder to detect in the urban centres of Greece proper. Here the exercise of town planning was frustrated by the pre-existing structures, and the best that we can usually hope for is that the general layout of the settlement will bear some trace of reorganisation and re-location. The most fruitful investigation of this has been conducted in respect of the town of Argos,[1] but under severe handicaps of modern building and heavy dependence on burial evidence (fig.3). Otherwise, as with the abandonment of the fortified island sites, the clearest sign may be a negative one. Where, as at Athens, the site of the subsequent *agora* had previously been given over to indiscriminate activities including burial, then the cessation of these activities may herald the new political order. In the case of Athens, this is detectable from shortly after 700 BC, when graves are progressively eliminated from an increasing area of the Agora site.[2]

But it is time to turn away from the urban centres, and look instead at territories. The territorial aspect is at once the most basic and the most neglected element of polis organisation. The frankest illustration of this neglect is to be found in the pages of almost any Classical atlas. Here you will look in vain for many features that one might expect to find in a map of a well-documented historical civilisation. The traditional atlas is constrained by its format to mark only the known and firmly located ancient toponyms, and such other data as the written sources convey. This excludes, most obviously, the unnamed sites excavated or otherwise investigated through archaeological means; but it excludes much else as well. There is unlikely to be a map showing the boundaries of the individual poleis of the Archaic and Classical periods. Then there are the second-order settlements, which must in reality have far outnumbered the *astea* themselves, but which in most atlases appear if anything less

[1]   Hägg (1982).

[2]   Thompson and Wycherley (1972), 10, 12, 19; Camp (1985), 28, fig. 11, and 34; neither account, however, brings out clearly the fact that from the end of the eighth century BC burials are excluded from the central area of the Agora and banished to locations on the periphery, where in turn they die out (apart from a couple of late burials in a family plot) at the end of the seventh.

numerous; internal, district boundaries are correspondingly absent. Here the findings of epigraphy have proved invaluable, at least in the case of Attica,[1] but these too are generally not taken into account in an atlas. All of this explains why most Classical maps, unless they are drawn on a small scale, wear such a sparse look. You do not need a map of an abstraction and that, as we have seen, is exactly how the polis was seen by most of its earlier students.

It should be a primary aim of archaeology to fill in these blank spaces on the map and, as we have seen, the development of the technique of intensive area survey has given it the instrument that the task requires. The survey has to be intensive if it is to achieve two joint objectives: first, to discover the full range of settlement, in at least a sample area, from the *astu* itself down to the smallest isolated habitation; and secondly to estimate the frequency of settlements, of each level of importance, as it varies from period to period. A large-scale or 'extensive' survey will of course cover a much wider stretch of terrain, but at the cost of picking up only the most conspicuous - that is normally the larger - settlements, with the consequence that the settlement range is truncated, and the settlement distribution possibly also distorted, through neglect or unpromising (e.g. infertile or overgrown) terrain. By its total or near-total coverage of a given piece of territory, the intensive survey should be capturing a very large part of the history of occupation there; yet even the most intensive survey is not a precision instrument. For example, the level of chronological definition can never be sufficiently high to establish that a group of sites was in exactly simultaneous, rather than broadly contemporary, occupation; one needs further supporting indications, such as are provided in the case of the colonial land-allotments at Metapontum,[2] where the sites are not only contemporary but also very regularly spaced and located with respect to field-boundaries.

But at a less specific level, the broad trends of settlement between one period and the next can emerge very clearly from survey. Consider, for example, the maps and tables published by Dr John Bintliff and myself from the limited area covered by our first four

[1]   See for example Eliot (1962) and Traill (1975), with their associated maps.

[2]   See especially Adamesteanu (1967).

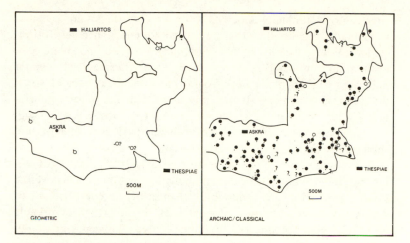

Figure 4: Boeotia survey:
Distribution of Geometric sites (left) and Classical sites (right)
(Slightly updated from Bintliff and Snodgrass, 1985)

seasons of survey in Boeotia (fig.4).[1] These show, in a space of 21 square kilometres, a maximum total of only 7 sites with occupation in the Geometric period, rising to a maximum of 23 in the Archaic, and a maximum of 76 in the Classical and earlier Hellenistic periods. Once one learns that the great majority of these are small, isolated rural sites, it becomes an inescapable conclusion that dispersed rural settlement took place over the first few centuries of the historical period and accelerated in the fifth and fourth centuries BC. Results like these can be first checked against those obtained by other surveys in Greece (which in several cases show similar patterns), and then monitored by the continuation of survey in the same area. In our case, three further field seasons (1984-86) have reinforced the overall proportions, but added more specific nuances. Thus, the seventy-odd additional sites investigated since the publication of the preliminary report include the two actual *astea* of Haliartos and Thespiai, in whose territory we have mainly been operating. These can now be added to the small group occupied from Geometric times onwards, showing that the population then existing was relatively nucleated. Thereafter, Thespiai provides the fuller sample, since at least two-thirds of our

[1]   For a preliminary report, see Bintliff and Snodgrass (1985).

sites can be confidently allocated to its territory. This sample makes it virtually certain that there was no major dispersal of rural settlement from the city in the eighth, the seventh, or the greater part of the sixth centuries BC; nor was the *astu* of Thespiai itself a major nucleated settlement in these years, but rather a cluster of small village-sized settlements. It was only in the fifth and fourth centuries that Thespiai grew into a sizeable city, and (perhaps in concert with its second-order settlement of Askra) generated a dense scatter of rural settlement within its territorial boundaries.

This pattern is the more interesting because of the contrast that it presents with certain other cases, notably that of Athens. Whatever its precise explanation, an undoubted feature of the early growth of Athens is the proliferation of new sites in the Attic countryside during the eighth century BC, and an accompanying concentration of occupation in Athens itself.[1] Since we have already seen one reason for associating with this general period the rise of Athens to statehood, and shall shortly consider another, it does seem likely that this process in Athens was accompanied by a sharp increase in the size of the city, and the number of rural settlements. Where, though, does this leave Thespiai? Is it simply an illustration of the fact that the physical processes attendant on state-formation could be utterly different in different places? Are there grounds for the surmise that, in terms of power rather than of political form, Thespiai and perhaps other Boeotian cities developed late, and for that reason may have espoused the loose form of ethnic confederation that appears in later history as the Boeotian League? Politically, there can have been no significant time-lag, since we are fortunate enough to have the first-hand testimony of Hesiod as to the function of his own polis.

Our reconstruction will partly depend on the view taken of the dispersed rural sites. In eighth-century Attica, they look like a successful attempt to consolidate, by internal colonisation, an unusually large territory for which a single city now took responsibility. In Thespiai, with a territory of perhaps one-twentieth of the size, this move may have appeared neither necessary nor perhaps feasible with the available resources of population. This brings us directly to the obvious demographic question: had Athens experienced a dramatic rise in population, which aided and even partly

[1] Snodgrass (1977), 16-17, fig. 3, and 29, fig. 5.

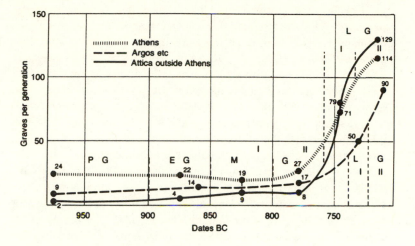

Figure 5: Unadjusted figures for the frequency of burials in
(i) Athens, (ii) The Argolid and (iii) The Attic Countryside, c.950-700 BC

caused the rise of the Athenian state? Ten years ago, I favoured a positive answer to these questions;[1] but there is little doubt that the interpretation then given was too simplistic. By calculating the numbers of extant burials, within and outside Athens, apportioned between successive generations (fig.5), I sought to show that the Attic population had risen exceptionally steeply, precipitating in at least this one case a political change. But one of the hypothetical or potential factors involved, which was explicitly left out of account, was an important one: the possibility of changing eligibility for formal burial. If the extant burials were not, at all periods, equally representative of both sexes, of all age-groups, and of all levels of society, then the count of graves is not a reliable indicator of the population of the settlement. In his new book *Burial and Ancient Society* (1987),[2] Ian Morris has argued convincingly that two at least of the above factors were indeed at work. From the mid-eleventh century BC to the mid-eighth, he believes, the extant burials from Athens show a suspiciously low proportion of child-burials, and an equally suspicious predominance of rich grave-goods. The great

[1] Snodgrass (1977), 10-14 and, more fully, (1980), 21-5, figs. 3-4.
[2] Morris (1987).

upsurge in numbers at the middle of the eighth century is partly, perhaps largely, accounted for by the suspension of these two exclusions. This finding carries with it an extremely problematic corollary: before about 750 BC, many poorer people and many children were being disposed of in some way that has not, so far at least, proved archaeologically traceable. Despite this very unexpected implication, I think that Morris' detailed arguments will convince most readers. He accepts that there was *some* increase in the Athenian population around the mid-eighth century; but this was on a much more modest scale than I had believed, and historically it was less significant than the abrupt change in the scope of the 'burying group'. Yet the most striking thing is that Morris' explanation of this major social change is in essence identical with the one that I had offered for the supposed upsurge in population: that the advent of the Athenian polis lies at the heart of it. What I had seen as a demographic explosion, helping to precipitate the formation of the state, Morris interprets as the newly-formed citizen body and their families, claiming their right to a formal burial of a kind which had hitherto been a fairly select privilege: a proximate cause has become an immediate result. Unless we are both wrong, it seems increasingly likely that critical changes began to take place in Athens in the eighth century.

In this survey of fortification, town planning, territorial settlement and demography, we have covered not only topics grouped by Ehrenberg under 'Land and Sea', but also some of those of his 'Tribe and Town', or at least of its second element. But can archaeology contribute anything to the question of tribalism, and of the pre-polis organisation of Greece? I think that today caution should be the watchword: since the publication of Denis Roussel's *Tribu et cité*,[1] it is difficult to sustain Ehrenberg's unquestioning faith in a 'tribal order' prevailing everywhere in the stage immediately before state-formation. The archaeologist must content himself with repeating that, in eleventh-, tenth- and ninth-century Greece, pottery styles, burial practices and some other criteria do project very clear regional divisions in Greece, larger in scale than most later polis-territories. Within each region, a degree of homogeneity prevails such that some kind of communal feeling is suggested. Were these regions early

[1] Roussel (1976).

political entities of a loose-knit kind? Caution is advisable not least because the sequel does not mark a very clear break with this early pattern, such as we would predict on a strictly political interpretation. The partial fragmentation of these regional pottery styles in the eighth century, to which Coldstream (1983) has drawn attention, never even approximates to the point where each pottery-producing polis has its own individual style. To this one might reply that, even after the adoption of the polis system, the regional allegiances still count for much: there was an expectation that, other things being equal, the Ionian or the Argolic or the Boeotian cities would follow a similar policy. These regional divisions, which ultimately derive from the closing stages of the Bronze Age, must have influenced many aspects of early Greek life, whether or not these included the directly political ones; and archaeology can claim to have done most to draw attention to them, if not yet to have interpreted their meaning.

So we come at length to 'The Gods'. Here, the contribution of archaeology, in the context of state-formation, is a relatively clear one. The realisation that communal state cults stood at the very heart of the polis should have prompted the archaeologists to make this contribution much earlier. For over a century now, major state and inter-state sanctuaries have been under intermittent excavation, and a striking feature of many cases - Olympia, Delphi, Delos, the Ptoion, the Athenian Akropolis, the Temple Hill at Corinth, to name but a handful - has been the flood of light thrown on the early phases of the sanctuaries. What this has shown is that, apart from an unsettled debate on the degree of continuity from prehistoric times, by far the clearest phenomenon in this area of religious history is the sudden access of activity near the beginning of the historical period. I shall not rehearse again the different categories of evidence which reflect this feature;[1] it is enough to say that sanctuary after sanctuary displays the sequence of an abrupt increase in the frequency of small dedications, followed (sometimes quite quickly) by the building of a first monumental temple. Roughly contemporary with the first phase at the older sanctuaries, the picture is compounded by the institution of a wave of new cults: sometimes these lie at new sites in the territory of a given polis; sometimes they mark the first such

[1]   Snodgrass (1980), 33, 52-65.

foundation in what is to become a new polis. They include the cults of heroes, particularly those sited at prehistoric tombs, as well as deity-cults. When the sanctuary belongs to a polis, the building of a monumental temple seems a particularly significant step, especially when (as is usual) the earliest temple is that dedicated to the god who became the presiding or patron deity of that particular polis. If Apollo in his sanctuary on Temple Hill was the guiding deity of Corinth, then the institution of a temple for him was, in some sense, retrospective proof of the institution of the polis of Corinth. The building of such a temple was, in addition, a communal undertaking of a substantial physical kind.

But this whole argument has been given a new dimension by the publication of François de Polignac's book *La Naissance de la cité grecque*.[1] While reviewers have quarrelled with his conclusions in detail, nothing can detract from de Polignac's achievement of bringing the *territory*, as well as the *astu*, into the religious argument. He has shown that, for many cities, the establishment of greater and lesser sanctuaries in the territory, sometimes including a major one deliberately located near its boundary, was of comparable importance to the formalising of the central polis cult in the city itself. Among other things, these extra-mural cults served to bind the *astu* to the outlying territory, by means of an annual festive procession from the former to the latter; to warn neighbours of the extent of the territorial claims of the polis; and generally to proclaim to every citizen the implications of what had been undertaken. This argument touches the very heart of the polis idea.

It remains to say something about Ehrenberg's 'Nobles and non-nobles'. It is well-known that a social dichotomy of this general form persisted long after the rise of the polis, until tyranny or democracy sapped its strength. But there is one very important step along the road away from 'noble' rule whose reality has, until very recently, been uncontested; and it is a step which has been primarily established by archaeological evidence. I refer, of course, to the 'hoplite reform'. Whatever the nature of pre-hoplite warfare in Greece - a subject on which there is still room for the most radical disagreement - it must surely be agreed that the formation of a citizen-army and, even more clearly, the rapid rise of this army to dominance

---

[1]   de Polignac (1984).

of Greek battlefields, was a decisive historical advance. Recent questioning of the reality of a 'hoplite reform'[1] cannot effectively detract from the historical consequences. Even if Homer's repeated use of the term *phalanges* implies the existence, in earlier times, of massed armies whose military effectiveness was greater than the Epic form allowed him to show, and even if these armies were well and uniformly equipped - a somewhat debatable inference from the text of the *Iliad* - the citizen hoplite embodied several major departures from such a system. The hoplite, in the first place, served primarily, and increasingly only, the state; secondly, he and his fellows comprised a substantial proportion (typically, about one-third) of the adult male population; thirdly he was, at his own expense, equipped and protected so well that for centuries he could only be resisted on the battlefield by other hoplites; fourthly, his pre-eminence sooner or later received the ultimate accolade, that nobles themselves came to fight as hoplites in the phalanx. Few if any of these attributes can have belonged to earlier mass armies. At whatever instigation they came into being, and at whatever point of time between the end of the eighth and the middle of the seventh century BC, hoplite armies shaped rather than merely echoed the history of the polis. The existence of hoplites is the clearest *a posteriori* proof of the existence of the polis, both in Greece generally and in each specific case; and the best evidence for hoplites remains the archaeological.

At a point rather earlier than the first clear evidence of the existence of hoplite armies, many communities in Greece had adopted another innovation that was closely linked with the hoplite phenomenon: the discontinuation of burial with arms (and of the corresponding provision of metal grave-goods for female burials). Everything about this change serves to underline its close connection with the rise of the polis: the fact that it primarily affected those of higher social status; the fact that it is not matched in other areas which rejected the polis idea (Lokris, Achaia and Thessaly continue to produce later warrior-burials); the fact that it finds a compensating feature in the sharp increase in dedications, of exactly the same classes of object, in the sanctuaries - the communal superseding the personal.[2] This change is most clearly dated at Athens and Argos,

[1]   e.g., by Pritchett (1985); Morris (1987), 196-201.
[2]   Snodgrass (1980), 52-4, 105-7.

where it coincides fairly precisely with the end of the local Geometric style around 700 BC, and at Knossos in Crete, where it is later or more gradual, with a few isolated cases persisting into the first half of the seventh century. Like the mustering of the hoplite armies, it shows how rapidly the ethos of the polis came to override what might be seen as the private interests of its members. Once again, however, it is essentially an archaeological phenomenon: the ancient sources do not record it, and indeed one interpretation of the Thucydides passage on the 'Carian' graves at Delos (1.8.1) would imply that, by the fifth century, the old practice of burial with arms had been forgotten.[1]

Greek historians may have begun to wonder where this catalogue of archaeological pretensions will end. So let me cut it down to size myself by acknowledging, first that many, though by no means all, of the contributions claimed here for archaeology relate to the single epoch of the rise of the polis. All the evidence here considered has pointed to a date in the eighth century BC for that episode, or at least for its inception. But that, after all, was the date to which Victor Ehrenberg had assigned it, largely on quite other kinds of evidence, as long ago as 1937.[2] What archaeology has added is a huge body of circumstantial and confirmatory detail, of many different categories. Secondly, let me acknowledge that many of the archaeological arguments depend ultimately for their validity on *a posteriori* reasoning from the statements of ancient authorities, or from the inferences made by historians of later periods in the history of the Greek city. This paper is designed to help concert, not to usurp, the most interesting line of enquiry in the contemporary study of Greek history.

Bibliography

Adamesteanu, D. (1967), 'Problèmes de la zone archéologique de Métaponte', *Revue Archéologique* 1967, 3-38.
Bintliff, J.L. and Snodgrass, A.M. (1985), 'The Cambridge/Bradford Boeotian Expedition: the first four years', *Journal of Field Archaeology* 12, 123-61.

[1]   So Cook (1955); for a somewhat different view, Snodgrass (1964).
[2]   Ehrenberg (1937).

Boardman, J. (1967), *Excavations in Chios, 1952-55: Greek Emporio*. London.

Cambitoglou, A. (1981), *Archaeological Museum of Andros*. Athens.

Cambitoglou, A., Coulton, J.J., Birmingham, J. and Green, J.R. (1971), *Zagora* 1. Sydney.

Camp, J.M. (1985), *The Athenian Agora: Excavations in the Heart of Classical Athens*. London.

Catling, H.W. (1983) and (1986), 'Archaeology in Greece, 1982-83' and 'Archaeology in Greece, 1985-86', *Archaeological Reports* 29 (1982-3), and 32 (1985-6).

Cherry, J.F. (1978), 'Generalisation and the archaeology of the state', in D.R. Green, C.C. Haselgrove and M.J.T. Spriggs (eds.), *Social Organisation and Settlement. British Archaeological Reports* (S) 47. Oxford.

Cherry, J.F. (1984), 'The emergence of the state in the prehistoric Aegean', *Proceedings of the Cambridge Philological Society* 210, 18-48.

Claessen, H.J.M. and Skalnik, P. (eds.) (1978), *The Early State*. The Hague.

Cohen, R. and Service, E.R. (eds.) (1978), *Origins of the State: the Anthropology of Political Evolution*. Institute for the Study of Human Issues. Philadelphia.

Coldstream, J.N. (1983), 'The meaning of the regional styles in the eighth century B.C.', in R. Hägg (ed.), *The Greek Renaissance of the Eighth Century B.C.: Tradition and Innovation. Skrifter utgivna av Svenska Institutet i Athen* (Series 4º) 30. Stockholm.

Cook, R.M. (1955), 'Thucydides as archaeologist', *Annual of the British School at Athens* 50, 266-70.

Ehrenberg, V. (1937), 'When did the *polis* rise?', *Journal of Hellenic Studies* 57, 147-59.

Ehrenberg, V. (1969), *The Greek State*. London.

Eliot, C.W.J. (1962), *The Coastal Demes of Attica*. Toronto.

Gesell, G.C., Day, L.P. and Coulson, W.D.E. (1983), 'Excavations and survey at Kavousi, 1978-81', *Hesperia* 52, 389-420.

Gesell, G.C., Day, L.P., and Coulson, W.D.E. (1985), 'Kavousi, 1982-1983: the Kastro', *Hesperia* 54, 327-55.

Hägg, R. (1982), 'Zur Stadtwerdung des dorischen Argos', in D. Papenfuss and V.M. Strocka (eds.), *Palast und Hütte*, 297-307. Mainz.

Hall, E.H. (1914), *Excavations in Eastern Crete: Vrokastro*. Philadelphia.

Levi, D. (1961-2), 'Le due prime campagne di scavo a Iaso', *Annuario della Scuola archeologica di Atene* 39-40 (n.s. 23-4), 527-34.

McDonald, W.A., Coulson, W.D.E. and Rosser, J. (1983), *Excavations at Nichoria in Southwest Greece* 3: *Dark Age and Byzantine Occupation*. Minneapolis.

Malkin, I.S. (1987), *Religion and Colonization in Ancient Greece. Studies in Greek and Roman Religion*, 3. Leiden.

Morris, I.M. (1987), *Burial and Ancient Society*. Cambridge.

Philippaki, B. (1970), 'Agios Andreas Siphnou', *Arkhaiologikon Deltion* 25, Chroniká, 431-4.

Polignac, F. de (1984), *La Naissance de la cité grecque*. Paris.

Popham, M.R., Sackett, L.H. and Themelis, P.G. (1979-80), *Lefkandi* 1: *The Iron Age*. London.

Pritchett, W.K. (1985), *The Greek State at War*, Part iv. Berkeley and Los Angeles.

Renfrew, A.C. (1975), 'Trade as action at a distance: questions of integration and communication', in J.A. Sabloff and C.C. Lamberg-Karlovsky (eds.), *Ancient Civilization and Trade*, 3-59. Albuquerque.

Renfrew, A.C. and Cherry, J.F. (eds.) (1985), *Peer Polity Interaction and the Development of Sociopolitical Complexity*. Cambridge.

Robertson, C.M. (1951), 'The place of vase-painting in Greek art', *Annual of the British School at Athens* 46, 151-9.

Roussel, D. (1976), *Tribu et cité*. Paris.

Schilardi, D. (1983), 'The decline of the Geometric settlement of Koukounaries at Paros', in R. Hägg (ed.), *The Greek Renaissance* [see above, under Coldstream 1983), 173-83.

Snodgrass, A.M. (1964), 'Carian armourers: the growth of a tradition', *Journal of Hellenic Studies* 84, 107-18.

Snodgrass, A.M. (1977), *Archaeology and the Rise of the Greek State*. Inaugural Lecture. Cambridge.

Snodgrass, A.M. (1980), *Archaic Greece: the Age of Experiment*. London.

Thompson, H.A. and Wycherley, R.E. (1972), *The Agora of Athens. The Athenian Agora*, 14. Princeton.

Traill, J.S. (1975), *The Political Organization of Attica. Hesperia Supplement* 14. Princeton.

Vallet, G., Villard, F. and Auberson, P. (1976), *Mégara Hyblaea* 1: *le quartier de l'agora archaïque*. Paris.
Zaphiropoulou, Ph. (1967-71), 'Donoussa', *Arkhaiologikon Deltion* 22, Chroniká, 467; 24, Chroniká, 390-3; 25, Chroniká, 426-28; 26, Chroniká, 465-7.

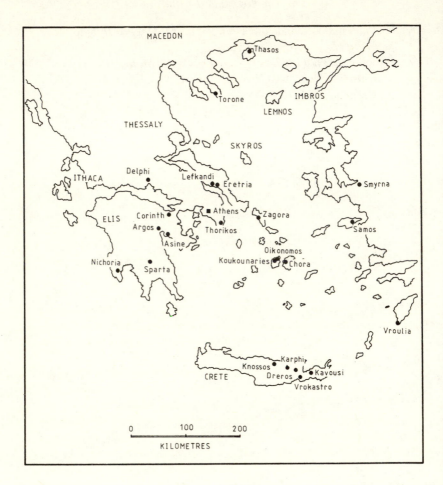

Figure 1: Sites mentioned in text of Morris (ch. 2).

The early polis as city and state

Ian Morris

Aristotle is not known for his sense of humour.[1] So, when he poses what look like frivolous questions, we should be ready to seek more serious problems behind them. At one point in his musings on the constitutional change he suddenly asks: 'How are we to tell whether a state is still the same state or a different one?' We could, he suggests, divide its physical territory and population into two, to see if that makes them two different states - but that, he decides, would be silly. He concludes: 'That perhaps is not a very serious matter: it arises from our use of the word polis to mean both the state and the city' (*Politics* 3.1276a 19-25, adapted from Saunders' translation).

Aristotle's problem was how to define the essence of the polis, the form of political association for which, he thought, mankind was peculiarly suited. The same problem haunts discussions of the polis 2,300 years later. For most historians, the expression 'the rise of the polis' is synonymous with both 'the rise of the city' and 'the rise of the state', and the sort of confusion Aristotle noted is deepened by the conventional translation of polis as 'city-state'. Classicists regularly point out that this is a poor translation, but few bother to ask themselves why. This ambiguity has obscured central questions in the history of the early polis.

---

[1]   Finley (1981, 83) claims to identify 'the only joke ... in his entire corpus' at *Constitution of Athens* 16.8. The joke is not very funny, and anyway, the Aristotelian authorship of this work is disputed. [Aristotle]'s point, as usual, is perfectly serious.

In this paper, I look at the evidence for urbanisation and state formation in the Dark Age (c.1100-750 BC) and Archaic periods (c.750-500 BC). There is some consensus that the late eighth century was the crucial time in the rise of the polis. I share this point of view, but I question its significance as a period of political centralisation or urban growth. I take a gradualist, or perhaps even primitivist, perspective on both these processes. In the first part of the paper I argue that settlements did grow in and after the eighth century, but the scale of the changes was so small that we cannot meaningfully describe it as 'urbanisation'. I then suggest that the development of political institutions also accelerated in the eighth century, but that Dark Age society was already very hierarchical, and the process of state formation was in no sense a quantum leap into complexity.

What, then, was the rise of the polis? While it can be usefully studied as a process of centralisation (e.g. Snodgrass 1986), I have argued that its historical importance is that it was a revolution in social structure, a complete transformation in the way people saw the world around them (Morris 1987). This is indeed much the way that Aristotle ultimately defined the polis - not as a territory or a group of political offices, but as a relationship between its constituent citizens.

To speak of 'the polis' at all is of course to deal in abstractions. There were hundreds of communities in ancient Greece, constantly changing throughout their histories. I use polis in this paper as an 'ideal type', to describe a form of society which existed in parts of Greece in the eighth to first centuries BC. The polis was a complex hierarchical society built around the notion of citizenship. It was made up of hundreds or even thousands of independent peasant households, which neither paid impersonal dues to a centralised government, nor depended on the state for the means of life. In contrast with most equally complex societies of its day, the primary producers owned (in all the most important senses of the word) the means of production. The wealth of the polis elite and the finances of such centralised government as existed was not based primarily on direct exploitation of a peasantry through tax or rent. The equation of the polis with the whole citizen body, even if governmental functions were often reserved to a smaller group, marks it off from other ancient states. All citizens had a share in the polis, which in its most developed form was based economically on the institution of chattel slavery. If the citizens became subjects, their community ceased to be a polis (Wood 1988 suggests a rather different model).

The polis world was preceded by the Mycenaean civilisation, typified by palace-centred economies. The Mycenaeans probably had a word *'ptolis'*, but it did not have the same connotations as the classical polis. By the end of the Hellenistic period, in the first century BC, polis seems to have lost its classical sense of a citizen community. It sank into being merely a town within a larger royal state, although there is controversy over the rate at which this happened (see Veyne 1976; Davies 1984; Gauthier 1985; Bernhardt 1985; Will 1988).

By examining the processes of urbanisation and state-formation implied by our translation of polis I am not waging a boundary war. I will not suggest that we talk about Dark Age cities or states, or that we abandon these perfectly good words as descriptions of the developed polis; arguments about categorisation are rarely useful. Rather, I hope to cast some light on the Dark Age, where it is most needed. The preceding Mycenaean world was one of small cities and state-level hierarchies (but not city-states). Following the destructions of the palaces around 1200, Mycenaean culture gradually faded away. Monumental architecture, writing, and the palace as a redistributive centre all disappeared by 1100. I will suggest that this was not a complete collapse, arguing (i) that quite substantial nucleated settlements survived, (ii) that a complex, ranked society continued to exist in Greece from the eleventh to the eighth century, and (iii) that the Mycenaean and Dark Age heritage is vital to the way we look at the classical polis.

The emergence of the Greek city

A city is defined by its political, economic and social relationships to the surrounding countryside. Many universalising criteria have been offered, but no set has proved acceptable. In this section, I will consider the evidence for growth in the size of the largest Greek communities from the eleventh to sixth centuries, and the effects this growth had. Our evidence is mainly archaeological. No texts survive from the period between 1200 and 750 BC, and Homer, our earliest source, is difficult to interpret. Small nucleated settlements are taken for granted in the poems, especially in the description of the shield of

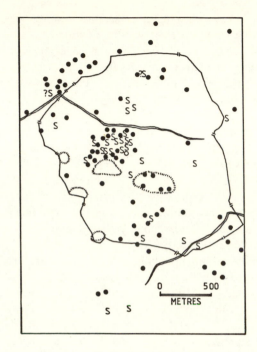

Figure 2: Area occupied at Athens, 1100-700 BC. Circles represent cemetery remains; S represents settlement evidence. The continuous line marks the course of the fifth-century wall. After Morris (1986) figures 17, 18 with additions from *Arkhaiologikon Deltion* 34:2 (1979 [1987] 11-33).

Achilles (*Iliad* 18.483-607), but much is disputed (see Luce 1978; Scully 1981).

The only way to approach growth is through the remains of the habitation sites themselves. Anthony Snodgrass, more out of desperation than choice, used graves to argue that population grew at about 3% per annum in late-eighth-century Athens (1977, 10-18; 1980, 23-4; 1983), but this class of evidence is open to many distorting factors. In this case it is unreliable (Morris 1987, 57-155), and the rapid increase in numbers of graves at Athens is followed by an equally rapid decline after 700, which cannot plausibly be associated with a depopulation (Camp 1979; Snodgrass 1983; Morris 1987, 156-69).

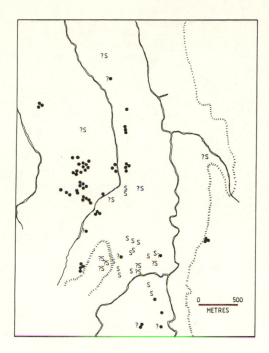

METRES

Figure 3: Area occupied at Knossos, 1100-700 BC. Circles represent cemetery remains; S represents settlement evidence. Whitley (1987, 264-66) suggests that the settlement covered a rather smaller area. After Hood and Smyth (1981) figure 4, with additions from *Archaeological Reports* 1980/1 to 1986/7.

It is not easy to study Dark Age settlements. Most of the major sites lie deeply buried or even destroyed by later occupation, and those few which are available are still poorly known. We can establish the area of sites, but not their internal layouts. Population estimates therefore have a very wide margin of error; but the results are, I think, still very significant.

The location of the Dark Age cemeteries at Athens, Knossos and Argos suggests that these settlements occupied roughly 200, 100 and 50 hectares respectively (see figs.2-4). These are very large areas. Snodgrass has argued that such sites consisted of small clusters of houses or separate hamlets divided by open areas, sometimes used for burials (1980, 155-6). This is probably true for most mainland sites,

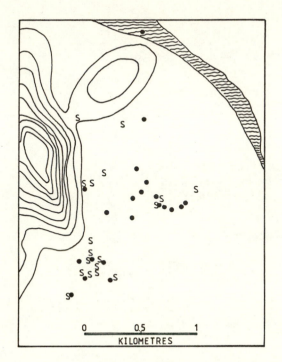

Figure 4:   Area occupied at Argos, 1100-700 BC. Circles represent cemetery remains; S represents settlement evidence. After Hagg 1974; 1982; Foley 1988.

although at Knossos the picture is now being replaced by one of a single nucleated settlement (Coldstream 1984; Whitley 1987, 266).

This pattern raises the question of whether Athens, Argos, Lefkandi and other sites were single communities. The inhabitants shared the same refuges and sources of water, worked adjacent lands, and constantly entered into all forms of face-to-face interactions and exchanges. It would surely be wrong to see these groups of houses, separated by only a few metres of ground containing their dead, as distinct, self-contained communities, like the caves of the inhuman Cyclopes in the *Odyssey* (9.114-15). Naroll (1956, 692) suggested taking open spaces of 200 metres as defining boundaries between communities. This is an arbitrary ruling, but even so, the open spaces in Greek settlements seem to be much smaller. I shall assume that all areas of housing on one site belong to a single community, unless there is evidence to the contrary.

It is never easy to calculate populations from house remains. Naroll (1962) again sought a cross-culturally valid equation, this time of 10 square metres of roofed space per person. The reality is more complex, and recent research shows this to be more a minimum than a mode (Hodder 1982, 193-4; Whitelaw 1984; Colb 1985). Classical Greek houses average two to four times as much space per person (Lauter-Bufe and Lauter 1971; Thompson and Wycherley 1972; Graham 1974; Hoepfner and Schwandner 1986). Literary sources from the eighth century assume nuclear families as normative residential units (e.g. Homer, *Odyssey* 4.302-5; Hesiod, *Works and Days* 405-13), and Dark Age structures average 40-70 square metres. I assume four or five people as the normal group, with only a small area of roofed space per person, close to Naroll's figure - an interesting detail on the quality of life in early Greece.

Moving from this figure to population densities presents further problems. First, we must establish what proportion of the structures on Dark Age sites were typically non-residential. There is little variety in the finds from different parts of most settlements. Each structure has traces of spinning and weaving, preparation of food, storage, basic craft activities, and occasionally more specialised ones.

A few examples may help. In the ninth-century house at Thorikos, room XXI contained coarse and fine wares, in both open and closed shapes; stone tools; and debris from the cupellation of silver. Next door, room XXII held a very large pithos and several other domestic pots. Outside, area III was probably an open court; in it a hearth, with animal bones and shellfish, and numerous flints. The general impression is of a domestic unit, with small-scale metalworking (Bingen 1967a; 1967b).

Eleventh- to ninth-century houses at Asine, Smyrna and Nichoria confirm this picture, with plenty of evidence for all domestic activities taking place under each roof, and few specialised buildings (Wells 1983; Akurgal 1983; MacDonald *et al.* 1983). In large houses, some rooms were set aside for particular functions, such as room XLI at Smyrna, which was probably solely for storage and cooking (Akurgal 1983, 22-4).

The clearest evidence is from the eleventh-century site of Karphi on Crete. Here, of about thirty houses, all except house XXI (the intriguing 'Baker's House', rooms 71, 73, 74) contained spindle whorls or loomweights, pithoi, coarse and fine pottery in a ratio of about ten sherds to one, and stone or bone tools. The larger houses also contained fragments of figurines, and showed more specialisation by rooms; house XIV (the 'Great House') had a large number of pithos sherds in room 9, and in room 12 quantities of fine pottery and fragments of bronze. In one- or two-room houses like II, III and IV a little of everything was found in each room (Pendlebury 1937/8; Nowicki 1987).

Specialised temples began to be common in the eighth century, but structures were still predominantly domestic. A partly dug house at Lefkandi had a floor deposit with stone tools, numerous open vases and loomweights; outside were stone circles which may have been oil presses or bases for granaries (Popham *et al.* 1980, 11-25). A roughly contemporary parallel at Smyrna (room XXII) was probably an olive press, with a channel running away from it (Akurgal 1983, 44). Another olive press has been found cut into the natural rock at Koukounaries, probably of eighth/seventh-century date (Schilardi, forthcoming). Zagora (Cambitoglou *et al.* 1971; Cambitoglou 1981) is particularly revealing. The earliest houses on the upper plateau tended to be one-room structures, with traces of all typical domestic activities in each; later in the eighth century many had extra rooms added, with some variability in finds between the rooms, but still no major differences between the houses.

Most Dark Age and Archaic houses have been excavated in isolation, and the relationships between structures are obscure. The exceptions come mainly from Crete and the Cyclades, where for a variety of reasons Dark Age sites are well preserved and accessible. However, they are often on hillsides or plateaux, which perhaps encouraged denser occupation than on mainland sites, which tended to be on level ground near an acropolis. At Asine, for instance, none of the four excavated eleventh- to ninth-century structures were contemporary. All were surrounded by open areas, perhaps gardens used for horticulture (Wells 1983; cf. *Odyssey* 7.112-32). At Nichoria, units IV-1 and IV-5 were also of different dates, and this tiny hamlet had a very low density (MacDonald *et al.* 1983). Another problem is that the excavated sites are often very small ones, and, as Fletcher has shown (1981), density within a site varies with its overall size. Both small villages and modern 'super-cities' allow far higher densities than middle-sized agrarian towns.

Densities were high in the excavated parts of some sites, like Karphi (Pendlebury 1937/8), Vrokastro (E. Hall 1914; Hayden 1983) or Kavousi (Boyd 1910; Gesell *et al.* 1983; 1985), all on Crete. There is some confusion over chronology at the last two sites, and little of their plans need be pre-750. Densities of course varied across sites; the houses on the upper plateau at Vrokastro suggest 200-250 per hectare, with at least ten units in an area of 0.2 hectares, while the houses on the lower terrace were smaller and may have reached 250-300 per hectare. At Karphi, 0.7 hectares has been exposed. The density here must have exceeded 200 per hectare when the site was abandoned around 950 BC, although earlier it may have been rather less (see Nowicki 1987, 246).

At Smyrna, less than 0.1 hectares of the tenth/ninth-century housing has been excavated. Six rooms were in use in the ninth century, grouped around a courtyard. Room XLI may have formed a single unit with XLVI. XLVII and XLIX are on different alignments, and may have been separate houses. Their areas would have been about 50 square metres, quite typical for the Dark Age. XLV and XLIV form a single unit. If we do have four units here, their density would be the equvalent of nearly 300 per hectare.

The evidence from mainland sites is much poorer, but if we assume lower densities within those areas which were actually used for housing - say, typically, 50-100 per hectare - and further assume that only about one quarter of each site (as delimited by its cemeteries) was normally used for housing, we get overall parameters of 12-25 people per hectare. These are very low figures (compare Renfrew's estimate of 100 per hectare for Neolithic sites, 1972, 251) and they may well be an underestimate, but even so they give us totals of 600-1,200 people at Argos, 1,250-2,500 at Knossos (where the density was probably much higher), and 2,500-5,000 at Athens. There has been sharp debate over the population of Dark Age Lefkandi, but at present the area of the settlement is unclear. Smaller but more densely peopled sites like Karphi, Vrokastro and eighth-century Zagora on Andros must have numbered several hundreds.

The figures for Athens, Knossos and Argos are generalised ones for the whole period 1100-750; population probably fell sharply from about 1,200 to 1,000, then grew gradually until the early eighth century. Nearly all known sites expanded rapidly between 750 and 700, whether large centres like Corinth or small villages like Koukounaries on Paros. Many of the villages were abandoned in the seventh century, the population either moving to a main regional settlement, or emigrating overseas. Population continued to grow through the Archaic period. By 500 BC Athens may have numbered 25,000 souls, and by 450 it was probably around 35,000, with a density of 170 per hectare - seven to fourteen times that suggested for the Dark Age (Morris 1987, 99-101). No other Greek city was so large, but several may have had as many as 10,000 residents.

A ten-fold increase in 500 years is an important long-term process, but is 'urbanisation' an appropriate concept? Finley (1981, 8) accused ancient historians of reducing urbanism to 'the mere arithmetical total of layout and drains and inhabitants', providing nothing more than descriptions of particular cities. Instead of offering a catalogue, I will draw on the approaches to urbanism outlined in a classic article by Wheatley (1972), considering the emergence of the early Greek city under five headings.

1   Economic relationships to the hinterland

The city must eat. High inter-annual variability in crop yields around the Mediterranean inevitably meant that all Greek communities, even in the Dark Age, had to import food in some years (Garnsey 1988, 8-16; Garnsey and Morris 1989). The main Dark Age towns were small enough to ensure that when crops did not fail, they could feed themselves from their own catchment area. What we are concerned with is the conversion of rural areas to a *permanent* supply role. The extreme case is fifth- and fourth-century Athens, where not only was the hinterland drawn on, but grain imports from overseas were needed every year to sustain the population (e.g. Demosthenes 20.31-2). However, Athens was unique. By the late fifth century several states may have been regular importers (Thucydides 3.86), but by and large Archaic settlements fed themselves, except in the inevitable bad years.

Starr argues that the 'industrial and commercial sectors of sixth-century Athens' numbered about 6,000, and that Athens 'would have required seaborne grain for its support' (1977, 104-5).[1] Starr's

---

[1]   Starr also cites Aristotle fr.510 Rose (Athenaeus 8.348b-c) to prove that 'nearby farmers, fishermen and other non-urban elements became bound to urban markets' (1977, 107). The passage describes how sixth-century Naxians regularly gave fish from their catch to a local lord, rather than sell it to townsmen, and that this led to a pitched battle between those wishing to buy and those not wishing to sell. If this shows

estimate of the agricultural potential of Attica (1977, 153-6) is far too low (Garnsey 1988, 107-19), and his case is weakened by assuming that the craftsmen of Archaic Greek communities were full-time specialists. Even in the fifth century a high proportion of Athenians were landholders.[1] In the late fourth century, Aristotle (*Politics* 2.1265a 14-19) argued that it would be impossible for any polis to support 5,000 non-agricultural producers. If we assume instead a much smaller group of non-producers - just a few hundred, or even a thousand, with a larger number of part-timers - there is no need to project the fourth-century situation back into Archaic times.

As always, Athens is the extreme case. If there were only small changes there, it is unlikely that urbanisation would be more pronounced elsewhere. The growth of Rome to a population of about one million in the first century BC transformed agricultural production in large parts of the empire (Hopkins 1978; Garnsey 1988, 182-268), but the scale of Greek 'urbanisation' was totally different. In this respect, the town/country relationship changed little between 1100 and 500 BC.

2 The growth of the market

This links up with the last point, and with a later one, via the relationships engendered by market exchange. The increasing scale of Greek society, especially at Athens, probably went hand-in-hand with the spread of market exchange. By the fifth century, the extent of market relationships distinguished the way of life in the city of Athens from that in the surrounding countryside (e.g. Aristophanes,

---

anything, it is villagers refusing to be part of any such marketing network; and as Gallant (1985) points out, fish probably played a relatively small part in subsistence anyway.

[1] The sources are poor, but see Thucydides 2.16; Aristotle, *Politics* 1.1256a39. The controversial passage in Dionysius of Halicarnassus, *On Lysias* 34, is the only quantification, saying that in 403 BC only 5,000 Athenian citizens were not landholders. Many 'urban' Athenians were of course farmers; e.g. Xenophon, *Oeconomicus* 11.15-16; Lysias 1.11, 20, 23; Menander, *Kitharistes* 54-5; *Perikeirome* 364; *Samia* 38-9; *Phasma* 16. On residence, see Osborne 1985a; and for other poleis, Thucydides 4.84, 88; 5.4; Xenophon, *Hellenica* 7.5.14. Strabo's association of urban and agricultural life (4.1.5) may be relevant.

Acharnians; *Clouds*), but the earlier stages of this process are obscure. In Homer, more personalised exchange forms seem to be the norm, particularly what anthropologists call gift exchange (Donlan 1982). Again, the evidence is hard to interpret. I have argued that market exchange played little part in the lives of most Greeks before 500 BC (Morris 1986). James Redfield (1986) suggests that Homer is archaising and generalising an ideal, and that the market displaced other exchange forms by 700 BC. Homer can certainly be read in many ways, but Redfield's arguments rest largely on the kind of assumptions about early Greek urbanism which I am attacking here.

3 *Political, religious and social relationships with the hinterland*

The political and religious services which a city supplied to its hinterland are important in any study, but in this case the problem is complicated by the extent to which these services were products of the rise of state-level organisation as well as urbanism, and how far cities can develop in this respect without state institutions (and vice versa).[1]

The relationships between politics and settlement could be complex. Osborne (1987, 113-36) distinguishes between the democracies of Thasos, where the country was subordinated to the city, and Elis, where villages negotiated with the town almost like independent communities. He suggests that in fourth-century Athens there was a *de facto* separation, with those living in or near Athens achieving such political dominance that 'what was in theory a direct democracy was in practice a subtle representational one' (1985b, 92). The same evidence can be used to produce a different picture (e.g. Hansen 1983; Whitehead 1986a, 256-326), but even Osborne's model makes the Athenian polis an open city, without legal distinctions between those of rural or urban origin. In this, it differed from medieval or early modern cities (Braudel 1981, 515-20; Hohenberg and Lees 1985). We certainly cannot speak of urbanisation in the sense of the increasing separation of the city from the country. There may have been differences in political attitudes between city and country dwellers (e.g. Ps.-Xenophon, *Constitution of Athens* 2.14;

---

[1] This question has been faced most explicitly in Egypt: see Wilson 1960; Hoffman *et al.* 1986.

Xenophon, *Hellenica* 5.2.7), but the only evidence for real distinctions are stories that some Archaic tyrants attempted to keep countrymen out of the towns (Aristotle, *Constitution of Athens* 16.3; *Politics* 5.1305a 18-22; 1311a 13-15; 1313b 1-7). We may also note that when Aristotle described his 'best democracy' - that least like Athens - the citizens are too busy farming to come into town for politics; but he does not refer to any polis having laws to keep them out (*Politics* 6.1318b 10-17).

De Polignac (1984) has shown that the city was not always the primary religious focus within a polis. He argues that it was establishing a major rural sanctuary, rather than sanctuaries in the city, which defined the polis. Rural hero cults (Whitley 1988) were also important in polis religion.

On the other hand, from Homer on we find that city dwellers despised villagers as rustic boors, while countrymen despised their urban neighbours for their softness and decadence (Walcot 1970; Lloyd 1983). There was no real change in this pattern throughout antiquity, and it corresponds to what Redfield (1953, 23-29) called 'the great and little traditions', the typical double conceptual universe of peasant society. Given the ubiquity of this framework, and the considerable size of some Dark Age settlements, it is probable that there were similar bigotries in that period too. The significant thing is not that these prejudices appear in Archaic and Classical literature, but that no stronger urban/rural opposition evolved.

4 The urban way of life

According to Tönnies and Wirth, the growth of cities can produce a distinctively urban mentality, where ties of kinship and face-to-face association decline, and are replaced with single-stranded contracts and rationalising behaviour - what Tönnies called the substitution of *Gesellschaft* for *Gemeinschaft*, and Wirth characterised as the rise of 'urban anomie', where stress increases as the family declines (Tönnies 1955 [1887]; Wirth 1938; 1940).

Ancient Greeks were of course conscious of differences between life in the city and the village, but there is never a hint of an 'urban way' at the level which Wirth described. Scale is again vital. No Archaic Greek settlement grew so large that even the seeds of urban anomie were planted. While Athens was no 'face-to-face' society

(Osborne 1985b, 64-5), it is reasonable to say that life in an 'average' Greek city did have a great deal in common with that in a large village. Athens, as always, is the extreme case: and again, there was little change from the Dark Age to the sixth century.

5   *Spatial structure*

The internal layout of sites offers another approach. Various spatial models of a generalised 'pre-industrial city' have been proposed (e.g. Sjoberg 1960; Vance 1971). However, as Collis points out, these at best apply to new foundations; settlements which were 'natural growths' will have far more complex structures (Collis 1984, 121-36. On Sjoberg, see Finley 1981, 251 n.8; Braudel 1981, 495-8).

In Plato's ideal city of Magnesia, artisans and citizens had their own quarters (*Laws* 8.848e 5-7, with Vidal-Naquet 1986, 224-45). Archaeologists have tried to identify 'Industrial Quarters' in Archaic Greek sites, but without much success. The material record does not allow us to distinguish between full-time and part-time specialists with any confidence, and full-time artisans could of course live in their workshops (e.g. Demosthenes 21.22, if the deposition has relevance); but there is little to suggest concentration of industrial activities in special districts before the late sixth century. Traces of Dark Age silver casting at Argos (Courbin 1963, 98-100) and bronze casting at Lefkandi (Popham *et al.* 1980, 93-7) have no clues as to context, but silver extraction was carried out in a domestic area at Thorikos in the ninth century (Bingen 1967a, 26-34). The evidence cannot be decisive, but it suggests little functional specialisation in settlements. The so-called 'installation de caractère artisanale' in eighth-century Argos consists solely of three clay storage bins and a pithos found in a very narrow trench (Daux 1959, 755). At Corinth, the ironworking in seventh-century House I was accompanied by plenty of domestic pottery, and the 'Trader's Complex' of around 600 BC was identified as such solely on the basis of imported pottery (Williams *et al.* 1971, 3-10; 1974, 17-24). Even the famous seventh-century 'Potters' Quarter' has been shown to have been a normal domestic area, not an industrial complex (Williams 1982). The Mazzola area of Pithecusae is often taken as evidence for an 'ironworking quarter' of about 700 BC, but one of the structures was definitely domestic, and ironworking slag was also found in the main settlement area (Buchner 1970/1, 64-7).

In the *Odyssey* (3.430-8) Nestor summons a goldsmith to his home to gild a cow's horns, and most early craft activity may have been on such an *ad hoc* basis. Hesiod's references to potters and a smithy (*Works and Days* 25, 493) are not much use. The earliest-known Dark Age kiln was in a cemetery (Cambitoglou 1982), presumably producing for funerals. Many early sanctuaries included areas where metal votives were cast on the spot.[1] Excavations at Istria on the Black Sea coast illustrate the change through time. Several houses had traces of sixth-century and later craft production (Coja 1962); and there was also a sequence of Classical and Hellenistic pottery kilns, apparently post-dating the residential use of that part of the site (Coja and Dupont 1979, 15-62), representing a more specialised area. By the late sixth century many centres will have had some full-time potters and metalworkers, even if some areas of production were monopolised by a single polis, and small parts of many cities were probably given over to workshops. The most famous case is the Athenian Potters' Quarter, where a number of Classical kilns have been found (e.g. Gebauer and Johannes 1937, 185; Gebauer 1938, 609; 1940, 357; 1942, 204-8; Alexandri 1968, 39). However, craft production remained on a very small scale, probably as a part-time household operation (Ehrenberg 1951, ch.3; Mossé 1969, chs.6,7). Finley (1985a, 137-8, 195-6) stresses that no ancient city had an industrial quarter comparable to those of medieval cities.

No other criteria suggest a greater level of urbanisation in the emergent polis. Snodgrass looked at fortification and town planning, and concluded that 'whatever factors made possible the achievement of Archaic Greece, an advanced urban culture was not one of them' (1980, 157-8). Walls were being built for protection from at least 900 BC, often for small Cycladic villages (e.g. Cambitoglou 1981,

---

[1] Possible kilns of the eighth century were found in houses at Delphi (Amandry, Lerat and Pouilloux 1950, 328; Coja and Dupont [1979, 43] treat them as certain), and an early seventh-century example from a house in Athens (Thompson 1941, 3-8). Other seventh-century cases are known from Amendolara and Gela, and at least eight sixth-century examples. The context is clear only in the case of a kiln in a temple temenos at Megara Hyblaea (Villard and Vallet 1953, 13-18). Evidence for sacred metal-working is abundant.

23, 103), and they are no index of urbanism. Town planning is more a sign of centralisation than of urbanism per se (in so far as it is legitimate to separate them). The first clear evidence comes in the seventh century, although Megara Hyblaea may have had a regular layout in the 720s (Vallet and Villard 1976; Svenbro 1982). All planned sites are new foundations; those which were settled earlier, such as Eretria, c.850, or Corinth, c.925, show no such planning. Before 600, even small villages like Vroulia on Rhodes (Kinch 1914)[1] or Oikonomos on Paros (Schilardi 1983, 205-9) could be strictly planned.

The evidence for the planned agora, the assembly-cum-market place, is mixed. In Homer, the agora at Phaeacia had 'polished stone' seats (*Odyssey* 8. 6-7), and in Ithaca, Odysseus had his own seat (*Odyssey* 2.14). The descriptions are vague, but neither sounds like a carefully planned urban centre. Dreros may have had an agora from c.700 (Demargne and Van Effenterre 1937, 10-15), and Megara Hyblaea from c.650 at the latest (Vallet and Villard 1976). Snodgrass suggested that the agora was a late development at Athens and Corinth (1980, 154-8), but subsequently offered arguments for a date around 700 at Athens (1983). There may have been a seventh-century agora east of the acropolis (Dontas 1983; Robertson 1986). The monumental agora was generally a late-sixth-century phenomenon (see Hoepfner and Schwandner 1986).

We must conclude that urbanisation was slow and limited in early Greece, and that if we wanted to draw a line between 'city' and 'non-city' stages, it would probably be in the late sixth century. The rise of the polis and the rise of the city were anything but synonymous.

The rise of the Greek state

'The State' is notoriously difficult to define. I will come back to this later; for now, I make an 'innocent' reading, that a state is a complex, permanently hierarchical social and political organisation, with

---

[1]   Vroulia is often erroneously dated as c.700. For the earliest pottery, see Hopper (1949, 173-4, n.48). Recent excavations at Koukounaries have also shown that the incised-and-stamped pithoi only begin on Paros in the seventh century, and that Oikonomos must have been founded after 700.

formal offices of government. What was the path to this level of complexity in ancient Greece? Most historians agree that Homer's Ithaca does not merit the title 'state' (e.g. Runciman 1982; Halverson 1986), but there is no consensus about how to interpret the poems as historical sources. Again, archaeological data are needed.

Our evaluation of state-formation depends on our assumptions about the Dark Age. Most British and American scholars stress the profundity of the twelfth-century decline, and the poverty, small scale, and lack of hierarchy of Dark Age Greece. Dark Age society is often described as tribal and pastoral. The subsequent appearance of state institutions is seen as a sudden leap into complexity, accompanied by an agricultural revolution and the substitution of territoriality for blood ties. I want to offer a different picture - that the twelfth-century collapse did not destroy hierarchy in Greece, and that state-level institutions appeared in a gradual process of centralisation, with the state's penetration into civil society remaining very limited until the Hellenistic period.

To make this case, I return to my earlier point about the size of the largest Dark Age communities, and to a well-established sociological theme. A century ago, Herbert Spencer proposed that population size and social complexity were linked: 'as population augments, divisions and subdivisions become more numerous and more decided' (1885, 449-50). Developing this theme in the 1950s, Naroll concluded that

> The larger the group of people who interact, the more ramified
> their organizational structure needs to be ... where gatherings
> normally never exceed a few hundred, no authoritative officials are
> needed ... But my sample suggests that when settlements contain
> more than about five hundred people they must have authoritative
> officials, and if they contain over one thousand, some kind of
> specialized organisation or corps of officials to perform police
> functions.
>
> (1956, 690)

The splitting of groups because of their inability to cope with the pressures of social interaction, well before they reach the optimum carrying capacity of their environment, is well documented from all over the world. It seems that *homo sapiens* can only cope with a certain number of very intensive face-to-face interactions. Where no communities number more than 100 to 150 individuals, there is little differentiation; usually the most basic relationships of household, affinity and reciprocal assistance can order relationships. Above this size of community, where groups number roughly 150 to 350, it is harder to handle at a purely personal level all the relationships entered into in social life, and sub-groups of a higher level than the household appear. These may be demarcated residentially, and they allow members to enter into relations with a larger number of individuals. Intense personal relationships occur as before with people both inside and outside the individual's own group, while these 'mediating structures' allow the individual to relate to a wider range of people in a less intensive way, on the basis of group or sub-group membership.

Societies where the largest communities are below a threshold of about 350-500 members are not usually associated with systems of organisation involving ascribed status. Rather, rank tends to be achieved without the aid of established offices, through a man's (or, less commonly, a woman's) own efforts. But where there are permanent settlements of 500 or more people, constituted offices begin to emerge, with access often restricted by birth. People in such communities obviously still have ties of blood relationship and affinity, just as in acephalous communities. The emergence of large groups does not substitute 'contracts' for personal contacts, but rather new higher levels of integration, including hierarchical status, encompass and redefine these aspects. Above 500 or so people, an agrarian community starts to take on the characteristic features of peasant society, including the division into socially stratified groups (see Carneiro 1967; Forge 1972; Smith 1976).

I argued earlier that after the fall of the Bronze Age civilisations, the largest Dark Age communities certainly never dropped below 500 members, and probably never below 1,000 or even 2,000. The implications are clear: permanent social and political hierarchy survived the Mycenaean collapse. A little more evidence can be found to support this. The thirteenth-century Linear B tablets mention fairly lowly palace officials with the title *pasireu*; in Greek poetry of the eighth to sixth centuries, the cognate *basileus* refers to the aristocratic leaders of the community. The most plausible explanation is that with the fall of the palaces, the *wanax* or prince disappeared, and the *pasireu* was the most powerful figure who still had a viable leadership role. His evolution into the *basileus* again suggests the survival of at least some hierarchy (see Andreev 1979; Drews 1983, 98-107).

The Dark Age burials which survive are not easy to analyse. I have argued that they were part of an ideology of a very stratified society from about 1050 to 750 BC (Morris 1987). Two recent finds should be mentioned here. A huge building, about 45 metres long and dated c.1000-950 BC, has been uncovered at Lefkandi. Its purpose is still unclear, but it may have been the house of an important leader. Beneath its floor were two burials. One was the cremation of a man, with his ashes placed in a bronze urn, accompanied by an iron sword and spearhead, and a whetstone. Hector Catling has identified the figured urn as a Cypriot import of the twelfth century BC, and thus already two centuries old when the burial was made. The other burial was a female inhumation, adorned with gold jewellery. Reynold Higgins suggests that her gold gorget was a thousand years old when it was buried. Next to the two graves was a second pit, containing the remains of four sacrificed horses. Shortly after the burial was made, the whole structure was covered over in a huge mound, and a series of rich burials began immediately to the east (Popham *et al*. 1980, 168-96; Catling 1981/2, 15-17; 1982/3, 12-15; 1983/4, 17; 1985/6, 15-16).

The finds of Professor Lambrinoudakis at Chora on Naxos are less spectacular, but just as important. A group of rectangular stone structures was uncovered in the middle of the later town. In one of them was a male inhumation of around 900 BC, marked by a grave stone. A vigorous cult was carried out on circular stone structures above the tomb. By the sixth century, an ash deposit over a metre deep had built up; the burial and the area around it were then covered by a mound, which was respected until late Roman times (Lambrinoudakis and Zapheiropoulou 1983; 1984; 1985).

These different sorts of evidence all point to some degree of hierarchy in Dark Age Greece. There is indeed evidence for greater centralisation in the eighth century, when monumental architecture, writing and more serious warfare appear (Snodgrass 1980); and if we wished to pinpoint the 'transition to statehood', it would probably be around 700. My point, though, is that it was quite a small step, from an already complex, stratified society to a state which was for centuries weakly developed.

I want to introduce two rather abstract models to describe the fragility of early Greek state institutions. The first was developed by

Flannery (1972), arguing that we should look at the rise of the state as a control system, reacting to various internal or external forces which he called 'socio-environmental variables'. Complex government, he suggested, evolves in two ways. The first he called *promotion*, when a low-level institution takes on more powerful responsibilities (fig.5). Examples might be the promotion of local aristocratic leaders to a ruling oligarchy through the establishment of permanent offices; or the elevation of shrines to state or even inter-state sanctuaries.

Flannery called his second path to complexity *linearization*, when lower-order institutions are absorbed by higher ones, centralising powers. Examples of this might be Pisistratus' travelling judges in the sixth century, bypassing local leaders in the administration of justice; or Pericles' use of state pay for jury service, superseding the more personal patronage of rich nobles like Cimon (Aristotle, *Constitution of Athens* 16.5, 27.3-4). Through a combination of promotion and linearization, the state takes over more and more of life.

In the polis, these processes did not go very fast or very far. Modern definitions of the state emphasise a central monopoly of force, but in Classical Greece this was strictly circumscribed. If we can believe Lysias (1.2), most poleis allowed citizens to kill other citizens to avenge crimes such as homicide, adultery or theft. The existence of any standing force to impose the decisions of office-holders and to carry out police functions was very rare. State authority rested to a remarkable extent on the willingness of individual citizens to fulfil their obligations, and did not constitute a power external to the citizens themselves. Direct taxation was a symbol of tyranny and felt to be out of place in the polis (even though exploitation of the subjects is also central to many definitions of the state). Although the Athenians imposed a direct tax of 8.3% on grain production in their dependencies of Lemnos, Imbros and Skyros in 374/3 BC (Shear 1987) this was never extended to Attica proper or established on a regular basis. Most taxes were raised in wartime, and it was mainly the taxpayers themselves who decided that it should be done. In the fourth century, wealthy Athenians assessed their own liability for tax (Demosthenes 14.19,30). There were of course problems. Demosthenes says that by 355 there were massive arrears going back twenty years (22.42-68), and at Sparta things were worse still (Aristotle, *Politics* 2.1271b.14-15). But why did anyone pay at

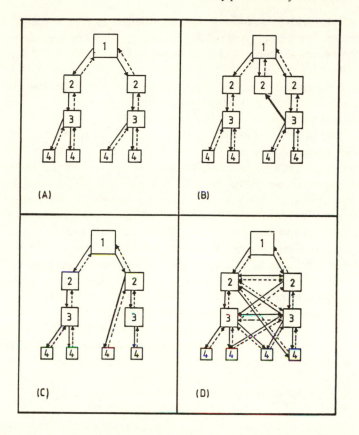

Figure 5: Flannery's model of the state as a control hierarchy. (A) The model for the control hierarchy, with socioenvironmental variables regulated by low-level institutions (4), and each successively higher level (3-2-1) regulating the output of the level below it (solid arrows represent policy or commands; broken arrows represent 'output'); (B) an example of 'promotion', with one function of a third-level institution rising to assume a position of importance on the second level; (C) an example of 'linearisation', with a second-level control bypassing level 3 and directly regulating the output of a fourth-level institution; (D) 'hypercoherence', when an early state becomes unstable through too complex linking of institutions at different levels - a situation which never developed in the polis, due to the simplicity of the institutional structures (after Flannery 1972).

all? As with so much else, the state left it in private hands, as a matter of personal honour. Rich men boasted that they not only paid their taxes and performed liturgies, but did so more lavishly than was asked (e.g. Lysias 21.3-5; [Demosthenes] 50). Patriotism had a role, but Athenians competed through their lavishness to win clients, political support, and sympathy from the jury (see Davies 1981, 91-105; Whitehead 1983; Rhodes 1986, 135-8).

The state had a minimal role in trade. Even in the case of life-sustaining imports such as grain its actions were largely *ad hoc*, responding to a particular emergency (Garnsey and Morris 1989). For example, as late as the 240s BC, while Samos had instituted state grain commissioners to safeguard the supply, it gave them no powers, and it was left to benefactors like Boulagoras to provide money to import food (Austin 1981, no.113). The Samians only 'linearized' this vital institution in the 180s, setting up a state fund for commissioners to buy grain (Austin 1981, no.116). Shipley (1987, 221) points out that even this was more for cultural than subsistence purposes, with the fund being used for 'luxury' wheat rather than more practical but less desirable barley.

This was 150 years after Alexander conquered Persia. How much weaker the states of the eighth and seventh centuries must have been! An *archon* at Athens or a *damiorgos* at Argos would have had wider responsibilities and some greater powers than a ninth-century *basileus*, but most aspects of life remained beyond the reach of the state.

A second set of abstractions is useful, drawing on Gellner's idea of the 'agro-literate state' (see fig.6, cf. J. Hall 1985). Gellner suggests that in most literate, pre-industrial societies, we find that 'the ruling class forms a small minority of the population, rigidly separated from the great majority of direct agricultural producers, or peasants' (1983, 9). The members of this class control state institutions, are internally stratified, and use culture to underwrite social structure to distance themselves from the subjects of the state. 'Below the horizontally stratified minority at the top', Gellner continues, 'there is another world, that of the laterally separated petty communities of the lay members of society... The state is interested in extracting taxes, maintaining the peace, and not much else' (1983, 10).

Gellner comments that small city-states tend to be less unequal than large empires, and depend more on face-to-face contacts (1983, 13-14; 1988, 22), but the contrast between his generalised model and

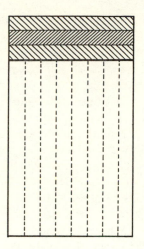

Figure 6: The agro-literate state. Stratified, horizontally segregated layers of military, administrative, religious and sometimes commercial personnel are rigidly divided from laterally insulated communities of agricultural producers (after Gellner 1983).

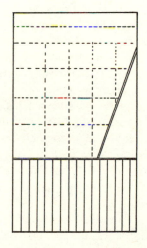

Figure 7: Model of the ideal polis structure. The weakly stratified and slightly laterally insulated citizen body is rigidly divided from both the strongly insulated chattel slave population and a group of sometimes wealthy resident aliens. The most problematic features of such a model of status are the location of the metics and the women of the citizen group.

the internal structure of the polis is very revealing. There were aristocrats, who sometimes monopolised office, but no segregated military, administrative and clerical classes, and writing did not function to set them apart as in Gellner's model. *The polis was a community of citizens*, not a mass of subjects under a differentiated elite. The main horizontal line in this model comes between the citizens and the slave population, which was even more 'laterally insulated' than the subjects in Gellner's scheme (Cartledge 1985; Vidal-Naquet 1986, 159-67), and even less capable of challenging the order. Even this line is cross-cut by an equally firm division between citizens and free resident aliens (fig.7), who suffered many legal disabilities but could be among the richest men in the state (Whitehead 1977; 1986b).

These two models can be seen as the extremes of a continuum of possible forms for the Greek state, with the various communities ranged between them. Gellner's model may be taken as fairly representative of the Greek state structure called the *ethnos*, typified by Thessaly or Macedon, where citizenship was not such a central force. The Athenian democracy would come closest to the other ideal type, with citizens and state a unity, opposing any separation of a ruling class at all. The Spartans were somewhere in between. It was in the interests of the aristocrats in the cities to struggle against the Athenian idea of the polis, trying not just to turn democracy into oligarchy, but to monopolise state power, extending it into citizen society; it was in the interests of the *demos*, the common citizenry, to resist. The conflict between these tendencies was one of the central tensions and driving forces in the history of the polis. The balance varied in time and space. As the structural centrality of citizenship weakened in the face of aristocratic power, the polis could gradually shade towards and into the 'Gellnerland' model. The oppositions frequently erupted into violence and a savage form of civil war which the Greeks called *stasis*.

This tension could be resolved in several ways. One, particularly common in Archaic times, was the rise of a tyrant, an absolute ruler. The tyrant monopolised access to state mechanisms, often coming to power as the champion of the *demos* against the nobles, but once there, operating against the interests of all (or so the sources say). Tyranny was the antithesis of the polis. It is no accident that most tyrants are credited with centralising state power. Some are said actively to have increased the 'lateral insulation' of their subjects at the same time as purging or placating the aristocrats to prevent them from challenging for power. It is also no accident that most tyrannies were short-lived, trying to balance such powerful forces (Aristotle, *Politics* 5.1313a 34-16a 1). The tyrants were critical figures in the growth of state institutions in the early polis, but their rapid collapse generally stopped them from so centralising power and extending the state as to leave those who succeeded them in possession of a social structure more like Gellner's model than a polis.

A second response was to call in outsiders. Both democrats and oligarchs found allies only too eager to help, particularly as the scale of warfare increased (Thucydides 3.82-4). The elites of the poleis were at an advantage here. Ties of ritualised friendship between the wealthy were often felt to be more binding than loyalty to the state. Herman (1987, 162-5) shows that when seen as a system of states, rather than from within the individual polis, ancient Greece does look rather like Gellner's model, with a stratified elite separated from the world of laterally insulated producers below; although we should note that even so, the Greek elite was only weakly marked off by cultural boundaries such as monopolies on reading, religion or fighting. Another part of the aristocrat's attack on the polis model of the state was to downgrade the local state boundaries. 'Patriotism' was largely a lower-class phenomenon in the polis (Herman 1987, 156-61).

I have argued that the evolution of state mechanisms in the early polis was fairly gradual, and that the state only began to accrue the sort of powers we find in most anthopological definitions well into the Hellenistic period. To borrow Clastres' phrase (1977), the polis was a case of 'society against the state'.

Conclusion

An appreciation of the emergence and the structures of the polis has to begin with the collapse of the Mycenaean world, and the depopulation and confusion of the twelfth and eleventh centuries. The societies which came out of this were complex but materially impoverished. They were very different from those of the palaces, and their ritual practices suggest that they may have actively been trying to define themselves in opposition to this historical background. There was perhaps a considerable growth in scale and increase in competition between 925 and 800 BC, but a crucial set of transformations in burial practices, cult activity and spatial organisation accompanying the introduction of writing around 750 BC might be taken as the material expressions of the ideology of the citizen state (Morris 1987, 171-210). I have argued that the emergence of the polis, the city and the state are related in a much more complex pattern than the conventional translation 'city-state' would lead us to expect, and can only be understood on a much longer time scale than ancient historians normally use.

On the last page of his last book, the late Moses Finley urged that both the structure of the state and the history of ancient urbanism should be explored more fully, and that 'The objective, in the final analysis, is the paradoxical one of achieving a more complex picture by the employment of simplifying models' (1985b, 108). This volume is a step towards realising that goal.

Acknowledgements

I would like to thank Paul Cartledge, Peter Garnsey, Anthony Snodgrass and all who took part in the Leicester-Nottingham seminar in January 1987 for their comments on an earlier version of this paper, without incriminating them in the final results.

Bibliography

Akurgal, E. (1983), *Alt-Smyrna I: Wöhnschichten und Athenatempel*, Istanbul.

Alexandri, O. (1968), 'He ephoreia klassikon arkhaiotiton Athinon', *Arkhaiologikon Deltion* 23:2, 33-109.

Amandry, P., Lerat, L. and Pouilloux, J. (1950), 'Delphes', *Bulletin de correspondance hellénique* 74, 316-28.

Andreev, Y. (1979), 'Könige und Königsherrschaft bei den Epen Homers', *Klio* 61, 361-84.

Austin, M.M. (1981), *The Hellenistic World*. Cambridge.

Bernhardt, R. (1985), *Polis und römische Herrschaft in der späten Republik*. Berlin and New York.

Bingen, J. (1967a), 'L'établissement du IXe siècle et les nécropoles du secteur ouest 4', *Thorikos II, 1964*, 25-46. Brussels.

Bingen, J. (1967b), 'L'établissement géométrique et la nécropole ouest', *Thorikos III, 1965*, 31-56. Brussels.

Boyd, H. (1901), 'Excavations at Kavousi, Crete', *American Journal of Archaeology* 5, 125-57.

Braudel, F. (1981), *The Structures of Everyday Life*. London.

Buchner, G. (1970/71), 'Recent work at Pithekoussai (Ischia)', *Archaeological Reports for 1970/1*, 63-7.

Cambitoglou, A. (1981), *Archaeological Museum of Andros*. Athens.

Cambitoglou, A. (1982), 'Anaskaphi Toronis', *Praktika tis Arkhaiologikis Etaireias kata to 1982*, 69-78.

Cambitoglou, A. Coulton, J.J. and Green, R. (1971), *Zagora* I. Sydney.

Camp, J. McK. (1979), 'A drought in the late eighth century BC', *Hesperia* 48, 397-411.

Carneiro, R. (1967), 'On the relationship between size of population and complexity of social organization', *Southwestern Journal of Anthropology* 23, 234-41.

Cartledge, P.A. (1985), 'Rebels and sambos in classical Greece: a comparative view', in P.A. Cartledge and F.D. Harvey (eds.), *Crux*, 16-46. London (also published as *History of Political Thought* 6/2 [1985] 16-46).

Catling, H.W. (1981/82), 'Archaeology in Greece, 1981/2', *Archaeological Reports for 1981/2*, 3-62.

Catling, H.W. (1982/3), 'Archaeology in Greece, 1982/3', *Archaeological Reports for 1982/3*, 3-62.

Catling, H.W. (1983/4), 'Archaeology in Greece, 1983/4', *Archaeological Reports for 1983/4*, 3-70.

Catling, H.W. (1985/6), 'Archaeology in Greece, 1985/6', *Archaeological Reports for 1985/6*, 3-101.

Clastres, P. (1977), *Society Against the State*. Oxford.

Coja, M. (1962), 'L'artisanat à Histria du VIe au Ie siècle avant notre ère', *Dacia* 6, 115-38.

Coja, M. and Dupont, P. (1979), *Histria V*. Bucharest.

Colb, C.C. (1985), 'Demographic estimates in archaeology: contributions from ethnoarcheology on Mesoamerican peasants', *Current Anthropology* 26, 581-99.

Coldstream, J.N. (1984), 'Dorian Knossos and Aristotle's villages', in *Aux origines de l'hellénisme. Hommages à Henri van Effenterre*, 311-22. Paris.

Collis, J. (1984), *Oppida. The Earliest Towns North of the Alps*. Sheffield.

Courbin, P. (1963), 'Fouilles stratigraphiques à Argos', in P.
  Courbin (ed.), *Études archéologiques*, 71-110. Paris.
Daux, G. (1959), 'Chronique des fouilles', *Bulletin de correspondance
  hellénique* 83, 367-793.
Davies, J.K. (1981), *Wealth and the Power of Wealth in Classical
  Athens*. New York.
Davies, J.K. (1984), 'Cultural, social and economic features',
  Cambridge Ancient History VII:1, 2nd edn, 257-320. Cambridge.
Demargne, P., and Van Effenterre, H. (1937), 'Recherches à Dréros',
  Bulletin de correspondance hellénique 37, 5-32, 333-48.
Donlan, W. (1982), 'Reciprocities in Homer', *Classical World* 73,
  137-75.
Dontas, G. (1983), 'The true Aglaureion', *Hesperia* 52, 48-63.
Drews, R.L. (1983), *Basileus: the Evidence for Kingship in
  Geometric Greece*. New Haven.
Ehrenberg, V. (1951), *The People of Aristophanes*, 2nd edn. Oxford.
Finley, M.I. (1981), *Economy and Society in Ancient Greece* (ed.
  B.D. Shaw and R.P. Saller). London. Reprinted Harmondsworth,
  1983.
Finley, M.I. (1985a), *The Ancient Economy*, 2nd edn. London.
Finley, M.I. (1985b), *Ancient History: Evidence and Models*.
  London.
Flannery, K. (1972), 'The cultural evolution of civilizations', *Annual
  Review of Ecology and Systematics* 3, 399-426.
Fletcher, R. (1981), 'People and space: a case study in material
  behaviour', in I. Hodder, G. Isaac and N. Hammond (eds.), *Pattern
  of the Past*, 97-128. Cambridge.
Foley, A. (1988), *The Argolid 800-600 BC. An Archaeological
  Survey* (Studies in Mediterranean Archaeology no. 80). Göteborg.
Forge, A. (1972), 'Normative factors in the settlement size of
  Neolithic cultivators (New Guinea)', in P.J. Ucko, G.W.
  Dimbleby and R. Tringham (eds.), *Man, Settlement and
  Urbanism*, 363-76. London.
Gallant, T.W. (1985), *A Fisherman's Tale* (Miscellanea Graeca 7).
  Ghent.
Garnsey, P. (1988), *Famine and Food Supply in the Graeco-Roman
  World*. Cambridge.
Garnsey, P. and Morris, I. (1989), 'Risk and the polis', in P. Halstead
  and J.O'Shea (eds.), *Bad Year Economics: Cultural Reponses to
  Risk and Uncertainty*, 98-105. Cambridge.

Gauthier, P. (1985), *Les Cités grecques et leurs bienfaiteurs (Bulletin de correspondance hellénique*, supp. vol. 15). Paris.

Gebauer, K. (1938), 'Ausgrabungen im Kerameikos, II', *Archäologischer Anzeiger*, 607-10.

Gebauer, K. (1940), 'Ausgrabungen im Kerameikos', *Archäologischer Anzeiger*, 308-64.

Gebauer, K. (1942), 'Ausgrabungen im Kerameikos', *Archäologischer Anzeiger*, 200-58.

Gebauer, K. and Johannes, H. (1937), 'Ausgrabungen im Kerameikos', *Archäologischer Anzeiger*, 184-203.

Gellner, E. (1983), *Nations and Nationalism*. Oxford.

Gellner, E. (1988), *Plough, Sword and Book*. Chicago.

Gesell, G., Day, L. and Coulson, W. (1983), 'Excavations and survey at Kavousi, 1978-1981', *Hesperia* 52, 389-420.

Gesell, G., Day, L. and Coulson, W. (1985), 'Kavousi, 1981-1983: the Kastro', *Hesperia* 54, 327-55.

Graham, J.W. (1974), 'The houses of classical Athens', *Phoenix* 28, 45-51.

Hägg, R. (1974), *Die Gräber der Argolis* I (*Boreas* 7:1). Uppsala.

Hägg, R. (1982), 'Zur Stadtwerdung des dorischen Argos', in *Paläst und Hütte*, 297-307. Mainz.

Hall, E. (1914), 'Excavations in eastern Crete, Vrokastro', *University of Pennsylvania, the Museum Anthropological Publications* III:3, 79-185.

Hall, J. (1985), *Powers and Liberties*. Oxford. Republished Harmondsworth, 1986.

Halverson, J. (1986), 'The succession issue in the *Odyssey*', *Greece and Rome* 33, 119-28.

Hansen, M.H. (1983), 'Political activity and the organization of Attica in the fourth century BC', *Greek, Roman and Byzantine Studies* 24, 227-38.

Hayden, B. (1983), 'New plans of the Early Iron Age settlement of Vrokastro', *Hesperia* 52, 367-87.

Herman, G. (1987), *Ritualised Friendship in the Greek City*. Cambridge.

Hodder, I. (1982), *Symbols in Action*. Cambridge.

Hoepfner, W. and Schwandner, E.-L. (1986), *Haus und Stadt im klassischen Griechenland*. Munich.

Hoffman, M.A., Hamroush, H.A. and Allen, R.O. (1986), 'A model of urban development for the Hierakonpolis region from

Predynastic through Old Kingdom times', *Journal of the American Research Center in Egypt* 23, 175-87.

Hohenberg, P.M. and Lees, L.H. (1985), *The Making of Urban Europe, 1000-1950*. Cambridge, Mass.

Hood, M.S.F. and Smyth, D. (1981), *Archaeological Survey of the Knossos Area* (British School at Athens supp. vol. 12). London.

Hopkins, K. (1978), 'Economic growth and towns in classical antiquity', in P. Abrams and E.A. Wrigley (eds.), *Towns in Societies*, 35-77. Cambridge.

Hopper, R.J. (1949), 'Addenda to *Neocrocorinthia*', *Annual of the British School at Athens* 44, 162-257.

Kinch, F. (1914), *Fouilles de Vroulia*. Copenhagen.

Lambrinoudakis, V. and Zapheiropoulous, F. (1983), 'Anaskaphi Naxou: Sangri', *Praktika tis Arkhaiologikis Etaireias kata to 1983*, 297-304.

Lambrinoudakis, C. and Zapheiropoulous, F. (1984), 'Naxos', *Ergon tis Arkhaiologikis Etaireias kata to 1984*, 77-9.

Lambrinoudakis, C. and Zapheiropoulous, F. (1985), 'Naxos', *Ergon tis Arkhaiologikis Etaireias kata to 1985*, 56-62.

Lauter-Bufe, H. and Lauter, H. (1971), 'Wohnhäuser und Stadtviertel des klassischen Athen', *Athenische Mitteilungen* 86, 109-24.

Lloyd, C. (1983), 'Greek urbanity and the polis', in R. Marchese (ed.), *Aspects of Graeco-Roman Urbanism*, 11-41 (British Archaeological Reports, International Series 188). Oxford.

Luce, J.V. (1978), 'The polis in Homer and Hesiod', *Transactions of the Royal Irish Academy* 78, series C, 1-15.

MacDonald, W.A., Coulson, W.D.E. and Rosser, J.J. (1983), *Excavations at Nichoria in Southwest Greece* III: *Dark Age and Byzantine Occupation*. Minneapolis.

Morris, I. (1986), 'Gift and commodity in Archaic Greece', *Man* 21, 1-17.

Morris, I. (1987), *Burial and Ancient Society: the Rise of the Greek City State*. Cambridge.

Mossé, C. (1969), *The Ancient World at Work*. London.

Naroll, R. (1956), 'A preliminary index of social development', *American Anthropologist* 58, 687-715.

Naroll, R. (1962), 'Floor area and settlement population', *American Antiquity* 27, 587-9.

Nowicki, K. (1987), 'The history and setting of the town at Karphi', *Studi Micenei ed Egeo-Anatolici* 26, 235-56.

Osborne, R. (1985a), 'Buildings and residence on the land in Classical and Hellenistic Greece: the contribution of epigraphy', *Annual of the British School at Athens* 80, 119-28.

Osborne, R. (1985b), *Demos: The Discovery of Classical Attika.* Cambridge.

Osborne, R. (1987), *Classical Landscape with Figures.* London.

Pendlebury, J. (1937/38), 'Excavations in the plain of Lasithi, III: Karphi', *Annual of the British School at Athens* 38, 57-145.

Polignac, F. de (1984), *La Naissance de la cité grecque.* Paris.

Popham, M.R., Sackett, L.H. and Themelis, P.G. (1980), *Lefkandi* I (British School at Athens supp. vol. 11). London.

Popham, M.R., Touloupa, E. and Sackett, L.H. (1982), 'The hero of Lefkandi', *Antiquity* 56, 169-74.

Redfield, J.M. (1986), 'The growth of markets in Archaic Greece', in B.L. Anderson and A.J.H. Latham (eds.), *The Market in History,* 29-58. London and Sydney.

Redfield, R.M. (1953), *Peasant Society and Culture.* Chicago.

Renfrew, A.C. (1972), *The Emergence of Civilization.* London.

Rhodes, P.J. (1986), 'Political activity in classical Athens', *Journal of Hellenic Studies* 106, 132-44.

Robertson, N. (1986), 'Solon's axones and kyrbeis and the sixth-century background', *Historia* 35, 147-76.

Runciman, W.G. (1982), 'Origins of states: the case of Archaic Greece', *Comparative Studies in Society and History* 24, 351-77.

Schilardi, D.U. (1983), 'The decline of the Geometric settlement of Koukounaries at Paros', in R. Hägg (ed.), *The Greek Renaissance of the Eighth Century BC,* 173-83. Stockholm.

Schilardi, D.U. (forthcoming), 'Anaskaphi stin Paro', *Praktika tis Arkhaiologikis Etaireias kata to 1988.*

Scully, S. (1981), 'The polis in Homer', *Ramus* 10, 1-34.

Shear, T.L. (1987), 'Tax tangle, ancient style', *American School of Classical Studies Newsletter,* Spring 1987, 8.

Shipley, G. (1987), *A History of Samos.* Oxford.

Sjoberg, G. (1960), *The Pre-Industrial City, Past and Present.* New York.

Smith, C.A. (1976), 'Exchange systems and spatial distribution of elites', in C.A. Smith (ed.), *Regional Analysis II: Social Systems,* 309-74. New York.

Snodgrass, A.M. (1977), *Archaeology and the Rise of the Greek State.* Cambridge.

Snodgrass, A.M. (1980), *Archaic Greece: the Age of Experiment*. London.

Snodgrass, A.M. (1983), 'Two demographic notes', in R. Hägg (ed.), *The Greek Renaissance of the Eighth Century BC*, 167-71. Stockholm.

Snodgrass, A.M. (1986), 'Interaction by design: the Greek city state', in A.C. Renfrew and J.F. Cherry (eds.), *Peer Polity Interaction*, 47-58. Cambridge.

Spencer, H. (1885), *Principles of Sociology* I. London.

Starr, C.G. (1977), *Economic and Social Growth of Early Greece, 800-500 BC*. Oxford.

Svenbro, J. (1982), 'A Mégara Hyblaea: le corps géomètre', *Annales économies, sociétés, civilisations* 37, 953-64.

Thompson, H.A. (1941), *The Tholos of Athens and its Predecessors* (*Hesperia*, supp. vol. 4). Princeton.

Thompson, H.A. and Wycherley, R.E. (1972), *The Athenian Agora, 14. The Agora of Athens*. Princeton.

Tönnies, F. (1955), *Community and Association*. London. First published as *Gemeinschaft und Gesellschaft*. Berlin (1887).

Vallet, G. and Villard, F. (1976), *Mégara Hyblaea: le quartier de l'agora archaique*. Paris.

Vance, J.E. (1971), 'Land assignment in the precapitalist, capitalist and postcapitalist city', *Economic Geography* 47, 101-20.

Veyne, P. (1976), *Le Pain et le cirque*. Paris.

Vidal-Naquet, P. (1986), *The Black Hunter*. Baltimore and London.

Villard, F. and Vallet, G. (1953), 'Mégara Hyblaea III: les fouilles de 1954', *École française de Rome. Mélanges d'archéologie et d'histoire* 65, 9-38.

Walcot, P. (1970), *Greek Peasants Ancient and Modern*. Manchester.

Wells, B. (1983), *Asine II. 4.2-3. The Protogeometric Period*. Stockholm.

Wheatley, P. (1972), 'The concept of urbanism', in P.J. Ucko, G.W. Dimbleby and R. Tringham (eds.), *Man, Settlement and Urbanism*, 601-37. London.

Whitehead, D. (1977), *The Ideology of the Athenian Metic* (Proceedings of the Cambridge Philological Society supp. vol. 4). Cambridge.

Whitehead, D. (1983), 'Competitive outlay and community profit: *philotimia* in democratic Athens', *Classica et Medievalia* 34, 55-74.

Whitehead, D. (1986a), *The Demes of Attica, 508/7-ca. 250 BC*. Princeton.

Whitehead, D. (1986b), 'The ideology of the Athenian metic: some pendants and a reappraisal', *Proceedings of the Cambridge Philological Society* 212, 145-58.

Whitelaw, T. (1984), 'The settlement at Fournou Korifi Myrtos and aspects of Early Minoan social organization', in O. Krzyszkowska and L. Nixon (eds.), *Minoan Society*, 323-45. Bristol.

Whitley, J. (1987), 'Style, burial and society in Dark Age Greece', unpublished PhD thesis, Cambridge University.

Whitley, J. (1988), 'Early states and hero cults: a reappraisal', *Journal of Hellenic Studies* 108, 173-82.

Will, E. (1988), '*Poleis* hellenistiques: deux notes', *Échos du monde classique* 32, 329-52.

Williams, C.K. (1982), 'The early urbanization of Corinth', *Annuario della scuola archeologica di Atene* 60, 9-21.

Williams, C.K. and Fisher, J.E. (1971), 'Corinth 1970: Forum area', *Hesperia* 40, 1-51.

Williams, C.K., MacIntosh J. and Fisher, J.E. (1974), 'Excavations at Corinth, 1973', *Hesperia* 42, 1-76.

Wilson, J.A. (1960), 'Civilization without cities', in C.H. Kraeling and R.McC. Adams (eds.), *City Invincible*, 124-64. Chicago.

Wirth, L. (1938), 'Urbanism as a way of life', *American Journal of Sociology* 44, 1-44.

Wirth, L. (1940), 'The urban society and civilization', *American Journal of Sociology* 46, 743-55.

Wood, E.M. (1988), *Peasant-citizen and Slave. The Foundations of Athenian Democracy*. London.

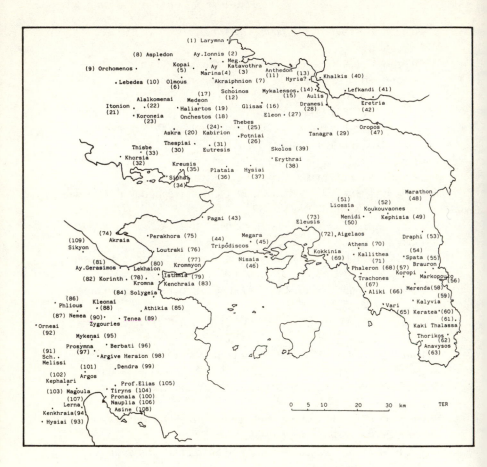

Figure 1: Rihll and Wilson survey area

∞ 3 ∞

Modelling settlement structures in Ancient Greece: new approaches to the polis

T.E. Rihll and A.G. Wilson

1   Introduction

> Had he asked himself the obvious question: why did that particular apple choose that unrepeatable moment to fall on that unique head, he might have written the history of an apple. Instead of which he asked himself why apples fell and produced the theory of gravitation. The decision was not the apple's, but Newton's.

Thus, with a literary flourish and a dash of popular folklore, Postan implies that the difference between history and physics is not intrinsic to the subject matter, but the question posed of it. Provocatively put, this is an extremely tendentious point of view. Apples are mindless. On the other hand, people are not just minds and history is not merely the history of ideas. Human life is rich and complex, and to catch and illuminate its many dimensions many approaches are necessary.

These approaches are, in the broadest sense, disciplinary: anthropology, archaeology, geography, history and sociology all have as their subject people and society. Their concurrence is apparent in, for example, ethnoarchaeology (see e.g. Binford 1983, and for anthropology and ancient history, Humphreys 1978), geoarchaeology (e.g. Butzer 1982), historical geography (e.g. Carlstein *et al.* 1978; Pred 1981), historical sociology (e.g. Giddens 1981; Abrams 1982; Skocpol 1984), and the *Annales* tradition (e.g. Febvre 1922). In this paper we bring together history and geography in a new and exciting way.

The emergence and evolution of the Greek polis has a strong spatial aspect. It involved the formation of a community in a territorial unit encompassing a number of settlements, and the development of a 'capital' city. To have things in common, and in particular to share a common identity, presupposes a relatively intense level of interaction amongst those who constitute a community *vis-à-vis* those who are excluded from it. When the poleis were coming into existence, did discrete communities align themselves with those with whom they had most in common - those with whom they experienced the most intense interaction? Did location *vis-à-vis* other settlements have a significant effect on their affiliation and union?

What role, if any, did the spatial dimension play in the development of one settlement, rather than another, into the undisputed capital of the polis? What role, if any, did it play in the development of some cities into great cities? In particular, did location *vis-à-vis* other settlements, rather than location in a particular type of environment,[1] have a significant effect on settlement growth and sociopolitical centralisation?

These questions can be explored through the construction of hypotheses on settlement interaction and growth in early Greece. The hypotheses can be rigorously evaluated by their translation into a mathematical model, which comprehensively tests those hypotheses in a simulation. In this paper we discuss such a project.

The mathematical model employed is one of a family of models developed over the last decade by a team of geographers at Leeds University; a programme of research and development in which the project here discussed represents the first attempt to apply the model principles and concepts in an historical context (cf. Clarke and Wilson 1985). Needless to say, like most pilot projects this one is prospective rather than definitive. But the results do suggest that this approach has some contribution to make toward an understanding of the ancient city. For a model embodies a set of hypotheses to explain

---

[1]   One could reasonably argue that the former subsumes the latter. An emphasis on settlements rather than on the landscape on which their residents live allows a more abstract approach and produces a model which is more widely applicable.

the patterns it identifies, unlike most spatial analysis techniques (for a survey of which see Orton 1982). This model may also hold out the promise of a more immediate and pragmatic value for historians and in particular for archaeologists, namely a potential to identify relatively large or important sites on the basis of location alone.

Whilst the essential principles and ideas expressed in the model are fairly simple, the mathematics by which they are expressed is not. Therefore we shall attempt to explain what the model does through analogies and simplifications; those for whom mathematics clarifies rather than mystifies the subject may find it helpful to consult the mathematical appendix (below, p.91) and Rihll and Wilson (1987).

In the next section we discuss the model. We begin with some general comments on the nature of mathematical models and simulation in order to clarify their aims and usage. We then discuss our model, describing in ordinary language what it is and how it works. Next we consider the data on which and with which it operates. The section concludes with a discussion of how the results are assessed. In section 3 we present some results which reproduce the general settlement structure of our survey area to a fairly high degree of accuracy, thus demonstrating that the simple hypotheses expressed in the model are sufficient to explain that structure. In section 4 we assess the value of the exercise, and suggest some of the main tasks for future research.

2   The model

A mathematical model consists of hypotheses concerning some real-world system of interest (in our case the settlement structure in Geometric Greece), which are formalised by mathematical equations. These equations allow the model to be quantitative and hence to be evaluated empirically, usually with the help of a computer. This process of experimental evaluation we may call simulation. It is a subtle process, both theoretically and practically.

It is subtle theoretically because the hypotheses and numerical data input to the model need considerable thought in their selection and interpretation. For example, a parameter like settlement importance is difficult both to define and to quantify. In historical contexts parameters and data are frequently difficult to quantify and when quantified are invariably estimates. Hence one must deal with a range of possible values, and consequently, as in any empirical work with a model, a large number of computations are necessary in order to evaluate variations in results as they are determined by variations in parameters or data. The outputs also present considerable and interesting problems of interpretation.

Simulation is subtle practically because obtaining input data can present problems. We have mentioned the problem of quantification. In addition, for analysing and interpreting settlement problems, scale is important; the number of settlements which need to be considered may be large, running into hundreds. This makes the use of computers essential, even if the mathematical models are extremely simple. The use of computers introduces further practical complications of course!

The purpose of a good model is to formulate simple concepts and hypotheses concerning them, and to demonstrate that despite their simplicity, they give approximate accounts of otherwise complex behaviour or phenomena. *If a model 'works'* (faithfully represents the known evidence) *then it shows that the assumptions and hypotheses built into the model contribute to an explanation of the phenomena.*

The aim of our model is to try to reproduce the settlement pattern in a fairly large area of central and southern Greece in the late Geometric period, using a small number of concepts and the small amount of data which is available. The basic concepts include site *size,* site *importance,* the *distance* between sites, and *interaction* between sites. Any explanation of an historical settlement pattern offered by the model will be exclusively in terms of these concepts and their hypothesised relationships.

The concept of interaction is modelled in a highly abstract sense; we make no assumptions about who or what is moving from A to B nor about purpose of movement. (The proper place for such conjectural details is during the interpretation of output, when the particular behaviour of the actors involved may be of concern.) The poleis and their predecessors were small societies coexisting side by side. By and large they spoke the same language, worshipped the same gods, and shared the same traditions as 'a people' (the nearest thing to a common history); interaction between them must have been relatively frequent. From sources of all periods we know that they begged, competed, fought, married, traded, travelled, worked and worshipped in, for or with other communities.

The hypotheses

Each site is considered as a place from which and to which interaction occurs. For clarity, a site is called an *origin zone* when it is considered as a place from which interaction originates, and a *destination zone* when it is considered as a place to which interaction is destined.

The basic hypotheses expressed in the model are that

(i) *interaction between any two places is proportional to the size of the origin zone and the importance and distance from the origin zone of all other sites in the survey area, which compete as destination zones;*

(ii) *the importance of a place is proportional to the interaction it attracts from other places.*

We require for each site an index or measure of its size and of its importance: its size is associated with its role as an origin zone; its importance is associated with its role as a destination zone. For its size, population is intuitively reasonable and is relatively easy to quantify, albeit as estimates. For its importance, however, population is not necessarily appropriate. To take an extreme example, Delphi's importance was not related to the number of its inhabitants. We need a more abstract index of the importance or attractiveness of a place; therefore we use the concept of resources. This too is modelled in a highly abstract sense; even the basic distinction between allocative and authoritative resources is left for the process of interpreting the output[1]. Clearly, getting numerical data for these components can be theoretically or practically problematic. We discuss this below in the section on data, where a further hypothesis is adduced which defers the need to tackle these problems, and mitigates them. This hypothesis results in a special case of our model which we call the egalitarian model; this is the model we apply to Geometric Greece.

---

[1] Allocative resources are *material* resources deriving from man's dominion over nature; the environment, physical artifacts and technologies.Authoritative resources are *non-material* resources deriving from the dominion of some people over others; the capability to organise or coordinate other people's activities. See Giddens 1979, 100f; 1984, 258-62, also 143f.

In order to 'fine-tune' the input data in the experimental evaluation of the model two further parameters are introduced, of which one relates to the distance between sites and the other to the resources available at a site. The former is used to simulate the ease or difficulty of communications, the latter to simulate the benefit or bane of a concentration of resources in one place.[1] These parameters are to be varied in the series of simulations. They are system variables, operating at the user-defined value right across the survey area. In varying them we seek an appropriate overall, or average, value.

Whilst we normally use these two parameters to vary the results, it simply is not the case that the model can produce any result one desires. To take an actual example, this model cannot reproduce in the same result a unified Attica and an independent Megara. The relatively vast polis of the Athenians can only be reproduced at parameter values which produce networks the size of regions, which is far too big a territory for a typical or even a large polis. Moreover, it is practically difficult (if not impossible) and more importantly it is theoretically invalid to try to manipulate the results to achieve some preconceived pattern.[2]

We assume for the purpose of modelling the settlement structure that the survey area is absolutely level and that the distance between sites is the shortest (i.e. straight-line) distance. This is a radical simplification of the real-world survey area and is completely counter-intuitive to historians trained to believe that the mountainous and

---

[1] 'Communications' is a very general concept covering both the means and the networks by which resources are transported from A to B. The resources in the real world may be, for example, people, goods or information; carried by foot, donkey, cart or ship. The network may be, for example, footpaths, roads, rivers or coastlines. 'Easing' communications in the simulation corresponds to real world improvements in the safety or convenience of movement brought about by, for example, peace, the partial or total elimination of bandits or pirates, better roads, or quicker or more reliable transport.

[2] It is probably impossible to alter significantly the 'performance' of one site without causing equally significant and probably undesirable side-effects on any other site, as the performance of each is interrelated to the performance of every other. We have experimented with this sort of manipulation and can assure readers that, partly because of these unpredictable side-effects, results are much better when the model operates on the egalitarian hypothesis.

fractured Greek landscape was in some way important to the development of the poleis. However, the actual landscape is to a large extent implicitly incorporated into the database through the location and density of settlements - none or few in mountainous or sterile areas, many or some in fertile and cultivable areas. It is nevertheless intriguing that this greatly simplifying assumption of an isotropic plain works as well as it does; all results discussed below assume it. In another application, we have modified this assumption (Rihll and Wilson, forthcoming).

The methods

These components and the hypotheses about their relationships are formalised and studied using mathematical methods known as *entropy-maximising methods* (see Gould 1972; Johnston 1979, 106-10; Thomas and Huggett 1980, 153-68; Wilson 1970). These methods are particularly useful in modelling types of social systems because they allow us to find the most probable overall state of the system whilst making the fewest possible assumptions about the particular actions and intentions of the people involved at the time. Entropy can be understood as an index of uncertainty - our uncertainty about the micro-level of the system being modelled, that is (in this case) the level of individual actors and actions. To maximise the entropy in a system is to maximise the possible configurations at the micro-level. The most probable overall state (or macro-state) is defined as that which results from the largest number of micro-states, of possible configurations.

For example, suppose that three people, A, B and C, move from place X to places Y and Z. If there are no constraints on the system - if, for examples, places X, Y and Z are equidistant and Y and Z are equally attractive destinations - then each of eight different possible configurations, or micro-states, of A, B and C's destinations are equally likely (see figure 2).These eight different configurations or micro-states result in four overall states or macro-states: 1. All three people go to Y and none to Z (= micro-state i); 2. Two go to Y and one to Z (= micro-states ii, iii and iv); 3. One goes to Y and two to Z (= micro-states v, vi and vii); and 4. None go to Y and all three go to Z (= micro-state viii). Macro-states 2 and 3 are more likely than macro-states 1 and 4 because 2 and 3 result from more micro-states.

Micro-states

	i	ii	iii	iv	v	vi	vii	viii
	Y Z	Y Z	Y Z	Y Z	Y Z	Y Z	Y Z	Y Z
A	1 0	1 0	1 0	0 1	1 0	0 1	0 1	0 1
B	1 0	1 0	0 1	1 0	0 1	1 0	0 1	0 1
C	1 0	0 1	1 0	1 0	0 1	0 1	1 0	0 1
	3 0	2 1	2 1	2 1	1 2	1 2	1 2	0 3

Macro-states

| 1 | 2 | 2 | 2 | 3 | 3 | 3 | 4 |

Figure 2: Micro- and macro-states

However, there are constraints on the system: for example, the size of the origin zone, the importance of the destination zone, and the distance involved. These constraints affect the definitions of possible micro-states and thus the likely macro-states. If, for example, Y is nearer than Z to X, and a constraint is imposed on the total distance travelled, then in more complex situations with larger numbers of travellers, the number of feasible macro-states like 2 will outnumber those like 3.

Thus the most probable overall state is at the same time the one about which we can be least certain at the level of historical configurations of actors and actions. Entropy-maximising methods accommodate the idea that at any point in history there are many possible futures, and that what generally happens is the (unintended) outcome of a multiplicity of contingent human actions.

Terminals and networks

Interaction is calculated between each site and every other in the analysis (not just near neighbours) according to the above hypotheses, each site being considered as an origin zone and then as a destination zone for every other site as it, in turn, is considered as an origin zone. (In fact the calculations are simultaneous, but the idea is essentially the same.) The total volume of interaction destined for a site may be called a site's credits. The volume of interaction which originates at a site - a figure which is constrained by the size of that site - we may call its debits. The largest single debit from a site can be compared with its total credit figure in order to establish settlement hierarchies. To be more precise:

(i)   if site A's greatest single debit is to site B, and this single figure is more than the total of A's credits, then A is a lower order settlement than B.

(ii) If site B's greatest single debit is to site C, and this single figure is less than the total of B's credits, then B is not a lower order settlement than C, and B is called a terminal.

Whereas A's debit to its 'chief creditor' B is more than all A's credits, B's debit to its 'chief creditor' C is less than all B's credits. To illustrate this idea dramatically, consider the units of interaction as people migrating: then this is to say that there are more emigrants from A to B than immigrants to A from everywhere, and fewer emigrants from B to C than immigrants to B.

By plotting links between each site and its chief creditor, except from terminals, we can identify settlement networks, each of which has one terminal, one centre. This way of representing results is based on the ideas of Nystuen and Dacey 1961. We extended this procedure so that interaction between an origin zone and its other creditors, as well as its chief creditor, can be presented graphically. Single debits at or above a user-defined percentage of the largest debit from any origin zone can be plotted to reveal visually more of the information contained in the results. For example, suppose that interaction from A to B is calculated at four units, and interaction from A to C at three units (see figure 3). If the user specifies that all debits at or above 75% of the maximum debit are to be plotted, then links will be drawn from A to B and from A to C. Consequently the figures reveal that whilst the maximum debit from A is to B, there is also a relatively significant debit from A to C. Or one might want to set the percentage very low, to see how extensive, if attenuated, a particular site's influence is; at or above 25%, links will be plotted from A to B, C, D and E.

Depending upon the scale and choice of the survey area (whether it is or is not a defined or definable territorial unit) a network may correspond to, for example, buildings within a settlement, settlements within a district, region or country, or settlements within a geographic area which is not coterminous with social or physical boundaries.

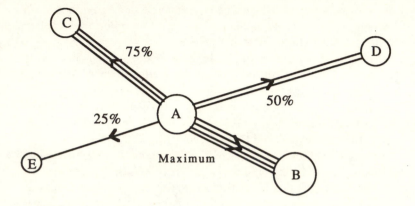

Figure 3: Proportion of maximum debit

The data

The survey area is part of central Greece; the period is the Geometric period. The area was chosen to include several major poleis about which a great deal is known to act as control sites, e.g. Athens and Corinth; two regions which are seriously neglected in the surviving documentary sources but which have recently received extensive archaeological attention, namely the the Argolid and Boiotia; and the general area in which the earliest poleis are thought to have emerged, i.e. the north-east Peloponnese. An extensive (but not exhaustive) search in 1985 revealed 109 sites within this area thought to have been occupied in the Geometric period (see figure 1).

For each site to be included in the analysis we need to know its location, and that it was inhabited in the period under consideration. The inclusion of sites which were not settlements but sanctuaries (or at least are renowned as the latter, even if there is evidence for habitation in the Geometric period, as in the case of Nemea for example) calls for comment at this point. Any study of the emergence of Greek poleis requires a definition of polis, however vague. One of the most fruitful contributions to this debate was the suggestion that the construction of a temple should be considered the watershed between pre-polis and polis status (Snodgrass 1977). Not all temples were built in settlements: two of the earliest stone temples in our survey area, namely the Argive Heraion and the temple of Poseidon at Isthmia, lie several kilometres from any settlement. This is consistent with the idea that the polis and its settlement hierarchy emerged through the unification of smaller units (synoikismos), rather than by the outward expansion and domination of a pre-existing principal settlement - originally at least.[1] These sanctuaries certainly attracted interaction; in some cases a considerable volume of it came from sites inside and outside the survey area.[2] Such sites should, therefore, be included in the analysis.

As stated above (Hypotheses), for each site in the analysis we require some figure to indicate its size and another to indicate its importance. In addition we require some figure to represent the ease or difficulty of communication across the survey area, and another to represent the benefit or bane of concentrated resources anywhere in the survey area. For ancient historians, this is a tall order. Even in the best-documented cases we can often only guess at the size of the population in a specific period. It is even more difficult to find numerical indices of settlement importance, the ease of communication, and the relative merits of concentrated resources. However, whilst our model needs numbers, we can begin, with the help of an additional hypothesis, by estimating them within the model.

In an extreme case we can start the simulation by assuming identical figures for the size and importance of each settlement and let the model determine distinctions between them by introducing a further hypothesis: that

(iii) *the size of a place is proportional to its importance.*

---

[1] For speculations on the role of non-settlement sanctuaries in the evolution of the polis see de Polignac 1984. One could argue that typically settlements incorporated by conquest were not considered part of the polis but subordinate to it, as seems to have been the case for some of the settlements in the Argive plain and was certainly the case for the Spartan perioikic communities.

[2] Dedications and debris at the Argive Heraion, for example, peak during the Geometric and Archaic periods, after which they very suddenly decline, see Waldstein 1902, especially 39; Mason 1976, 90 for summary. This suggests that its importance, in terms of attracting interaction from elsewhere, was greatest at this time.

This relatively innocuous hypothesis[1] in fact enables us to embed the entropy-maximising interaction model in a more powerful framework which allows site size and importance to be predicted.[2]

It should be noted that by using the model in this way we can assume that all sites were approximately equal in size and importance at the beginning of the period under consideration. This assumption we will call *the egalitarian hypothesis* and when applied to our model we will speak of *the egalitarian model*. Historically, of course, the sites were not equal in size, but in any case this hypothesis seems more valid than one that the Geometric settlement sizes approximated to those of the Classical period, about which we know little more (see further below).

The egalitarian model has two major advantages with respect to the data. First, the model is clearly independent of the evidence used to test the results: no data on site size or importance goes into it! The model does not 'know', for example, that Athens was bigger and more important than Plataia; all it knows is that there was a settlement at a place in Attica and there was another at a place in Boiotia. Second, we can use the model with a very inadequate database; all one needs to know about a site to include it in the simulation is its location. (One can even speculate about its occupation in the period under consideration by experimentation; by adding a dubious site and comparing the results with those of experiments using the same parameter values but without that site.) This gives the model a practical potential to identify important sites at a local or regional level, even if evidence is currently lacking, or exists but has yet to be organised or utilised to bear upon the problem posed. More concretely, the model can predict that sites which appear to be undistinguished were important (according to the criteria employed; see below) and, therefore, are worthy of closer investigation.

Thus by employing the egalitarian model we avoid the impossible task of gathering accurate quantitative data on the population and importance of the settlements investigated at the database construction stage. However, at the stage of testing and interpreting the results the same problem is just as acute, and apparently unavoidable. The output is necessarily quantitative, and approximate

[1] This hypothesis obviously requires a feedback loop in the programme.
[2] Cf. Harris and Wilson 1978, Wilson 1981, and the mathematical appendix.

in the same way that the input data is approximate. But historical judgments about the importance of, say, Khalkis, Corinth and Koroneia in the Geometric period are, and will probably remain, qualitative, based on more or less disparate quantities, qualities and types of evidence. We encounter the problem of assessing the model's results.

Assessing model output

As in any historical investigation of an hypothesis, we have an idea - perhaps only vague and certainly a tentative idea - of what it is we seek. Our model is designed to find the most probable *overall* settlement structure, and so it is ideas about the overall settlement structure in this area of Greece in late Geometric times which must be our guides.

The sites in our survey area fall into three broad categories:
(a) Those 'known' to have been important in the period in question, based on the qualitative and disparate types of evidence known to us. Although different scholars may accord different emphases to different items of evidence, a consensus may be expected on a number of the 'most important' sites. In this case, we expect agreement on the inclusion of Argos, Athens, Khalkis, Corinth and Thebes in the category of the, say, ten most important sites. (b) Those 'known' to have been unimportant[1] in the relevant period (debatable in the same way as the most important sites), e.g. Aulis, Eutresis, Kreusis, Perakhora, Potniai, Skhoinos, Zygouries. (c) Those which have been largely neglected by historians (ancient and modern) and archaeologists - the majority of the sites - whose relative importance is very difficult to ascertain. Amongst these are capitals of poleis or other territorial associations and a handful of individual settlements which were autonomous, at least for some of their known history, e.g. Akraiphnion, Anthedon, Haliartos, Kleonai, Kopai, Koroneia, Lebedeia, Megara, Mykenai, Nauplia, Orkhomenos, Oropos, Phlious, Plataia, Sikyon, Tanagra, Thespiai, Thisbe, and large non-capital

---

[1] It is difficult to identify somewhere as definitely unimportant as most sites are poorly served by surviving literary evidence and an archaeologically dull site is not likely to be excavated - those which are tend, for several and delicate reasons, to be sites which were important in another period.

settlements such as Akharnai, Myrrhinous and Tenea. It is about the sites in this category that the model may make predictions, given its power to identify the more important sites in the survey area. For if a series of results is 'correct' for the majority of those sites and networks about which we have good information, then they are *probably* 'correct' for those sites about which we know relatively little. One practical application of the model is to use its results to direct further historical and archaeological investigation toward particular known and little-known sites which are simulated as likely to have been more important than hitherto suspected.

Intrinsic to the nature of modelling is the performance of a large number of simulations to establish a range of results worthy of analysis. In our model the parameters used to simulate the ease/difficulty of communication (β) and the benefit/bane of concentrated resources (α) are used both to search for historically significant settlement patterns and then to focus them. It may be helpful to think of this process as analogous to focusing a microscope, where one must search for biological structures of interest on the slide, and bring them into sharp focus for close examination. We systematically work through a range of different parameter values, locating those which give historically acceptable results, which we then focus through finer variation.

Crude and initial criteria for acceptance of a result of a simulation include

(i)   a positive shortlist of control sites which we would consider to be the most important sites; category (a) above. We expect these sites to be amongst the most important of the hundred and nine in a simulation;

(ii)   a negative shortlist of control sites which we would consider to be the least important sites; category (b) above. We expect these sites to be identified as unimportant in a simulation;

(iii)   the correct identification of terminals, for we expect an emergent capital to be a terminal within a network;

(iv)   the network should correspond approximately to the historical structure of that polis or territorial association.

Any results which are not sufficiently 'accurate' according to the above criteria are rejected.

Since the model finds the overall settlement structure which is most probable given the initial structure and the parameter values chosen, it is unlikely that any result will be 'correct' in every detail, even allowing for the lax definition of 'accurate' which we must employ. But if the settlement patterns and, in particular, the centres which emerge at different stages of centralisation of the survey area are quite regular, with only minor variations over a series of simulations using significantly different parameter values (e.g. one or more settlements on the fringe of a network appear aligned instead with a neighbouring network, or isolated in their own territory; the centre shifts from one site to a neighbouring site, or becomes a subsystem centre in a larger network), then it confirms the probability of the basic structure, for it emerges as the most probable outcome even under different communication and resource conditions. That is why it is important to assess individual results as elements in a series of results.

A good result will identify as important sites the majority of those on the positive shortlist, and as unimportant the majority of those on the negative shortlist. In practice, in pioneering work of this kind and given the minimal input data, many scientists would be content with 40% accuracy. However, the data and the criteria by which they can assess accuracy are normally much fuller and more rigorous than we are able to adopt, and so we aim for 50% or better. If most of the positive control sites consistently appear in the ten most important sites and are identified as terminals or subcentres, and the negative control sites do not, then the hypotheses and assumptions expressed in the model are sufficient to explain the historical prominence or indistinction of those sites. If most of the networks consistently correspond to the historical settlement hierarchies at any one broad territorial level (e.g. small, medium, large), then the hypotheses and assumptions expressed in the model are sufficient to explain the formation and structure of those networks.

We then have to consider those sites and networks for which the same good overall results are in their cases 'incorrect' - particularly those for which the results are consistently 'incorrect'. Let us call them singular sites or networks. A site's result may be incorrect in one of two ways: it may be simulated to be more important than the record suggests, or it may be simulated to be less important than the record suggests. It is rather more complicated for an incorrect network, which may be simulated to be more extensive, more intense, less extensive or less intense than the record suggests.

There are five possible reasons for consistently incorrect results for a site:

(i)   the model is insufficient to explain that site's historical prominence/indistinction;

(ii)   the input data for each site is inadequate. The egalitarian hypothesis must be abandoned and differentials in site size at the beginning of the period in question must somehow be reflected in the input data;

(iii) the prominence/indistinction of that site as it appears in the historical or archaeological record is exaggerated/underrated;[1]

(iv)   the area in which the site lies has been unusually thoroughly surveyed/neglected relative to neighbouring areas or the survey area as a whole, so that there are disproportionately many/few sites in that area;

(v)   a site's prominence may derive from its position in a network which is, in our terminology, local, regional, national, or global. If its historical prominence derived from an area larger than or outside the survey area then it may not perform as well in simulation as it is expected to do. In such a case the extent to which it falls short of expectations in simulation may indicate the extent to which it attracted interaction from outside the survey area.

There are also five possible reasons for consistently incorrect results for a network:

---

[1]   This is a knotty problem. Consider the archaeological and literary evidence on Sparta, for example, which might have been a puzzle had not a passage of Thucydides survived: 'Suppose, for example, that the polis of Sparta were to become deserted ...' (1.10.2). What Thucydides did not predict was the capacity of literary evidence to mislead later generations merely by its unrepresentative production and survival, irrespective of the degree of bias of its content.

(i)   the model is insufficient to explain that network's extent or coherence;

(ii) as for sites;

(iii) the extent or coherence of that network as it appears in the historical record is exaggerated/underrated;

(iv) as for sites;

(v)   the topography of that area cannot be ignored. Either the barriers are so great or the routes so easy that some modification to the assumed isotropic plain is necessary to 'correct' the distances between sites inside and outside the area in question.

For any particular site or network reason (i) may be elaborated by known historical circumstances; for example, frequent or intense interaction between two sites may have been conducted most often under arms. Until resolved (if ever) there may consequently have been a fiercely observed, if mobile, border between the sites in question which is not explained by the model and consequently not reflected in the results. The most obvious example of this in our survey area is Khalkis and Eretria. Other examples in different survey areas would probably be Mantinea and Tegea, or Elis and Pisa.

3   Results

We now consider some results, recorded in figures 4 to 7, starting with a relatively devolved structure and proceeding towards a more centralised one. We only consider results which are acceptable according to the criteria stated above. In particular, we will not normally discuss sites appearing on the positive or negative shortlists, as satisfaction of the criteria for the majority of those sites is a prerequisite for acceptance of a result. Therefore most of the discussion will concern category (c) sites - those whose relative historical importance is uncertain, and singular sites and networks.

The legend for each figure gives the parameter values which produced the result: the smaller the β value, the easier communication across the survey area is simulated to be; the larger the α value, the greater the benefit of concentrated resources is simulated to be. Small β or large α tend to produce centralised structures; large β or small α tend to produce devolved structures. Also given is the number (Tn) of terminals (and therefore networks) predicted; this acts as a rough guide to the degree of centralisation in the survey area as a whole. The legend also carries the percentage of the largest single debit from any origin zone at or above which debits are plotted from origin zone to destination zone. The best compromise between a desire to see overlapping spheres of influence or dependence both within and between networks and a desire for clarity is 75%, so most figures conform to this standard. A site's maximum debit determines to which network it belongs (unless it is a terminal); such links are marked with an arrow where confusion could arise. This allows us to sketch the approximate line of the boundary between networks, even in relatively densely settled areas. The predicted rank of terminals, and occasionally other high-ranking but non-terminal sites, is given on the plot in larger figures (the small figures are the site numbers).

Consider figure 4. It shows thirteen networks. Given that all sites have identical input data, except their locations of course, and no modifications to the isotropic plain have been made, it is remarkable that even at this low level of centralisation the model should identify among the most important sites in the area Khalkis, Athens, the Argive Heraion, Thebes, Nauplia and Koroneia.

We also seem to have three 'near misses'. Nisaia is the simulated terminal instead of Megara just to the north. There may be several reasons why the terminal identification here is consistently incorrect, but the most obvious would seem to be our ignorance of this area and the relatively tiny number of known sites therein (reason [iv]). Koukouvaones is simulated to be the terminal in the area of Akharnai, where current hypotheses would prefer to see Menidi, just to the west; the identification is not secure but is based on the number of inscriptions concerning Akharnai found in the churches and houses of Menidi (Eliot 1976, 6). Finally Kromna is identified instead of Corinth, just to the west; this is particularly interesting. Since Roebuck's paper in 1972, reconciling the achievements of early Corinth with the site of early Corinth has been a well publicised problem. Kromna, situated approximately half way between Corinth and Isthmia, is as yet unexcavated. Extensive residential remains were discovered in 1960, and large cemeteries nearby: it was a substantial

settlement. The sherd-scatter suggested that it had been occupied for
about a thousand years, from at least the seventh century BC to the
fourth AD. Sporadic excavation over three days in 1938 turned up
nine poros sarcophagi (amongst other things), and a single grave
excavated in 1960 contained some 26 vases of fine quality closely

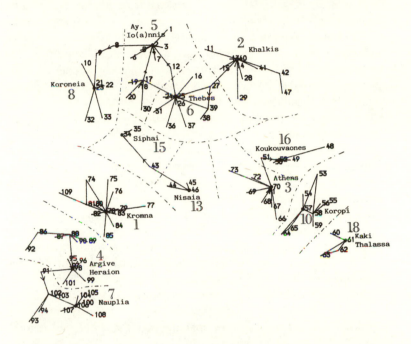

Figure 4: $\alpha = 1.025$ $\beta = 0.25$ T = 13 $\geq 75\%$ max. debit

dated to 560 BC.[1] Perhaps the collection of villages which was
'Corinth' in the early colonising period (Roebuck 1972, 101-3) was
more dispersed than commonly assumed. This site is predicted
regularly by the model as an alternative to Corinth in the company of
Athens, Thebes, and Argos or the Heraion, and some investigation of
the site and environs may prove worthwhile.

Another apparently anomalous 'important' site, Ay. Io(a)nnis, is
hardly known. It possesses a huge fortress, larger than Tiryns (Hope

[1] Wiseman 1978, 66. Wiseman 1976, 470 for summary; also Salmon
1984, 24, 35, 156.

Simpson 1965, 118), but has not yet been excavated. Koropi (ancient Sphettos) likewise is little known. One of the original twelve to synoikise with Athens (Strabo 9.1.20), it is the provenance of one of the most luxurious Geometric vases ever found (the Stathatou amphora, Coldstream 1977, 133).

Koroneia's network is somewhat anomalous. Koroneia is regularly simulated to be the terminal in a network stretching broadly north-south from Orkhomenos to Thisbe and Khorsia. She was an independent and fairly important state, and interacted frequently with Orkhomenos - often under arms. And whilst she seems to have preserved her independence into Classical times, perhaps in alliance with Lebedeia and Haliartos,[1] it was Thespiai, rather than Koroneia as in the simulation, which managed to subdue Thisbe when she did not retain independence (i.e. between 447 and 379 BC).[2] This erroneous network seems to be a consequence of the boundary of the survey area (which is a specific and drastic case of reason [iv] for incorrect networks), for the interests of Orkhomenos, situated right on our north-west boundary, went principally to the north and west, to Phokis and Thessaly, rather than to the south and east. The survey area is in Orkhomenos' case unfortunate and produces misleading results, both for herself and, to a lesser extent, for Koroneia: it would be interesting to compare the results with those of a survey area encompassing Phokis and Lokris (East and West).

Note the position of Nauplia before we leave this result. A member of the Kalaurian Amphiktyony, Nauplia is shown here as the terminal in a network of sites spanning both sides of the Argolid Gulf, including Asine, Tiryns, and Hysiai in the Thyreatis. If we lower the β parameter to simulate easier communications we see, in the next result (figure 5), that Nauplia is still a terminal but in a much reduced network consisting only of herself, Pronaia and Asine on the eastern bank.[3] Nauplia's loss is Argos' gain - not the Heraion's; Argos is now identified as a secondary centre in the

[1]   Hell.Oxy. 13.1; translation and commentary of § 11 (the Boiotian constitution) is conveniently available in Moore 1983, 127-34. See also Thucydides 4.93.4, and Roesch 1965, 37f.

[2]   Hennig 1974, Roesche 1965. Thisbe had a common border with Thespiai and Koroneia, Strabo 9.2.29.

[3]   Note that the parameter reflecting the benefit of concentrated resources (α) is also lower (i.e. less benefit) in this result.

network. Historically, Argive territory extended down the west bank
to Hysiai at least by c.669 BC when the Spartans there suffered a
heavy defeat (Pausanias 2.24.7). The Messenian Wars seem to have
given the Argives cause or excuse for conflict with the communities

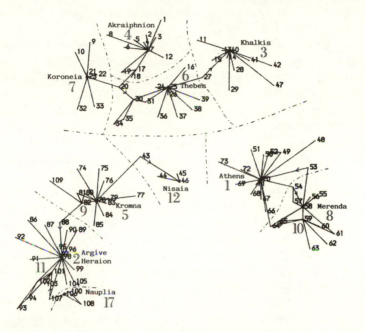

Figure 5: α = 1.005 β = 0.175 T = 10 ≥ 75% max. debit

in this southern Argolid network (later legend has it that Argos
supported the Helots and then the Messenians, whilst Asine and
Nauplia were allies of Sparta).[1] Argos ultimately defeated or subdued
them; the Asinians around 710 BC (Coldstream 1977, 154, 163), and
Nauplia during the latter half of the next century. Although the
sources[2] - which are very late - say that Nauplia was sacked and her

[1] According to Pausanias (4.27.8, 35.2) the Asinians and Nauplians
were allowed to continue to live in their new settlements (New Asine and
Mothone) in Messenia after its liberation; from this we deduce that their
allegedly pro-Spartan stance did not extend to subjugation of the
Messenians, at least in living memory.

[2] Strabo 8.6.11; also Pausanias 2.36.5; 3.7.4; 4.24.4.

people, like the Asinians, evicted, modern scholars are sceptical. Her history henceforth is meagre, but archaeological evidence suggests that she 'continued to exist, and possibly to flourish' (Tomlinson 1972, 44; see also 77). Not surprisingly the simulation fails to account for the fall of Asine, but suggests that the Nauplians' strength (relative to their neighbours) was their strategic position - strategic at least until the development of Temenion.

Other things to notice in comparison with the previous result (cf. figures 4 and 5) is that easier communications produce three fewer systems; two fewer in Attica and one fewer in Boiotia. The network centred on Athens now incorporates the system which centred near Akharnai; unification in the north of Attica produces one very dominant centre, Athens. Unification in the south of Attica, however, produces two nearly equal and neighbouring centres. The centre in the Mesogeia is pulled ESE from Koropi to Merenda (ancient Myrrhinous), and just to the south there is a secondary centre, only slightly less important, at Kalyvia (ancient Prospalta). Merenda, the new terminal, has an impressive archaeological record for Geometric times. Two vases reckoned with the Stathatou amphora as the most luxurious of their time were found here (Coldstream 1977, 133) and to date three cemeteries have been excavated: one described as 'vast' and another which has produced (amongst other things) an archaic kouros and kore (Leekley and Noyes 1976, 19).

In the Korinthia we see a similar dual focus pattern emerging. Kromna's influence is clearly diminished with the emergence of Corinth as a secondary centre. Kleonai (site no. 88) also deserves attention in this region. A subregional centre of an east-west network in figure 4, Kleonai is in both results united with the Argive network (although interaction between herself and Corinth is quite strong, >75% of the chief debit) which is consistent with her historical loyalties and, interestingly, contrary to the geography, i.e. topography of the area and the relative distances involved. This somewhat surprising historical alliance, reproduced in the result, has been noted by Tomlinson (1972, 29) and Adshead (1986, 4f., 35), who offer a political explanation. Note also in this respect Krommyon (site no. 77), which the simulations always unite with the Corinthian network. According to Strabo (8.6.22) Krommyon was in Corinthian territory, though it once belonged to Megara. Pottery and burial practices of Geometric date have been found to be almost wholly Corinthian (Coldstream 1977, 85f.; Salmon 1984, 25,

48), and there are no extant finds dated earlier than c.800 BC. This inevitably raises a question mark over the accuracy of Strabo's information. On the other hand we know very little of Megarian burial practices, or indeed, of anything Megarian in the Geometric period, when Megara is known better for her settlements abroad than in her homeland.[1]

The western sector of the Theban network has a subordinate centre at Thespiai (site no. 30), serving as the regional centre over Askra, Eutresis, Kreusis and Siphai. Thespiai was a large and independent state until Classical times; her decline was synchronous, not coincidentally, with the rise of Thebes. Her territory included Askra, Eutresis, Kreusis, and until c.386 Siphai (which gained independence only for a short time). According to Herodotos (5.79.2) Thespiai was a close friend of Thebes and had long been so, though presumably was not by 423 when Thebes destroyed her city walls.[2]

In the north of the survey area Akraiphnion is simulated to be a very important site. This is particularly interesting in view of the fact that, though long known to archaeologists, it has become a familiar name only recently. The cemeteries began to receive serious attention in 1974, and were quickly recognised as one of the most exciting discoveries of the decade in Greek archaeology. After one season some 400 richly furnished graves had been excavated, containing over 2,000 vases from Attica, Euboia and Korinthia, as well as from other areas of Boiotia. By 1986 the total number of graves revealed was in excess of 1,100.[3]The excavations and finds still await proper publication, so a detailed comparison with other sites is not yet possible, but this figure can be roughly compared with that of dated graves in Athens and Attica between c.1000-500 BC: namely, 1,226 (Morris 1987, Appendix 1). Had Akraiphnion not recently received this attention, which it clearly deserves, the model results would have suggested it as a prime site for investigation.

---

[1] Legon 1981 for regional survey; Biers 1976, 565 for summary; also Genière 1983.

[2] Roesch 1965, *ibid*. 1976, 101; Fiehn 1936. The Cambridge/Bradford Boiotia Expedition estimate the size of Thespiai at 140 ha., *AReps* 1986/7, 23f. See also the fuller account in Bintliff and Snodgrass 1985.

[3] Cf. *AAA* 7 (1974) 325-38; 10 (1977) 273-86; *AReps* 1974/5, 18; 1975/6, 16; 1980-81, 22. The 1986 figure was reported to me by Steve Hodkinson (pers. comm.).

Whether its performance in simulation is accurate in historical terms remains to be seen. The evaluation need not be confined to the city (not yet excavated) however: the Ptoion, about 2 kilometres east of Akraiphnion, calls for consideration here. Excavated intermittently by the French School for over a century, this double sanctuary (to Apollo Ptoios and the hero Ptoios) is well known. It very suddenly burst into life c. 640-620 BC. The imposing dedications, which include numerous marble kouroi and korai, bronze tripods, plaques and statuettes, suggest that the Archaic period was one of great prosperity in this region, and that the sanctuary was one of great importance (Schachter 1981, 52-73). By identifying Akraiphnion as one of the most important late Geometric settlements, the model goes some way to explain the 'unheralded' and dramatic development of the Ptoion sanctuary in the Archaic period.

Figure 6 shows the effect of increasing the simulated benefit of concentrated resources; the ease of communication is simulated to be the same as in figure 5. This change in conditions has scant effect in the northern half of the survey area, but causes a small number of significant changes in the southern half, including the absorption of two networks into larger neighbouring networks.

Corinth, Kalyvia and Argos benefit most from the different circumstances, in terms both of overall rankings (Corinth 9 - 1; Kalyvia 10 - 3; Argos 11 - 4) and of becoming the terminal in their respective networks (cf. figures 5 and 6). Nisaia and Nauplia suffer most, losing independence as their networks are incorporated into those of Athens and Argos respectively - Nisaia does retain secondary centre status, however. Kromna and Merenda also do much less well in the different circumstances of the simulation, losing terminal status and rank importance in their respective networks. The Argive Heraion remains an important centre but becomes subordinate to Argos.

Elsewhere in the survey area the settlement hierarchy and structure remains much the same, except that Thespiai loses subordinate centre status. Negligible changes in overall rankings occur and a handful of sites are aligned instead with neighbouring networks: Eleon with Thebes instead of Khalkis, Askra with Akraiphnion (via Medeon) instead of Thebes (via Thespiai), Siphai and Kreusis with Koroneia instead of Thebes (via Thespiai), Spata with Athens instead of Merenda, and Kleonai, Zygouries and Tenea with Corinth instead of the Argive Heraion. Note that half of these sites (Eleon, Askra,

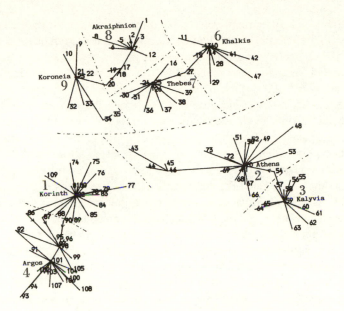

Figure 6: α = 1.05 β = 0.175 T = 8 ≥ 75% max. debit

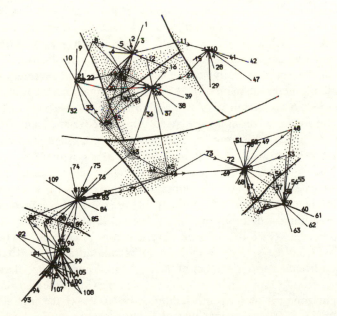

Figure 7: α = 1.05 β = 0.175 T = 8 ≥ 25% max. debit

Spata and Zygouries) are simulated to interact at least 75% as much with their former network as they do with their present one.

The overlapping and competing spheres of influence which the model simulates are revealed by plotting more of the debits for thesame result, which also helps to explain the changes in more detail. This is done in figure 7, which shows the same result as figure 6, but all of the simulated interaction debits from any origin zone (except terminals) which are 25% or more of the maximum debit from that origin zone have been plotted. Border zones are stippled where interaction goes over the border to a site in a neighbouring network; the density of the stippling is determined by the number of borders crossed (the maximum number is three, in the areas of Siphai [site no. 34] and Pagai [site no. 43]).

Almost all borders are fuzzy. Consider the Megarid which, whilst not identified as an independent network at these parameter values, is identified as an area of complex affiliations. Although its major interaction is simulated to be with Athens, at least 25% of that volume goes to Corinth, and at least another 25% goes to Thebes. By plotting other percentages we are able to calculate that about 55% of the interaction from Nisaia goes to Athens, and about 20% each to Corinth and Thebes. When an origin zone's interaction is dissipated like this, it would suggest that, unless some very powerful interests intervene, such a site's attachment or commitment to any particular terminal would be correspondingly weak. This also illustrates how the model simulates a large centre some distance from the origin zone attracting more interaction than a small site much nearer to it: it is the more distant terminals, Athens, Corinth and Thebes which attract interaction from Nisaia, whilst Nisaia attracts between 25 and 49% of the maximum debit from the closer but less important sites on the borders of their networks, Eleusis (site no. 73) and Krommyon.

The spheres of influence of the six highest-ranking terminals at these parameter values are summarised in Table 1. The complex relationship between the number of sites and the intensity of interaction in determining a terminal's (and any site's) rank importance is clearly indicated here. Khalkis' priority over Thebes arises from the greater volume of interaction attracted to Khalkis, albeit from a smaller number of sites, than is attracted to Thebes, albeit from a larger number of sites. The maximum debit from an origin zone can vary from, theoretically, 100% of the interaction leaving it to 40% or thereabouts, and a 100% credit from a small site may be less in volume, and therefore less significant, than a 20% credit from a large one. To complicate matters further, a subordinate centre may compete with the terminal for interaction from sites in and out of the network; it may also extend the territory of the network to which it belongs.

These effects are made more apparent by tabulating such

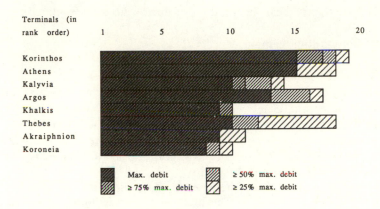

Table 1: Number of sites over which terminal exercises influence

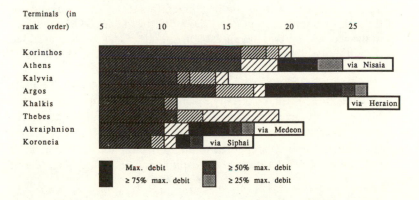

Table 2: Number of sites over which terminal exercises influence (indirectly)

subsystems separately, see Table 2. The subordinate centre Nisaia attracts maximum debits from three sites and brings them into the Athenian network, thus extending it west. But these sites' interaction debits go to Nisaia, not to Athens, and do not contribute directly to Athens' importance.[1] The relationships between Medeon and Akraiphnion and between Siphai and Koroneia are similar. In the Argolid, however, the Heraion is clearly a competitor with Argos for interaction from sites in the north and mid Argolid (also demonstrated in simulations which identify it rather than Argos as the terminal).

4 Concluding remarks

The model simulates settlement growth through a series of iterations from an initial egalitarian state: the hypothesis is that initially all sites are approximately equal in size and importance. Interaction between them is first simulated on the hypothesis that it is related to the distance between each site and every other. (Since at this stage all the sites are equal, the size of the origin zone and the importance of the destination zone are irrelevant.)

The communications parameter (β) determines the radius of any site's effective influence. The number of sites within that radius, combined with their proximity to the site in question and to all the other sites in their radii, determines the volume of interaction which arrives at the site. This gives a total credit figure for each site. The differential credit figures are then used to assign input values of size and importance for each site in the next iteration; i.e. the results of the first iteration are used to set the input for the next. Consequently in the second iteration the interaction hypothesis takes account of the (hypothetical) size of the origin zone and the (hypothetical) importance, as well as the distance, of the destination zones.

The degree to which the results are considered historically accurate is the degree to which these hypotheses are sufficient to explain the historical settlement structure. In answer to our original questions, the results show that location had a very significant effect on settlement affiliation and union in the formation and development of poleis; on the development of the capital; and on the development of

[1]   They contribute to Athens' importance only in so far as they make Nisaia a relatively large site on the first iteration, and this in turn makes Nisaia's debit to Athens in the second iteration more voluminous than that from a site at the same distance but simulated to be of smaller size.

some capitals in 'great' cities. The relative importance of Athens, Corinth, Argos, Thebes and Khalkis in the historical period need not be 'explained' by the supposition, implicit or explicit, that they were always (or at least, in the period *before* the period under consideration) relatively important: it can be explained largely by their location *vis-à-vis* other Geometric period sites. The sites in the survey area patently were not approximately equal in size in the early Geometric period. However, the fact that the egalitarian hypothesis reproduces the historical structure of the late Geometric/early Archaic period reasonably well suggests that those differences in size were not significant in political development, and it demonstrates that the historical structure can be largely explained without reference to them.

The Mesogeia area of Attica is the only outstanding error, where the simulations consistently predict the emergence of an important centre. Two reasons immediately present themselves to explain this error. First, the series of results shows that, whilst Athens is consistently identified as the terminal in the north Attica network, the terminal in the south Attica network is variously Sphettos (site no. 57), as in figure 4, Myrrhinous (no. 58), as in figure 5, or Keratea (no. 59) as in figure 6. Historically there may have been considerable competition between these sites for dominance in the area, which weakened the influence of each, whilst Athens' influence was unconstrained by any effective competitor in her area. This could conceivably underlie the second reason: that when the Athenians synoikised, they chose Athens as their 'capital'. In this case it would be interesting to compare the results with those of a survey area which covered the Archaic period, as a strong settlement produces its own penumbra of subordinate settlements. An important further experiment would be to see whether the inclusion of input data on late Geometric/early Archaic site size and importance would better reproduce the historical settlement structure than does the egalitarian hypothesis.

The period of analysis is important, since in Boiotia, to take another example, the early league (if 'league' is an appropriate word for the loose and informal grouping which it seems to have been) evolved in the sixth century, and the strong league with Thebes at its head was not in operation until about 447 (Demand 1982, 16-20). In order to model that settlement structure the sites in the survey area should be those of Classical, not Geometric, date.

There are basically three kinds of benefit to be gained from building a simulation model (Aldenderfer 1981).

1. *Conceptual*. Model building demands explicit structure and a clarity which forces one to rethink current concepts and assumptions, and to do so at the start of the exercise. It was at this stage, for example, that the weaknesses in the concepts polis and 'city' became painfully apparent. The problem had to be redefined; this redefinition involved the employment of the concepts of site size, site importance, resources, terminals and networks.

2. *Developmental*. This is the benefit arising from trying to translate a verbal hypothesis into a mathematical model, or, as in this case, trying to simplify and generalise a mathematical model and the verbal hypotheses it expresses to suit a society, space, and time very different from that for which it was originally developed. Either way, the process forces the model builder to give clear and sharp expression to his or her ideas and the relationships between them, and to work through the hypotheses in a consistent and coherent manner.

3. *Output*. This is the benefit which may arise if the model has been successfully tested and the results may be expected to be realistic, that is, usable. This model seems to have predictive power, but it cannot be demonstrated until sites which are consistently simulated by the model to be important, notably Akraiphnion and Kromna, are excavated.

The major benefits of model building at this time are, we believe, in the conceptual and developmental areas. Stale or inappropriate concepts, unfounded or unjustifiable assumptions, poorly formulated or poorly grasped hypotheses, gaps in knowledge or data, are all brought into sharp focus in the attempt to build a model, irrespective of whether or not it ultimately 'works'.

A model directs attention not toward what happened, but to why it happened. The aim is to construct a set of simple hypotheses which emphasise significant features of the system under consideration and which, when rigorously pursued, reproduce what happened. Our model has emphasised the features of space and interdependence; the interdependence of settlements within a polity and of polities within a region. We have emphasised space by initially and literally making 'all other things equal'. We have emphasised interdependence by making the differentiation of all other things dependent on interaction across space. The hypotheses in our model are simple, general, and abstract; the explanations it can offer are in consequence general and abstract. They aim to be sufficient, not complete, explanations of the norm, the trend, without which the peculiar and the remarkable in history cannot be appreciated.

Our apparent disregard for so-called 'urban theory' is based not on disciplinary parochialism or rampant empiricism (cf. Finley, 1985, 61-6), but on the futility of the majority of this difficult and often sophistic literature for students of ancient society. For a city does not exist independently of the society which produces it, and urban studies tend in consequence to be about society as a whole. The attempt to identify distinctively 'urban' phenomena (now abandoned) amounted to an attempt to identify a distinctively urban type of society, and problems with the definition of 'urban' left only the sort of societies traditionally studied by anthropologists out of the reckoning. (It is symptomatic of the field that in recent theoretical work what is properly called 'the sociology of consumption' continues to go by the name of 'urban sociology' in order to preserve intellectual continuity with earlier studies: Saunders 1985, 289.) Less ambitious theoretical and empirical work continues on types of city (and society), principally four types: the primary city (or 'first cities', e.g. Adams 1966, Wheatley 1971); the medieval city (e.g. Hohenberg and Lees 1985, Holton 1986); the contemporary city in post-industrialised nations (e.g. Berg 1982, Saunders 1985); or the contemporary city in underdeveloped or developing nations (e.g. McGee 1971, Reissman 1964). In each of these cases significant features of ancient society (such as those mentioned below) are largely or wholly absent, and the emphases are instead on features alien to and largely inappropriate to ancient society.

We have considered the city not as an urban form but as a locus of social interaction, a place where allocative and authoritative resources are concentrated and focused; our concern has been with the whole scatter of settlements rather than with the known centres (see Finley 1983, 5f.). Our model takes account of the theoretical desideratum to consider a polis not as a closed community, isolated in space and time, but as an open community interdependent to greater or lesser degree on other contemporary communities. Poleis were autonomous societies - or tried to be. But however much they disliked the fact, they were not independent, and they knew it: a common way of canvassing support when under threat was to point out the consequences of the plaintiff polis's defeat for other poleis - both for those which threatened it and for those which might support it (e.g. Thucydides 1.32-36; 1.120-24).

We believe that this approach begins to realise settlement archaeology's great potential for understanding social process and change (Snodgrass 1984, 229, and more generally Snodgrass 1987).

One of the most important tasks ahead in this kind of research lies in the construction of models (mathematical and non-mathematical) of other aspects of the ancient city, or more broadly, ancient settlement. This is necessary to identify more constraints which could be introduced into this model to produce an even better correspondence between the simulated results and the 'facts' as we know them, and thus to refine the hypotheses expressed in the model and the explanations it can offer. Very significant and distinctive features of ancient society which are pertinent include: land-ownership as a correlate of citizenship, where citizenship was neither universal (before AD 212 in theory at least) nor trite; 'hinterland' - however tiny - as a correlate of settlement - however tiny; and scale: polities huge by the standards of the time and the culture, such as Athens, which covered an area tiny by our standards - in this case smaller than the West Riding of Yorkshire. We need to construct a model to explain the size of networks or poleis: why c.70 sq. miles was the average size, and why some poleis were significantly smaller or considerably larger than this.

Acknowledgements

A version of this paper was presented at a seminar on the Ancient City at Leicester University; we wish to thank the participants for their comments. The paper has also benefited from full and constructive criticism by the editors. In addition, we wish to thank J.V. Tucker for extensive discussions on the scope and limits of models in historical contexts, and detailed criticism on the penultimate draft.

Mathematical Appendix: spatial interaction and location model

$$I_{ij} = A_i O_i W_j^{\alpha} e^{-\beta c_{ij}} \tag{1}$$

where

$$A_i = 1/\sum_k W_k^{\alpha} e^{-\beta c_{ik}} \tag{2}$$

Calculation of $\{W_j\}$: calculate [1] using a set of guessed starting values for W_j (for egalitarian start, set all values equal). Calculate

$$D_j = \sum_i I_{ij} \tag{3}$$

where D_j is the total credit to j. If $D_j > W_j$, the simulated credit to j is greater than the original guess, and the hypothesis is that W_j should be increased; if $D_j < W_j$ then it is less than the original guess and should be decreased. At equilibrium, we require

$$D_j = W_j \tag{4}$$

So, substitute for D_j from [3]

$$\sum_i I_{ij} = W_j \tag{5}$$

and for I_{ij} from [1] and [2]

$$\sum_i \frac{O_i W_j^{\alpha} e^{-\beta c_{ij}}}{\sum_k W_k^{\alpha} e^{-\beta c_{ik}}} = W_j \tag{6}$$

These non-linear simultaneous equations can be solved for given values of α and β to give $\{W_j\}$, the spatial pattern of settlement size. For the feedback version, $\{W_j^F\}$, set O_i equal to W_i and rerun.

Notation

I_{ij}	=	interaction from i, the origin zone, to j, the destination zone
O_i	=	the size of i
W_j	=	the resources at (or attractiveness of) j
c_{ij}	=	the distance from i to j
α	=	a parameter reflecting the benefit of concentrated resources
β	=	a parameter reflecting the ease of communications
$e^{-\beta c}{}_{ij}$	=	a negative exponential function arising from entropy-maximising methods and having the same effect as a distance-decay function.

Bibliography

Abrams, P. (1982), *Historical Sociology.* Shepton Mallet.

Adams, R.M. (1966), *The Evolution of Urban Society, Early Mesopotamia and Prehispanic Mexico.* Chicago.

Adshead, K. (1986), *Politics of the Archaic Peloponnese.* Aldershot.

Aldenderfer, M.S. (1981), 'Computer simulation for archaeology', *Simulations in Archaeology,* ed. J.A. Sabloff. Albuquerque.

Berg, L. van den *et al.* (1982), *Urban Europe: A Study of Growth and Decline,* vol. 1. Oxford.

Biers, W.R. (1976), *Princeton Encyclopaedia of Classical Sites,* 565 sv. Megara.

Binford, L.R. (1983), *In Pursuit of the Past.* London.

Bintliff, J.L. and Snodgrass, A.M. (1985), 'The Cambridge/Bradford Boiotia Expedition: the first four years', *Journal of Field Archaeology* 12, 123-61.

Butzer, K.W. (1982), *Archaeology as Human Ecology.* Cambridge.

Carlstein, T., Parkes, D. and Thrift, N. (eds.) (1978), *Making Sense of Time.* London.

Clarke, M. and Wilson, A.G. (1985), 'The dynamics of urban spatial structure: the progress of a research programme', *Transactions of the Institute of British Geographers* 10, 427-51.

Coldstream, J.N. (1977), *Geometric Greece.* London.

Demand, N. (1982), *Thebes in the Fifth Century*. London.

Eliot, C.W.J. (1976), *Princeton Encyclopaedia of Classical Sites*, 6 sv. Acharnai.

Febvre, L. (1922), *La Terre et l'évolution humaine, introduction géographique à l'histoire*. Paris.

Fiehn (1936), *RE* 6A 37-59 s.v. Thespeia.

Finley, M.I. (1983), 'The ancient city', in *Economy and Society in Ancient Greece*, ed B.D. Shaw and R.P. Saller, 3-23, London. Originally published in 1977 in *Comparative Studies in Society and History*, 19, 305-27.

Finley, M.I. (1985), *Ancient History: Evidence and Models*. London.

Genière, T. de la (1983), 'Megara Nisaea, Megara Hyblaea et Sélinonte', *Dialogues d'histoire ancienne* 9, 319-33.

Giddens, A. (1979), *Central Problems in Social Theory*. London.

Giddens, A. (1981), *A Contemporary Critique of Historical Materialism*. London.

Giddens, A. (1984), *The Constitution of Society*. Cambridge.

Gould, P.R. (1972), 'Pedagogic review: entropy in urban and regional modelling', *Annals of the Association of American Geographers* 62, 689-700.

Harris, B. and Wilson, A.G. (1978), 'Equilibrium values and dynamics of attractiveness terms in production-constrained spatial-interaction models', *Environment and Planning*, A 10, 371-88.

Hennig, D. (1974), *RE Supp.* 14, 290-355 s.v. Orchomenos.

Hohenberg, P.M. and Lees, L.H. (1985), *The Making of Urban Europe*. Cambridge, Mass.

Holton, R.J. (1986), *Cities, Capitalism and Civilisation*. London.

Hope Simpson, R. (1965), *A Gazetteer and Atlas of Mycenaean Sites*, BICS Suppl. 16. London.

Humphreys, S.C. (1978), *Anthropology and the Greeks*. London.

Johnston, R.J. (1979), *Geography and Geographers*. London.

Leekley, D. and Noyes, R. (1976), *Archaeological Excavations (II) in Southern Greece*. New Jersey.

Legon, R.P. (1981), *Megara*. London.

McGee, T.G. (1971), *The Urbanisation Process in the Third World*. London.

Mason, R.S. (1976), *Princeton Encyclopaedia of Classical Sites*, 90 sv. Argive Heraion.

Moore, J.M. (1983), *Aristotle and Xenophon on Democracy and Oligarchy*. London.

Morris, I. (1987), *Burial and Ancient Society.* Cambridge.

Nystuen, J.D. and Dacey, M.F. (1961), 'A graph theory interpretation of nodal regions', *Papers, Regional Science Association* 7, 29-42.

Orton, C. (1982), 'Stochastic processes and archaeological mechanism in spatial analysis', *Journal of Archaeological Science* 9, 1-23.

Polignac, F. de (1984), *La Naissance de la cité grecque.* Paris.

Pred, A. (ed.) (1981), *Space and Time in Geography.* Lund.

Reissman, L. (1964), *The Urban Process.* New York.

Rihll, T.E. and Wilson, A.G. (1987), 'Spatial interaction and structural models in historical analysis: some possibilities and an example', *Histoire et Mesure* 2 (1), 5-32.

Rihll, T.E. and Wilson, A.G. (forthcoming), *Modelling Historical Landscapes.*

Roebuck, C. (1972), 'Some aspects of urbanisation at Corinth', *Hesperia* 41, 96-127.

Roesch, P. (1965), *Thespies et la confédération béotienne.* Paris.

Roesch, P. (1976), *Princeton Encyclopaedia of Classical Sites*, 101 s.v. Askra.

Salmon, J. (1984), *Wealthy Corinth.* Oxford.

Saunders, P. (1985), *Social Theory and the Urban Question*, 2nd edn. London.

Schachter, A. (1981), *Cults of Boiotia I*, BICS Supp.38.1. London.

Skocpol, T. (1984), *Vision and Method in Historical Sociology.* Cambridge.

Snodgrass, A.M. (1977), *Archaeology and the Rise of the Greek State.* Cambridge.

Snodgrass, A.M. (1984), 'The Ancient Greek world', in *European Social Evolution*, ed. J. Bintliff, 227-33. Bradford.

Snodgrass, A.M. (1987), *An Archaeology of Greece*, Sather Classical Lectures 53. Berkeley.

Thomas, R.W. and Huggett, R.J. (1980), *Modelling in Geography.* London.

Tomlinson, R.A. (1972), *Argos and the Argolid.* London.

Waldstein, C. (1902), *The Argive Heraion.* Cambridge, Mass.

Wheatley, P. (1971), *The Pivot of the Four Quarters.* Edinburgh.

Wilson, A.G. (1970), *Entropy in Urban and Regional Planning.* London.

Wilson, A.G. (1981), *Catastrophe Theory and Bifurcation: Applications to Urban and Regional Systems.* London.

Wiseman, J.R. (1976), *Princeton Encyclopaedia of Classical Sites*, 470 s.v. Kromna.

Wiseman, J.R. (1978), *The Land of the Ancient Corinthians*. Göteborg.

∞ **4** ∞

Surveys, cities and synoecism

W.G. Cavanagh

Introduction

Dialogue between historians and archaeologists is valuable; yet it is obstructed by uncertainty arising from the language we employ. Archaeologists usually and prehistorians by definition must create their own categories and call them by such names as they can coin. Historians, on the other hand, have the language and terms of the ancients, and they use this vocabulary to refine their understanding and define their meanings. In the following it is proposed to investigate the use of certain terms and their identification with archaeological phenomena.

Settlement, nucleation and dispersion, the relation of city and country, are concerns of archaeology, and especially concerns of the archaeology of intensive survey (McDonald and Rapp 1972, Bintliff 1977, Cherry 1979, Bintliff and Snodgrass 1985, Macready and Thompson 1985, Runnels and van Andel 1987). In discussion of the Greek state Snodgrass has clarified the terms, in particular polis and ethnos (1977, 1980) which define the political entities whose settlements have been found. In what follows, however, it is proposed to start, as it were, at the bottom of the heap, with the term *oikos*, to move from there to *synoikismos*, and finally work up to the theme of hierarchy of settlement, that is to say the fabric of the polis. In this last context we are faced with a welter of terms which vary in content from one state to another: polis, asty, chora, kome, demos, chorion. Can archaeologists place such terms in the context of their finds?

The household

> Oikon men protista gunaika te boun t'arotera.
> (First find a house and wife and ox to plough.)
>
> (Hesiod, *Works and Days* 405)

This phrase is quoted by Aristotle (*Politics* 1252b) in that very 'theoretical reconstruction of the advent of the polis' (Snodgrass, *supra*) we are attempting to escape. Aristotle seems to see the oikos as the polis writ small, or a sort of building block from which the polis is constructed. This point must not, however, be overstated, for Aristotle's discussion is framed in terms of legal right, constitutional status or natural justice, not of the economic or social as such, nor of what might be termed the customary. It is possible, all the same, for the family to be viewed, at least in the later classical period, as almost the antithesis of the state:

> It seems to me that the elaboration of this related set of norms for behaviour in public, together with increases in urbanisation and mobility of residence and social position which made the oikos more isolated, made the Athenians newly conscious of polis and oikos as being separate and different.
>
> (Humphreys 1983, 21)

Humphreys has shown (1983, ch. 5) how archaeology can be used to illustrate the ideology, that is to say people's perceptions, of the family and of the state. Here, however, the intention is different, namely to stress the material. The house, the tomb and landholdings are the most material expressions of the oikos, and for that reason the most accessible to archaeology (see Donlan 1985 for a discussion of the philological background to the term and usage in Homer).

The first case to be examined arises from the excavation of the North Cemetery at Knossos (Catling 1979, Coldstream forthcoming). Even without the statements of Hesiod and Aristotle that the nuclear family was an essential unit in Greek society, the fact that relatively few people were buried in these collective tombs, and that men, women and children were admitted, would strongly suggest that they are family vaults. Thanks to the refined pottery chronology available in the Aegean the use of these tombs can be dated with reasonable precision. One striking feature is their relatively brief duration of use

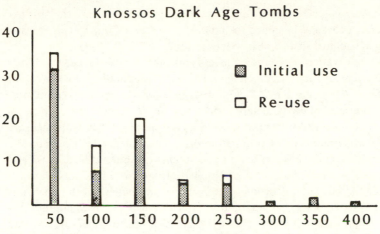

Figure 1: Histogram showing the duration in use of tombs from the North Cemetery at Knossos (c.1100-600 BC). 50-year intervals according to the conventional chronology.

(see fig.1): allowing 25 years per generation, some 44% of the chamber tombs lasted in continuous use for just two generations or less. 55% (these are cumulative totals) were in use for four generations or less, 78% for six generations or less, leaving a remainder of only 22% in use for more than six generations or 150 years. Now tombs can be abandoned for any number of reasons: the roof might collapse or the tomb become dilapidated, burial customs might change, or the family might decide they needed a new or more splendid vault. On archaeological grounds none of these explanations seems satisfactory in the case of the Dark Age tombs at Knossos. I am led to the conclusion that frequently the tombs were abandoned, either because that branch of the kin had come to an end, or because the family centre had moved elsewhere. A further point can be stressed on the basis of the Knossos tombs. Even given the very disturbed condition of the tombs, approximate figures can be calculated for the numbers interred in each. In the better preserved tombs the average per tomb per generation comes out as just over two individuals. This indicates an extremely restricted access, effectively perhaps the direct line of immediate descendants. In the eighth century the figure seems to rise to over three per generation, some support for the thesis argued by Morris (1987) that access to cemeteries was widened in contemporary Attica. These are two results concerning Knossos in the Dark Age. Is it possible to find further archaeological evidence to indicate a degree of impermanence and genealogical shallowness in the family?

Excavation of habitation levels and sites can be quoted. Snodgrass has already commented on the relatively short duration of a number of Dark Age settlements: Zagora, Emborio, Ayios Andreas on Siphnos, Lathuresa, Melie (Kaletepe) and a number of others. The foundation and later abandonment of these sites also indicate that some measure of impermanence of occupation was a fact of life in the ninth and eighth centuries BC. The new inhabitants certainly moved house and tomb from their place of origin (I shall return to this point later). I should be cautious of interpreting the abandonment of these sites as due to random changes of residence, both because Snodgrass has alerted us to the possibility of a pattern of abandonment of fortified sites in the late eighth century, and because villages tend to be permanent, and my argument here is that people and families would move from one village to another according to the vagaries of inheritance, fission and survival. The evidence of isolated rural settlements is therefore more apposite. Thus at Nichoria too (McDonald, Coulsen and Rosser 1983), the total occupation during the Dark Age does not exceed some 175 years, or seven generations, and the houses belong to at least two periods of occupation, and are built on different alignments. The chronology at Asine is clear in broad terms, and in the excavated plot published by Berit Wells (1983) again the three main phases of occupation might span no more than 175 years with several rebuildings.

Well deposits might provide further support, always bearing in mind that the abandonment of a well can come about for all sorts of reasons other than the abandonment of a house or plot of land. Unfortunately only one Geometric well from Knossos has been published, but in his account Coldstream summarises:

> Dug perhaps about 900 BC it was used to greatest advantage in the MPG and LPG periods, as is shown by the abundance of the water pots accidentally left at the bottom by their owners. In PGB the well declined in popularity, for a small amount of rubbish was evidently being thrown in. Then in the closing years of the ninth century the well-head either collapsed or was intentionally destroyed in a drought, and the well was used no more ...
>
> (Coldstream 1960)

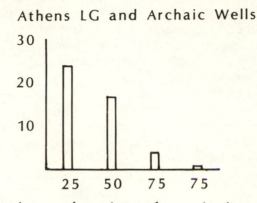

Figure 2: Histogram showing the duration in use of the wells of the Agora, Athens c.800-600 BC, at 25-year intervals according to the conventional pottery chronology.

The pattern of usage of wells in the Athenian Agora, during the Dark Age and Archaic period, on the other hand, shows shorter histories (Brann 1962, see also Camp 1979 and Snodgrass 1983): 56% seem to last in use for up to one generation, 33% for between one and two generations and only 11% last in use for a longer period (fig.2). This profile is completely different from that of the Knossos tombs.

> The assumption is that each well stood in the courtyard of a
> private house and that they can be used to indicate the probable
> location and density of prehistoric houses now lost.
>
> (Camp 1986, 33)

An insufficient number of wells has been published for us to say whether the pattern at Knossos is more typical of rural settlements, and that at Athens of the urban situation. Whether as an indication of habitation, industrial or agricultural activity, wells are a less reliable index for the *oikos* than tombs or houses. These scattered examples from a number of Dark Age sites do not lay a substantial foundation for further inference and further data are needed. Nevertheless they are sufficient to merit a comparison with written history.

    The issue raises questions of land tenure and movement of

population. The sort of movement I have in mind will, in a broad sense, have resulted from various factors. A number of authors have emphasised the consequences of partible inheritance and of dowry or marriage settlements in breaking up land-holdings (Davies 1978, Bintliff and Snodgrass 1985). Certainly death and marriage were critical moments for the transference of property, they might but do not need to coincide with the moment of fission. In families with several children it is possible in time that several families would reside together; but at some point a new household would be set up, and a new house built or an old one reoccupied. The opening of a new family tomb or burial plot, or the re-use of an old one, might coincide with this establishment or it might mark a more radical break.

Geographically at least, perhaps the closest we can approach Dark Age Knossos is the Gortyn Law Code (Willetts 1966). Here we have evidence for partible inheritance at the death of the father, and the principle, in medieval terms, of *paterna paternis* and *materna maternis*. Before the death of the father sons would normally be attached to the household, and daughters would marry out. On his death the household would be split up (V 28-54 stresses the partition of the property). The house in the polis and evidently such farm equipment and animals as did not belong to the serfs would pass only to the sons; the rest of the property would be inherited by sons and daughters at a ratio of 2:1 (IV 31-43; a difficult passage, Willetts is followed here). The *woikeus*, or serf, enjoyed security of tenure at the death of his master, and may on his own death have exercised a similar pattern of bequest (Aristotle, *Politics* 1264a, admittedly very vague). Now, as Hodkinson (1985) has proved, the termination of a line, whether heirless or with only a female legatee, would not be uncommon, perhaps of the order of 30-40% of all families; and the careful legislation at Sparta and elsewhere designed to cope with the problems of inheritance in the circumstances of failure of the direct line serves to confirm the point.

A similar point has been made by Davies in discussing the propertied families of Attica (Davies 1981). His figures (p.86) show a steeper rate of decline than that recorded above on the basis of the Knossos tombs, for they record not only the demographic effects of family nucleation, but the effects of partible inheritance on the continuity of wealth and status: in other words there is a financial threshold; and perhaps also the accident of survival biases the figures.

They are in fact remarkably similar to those found by Humphreys (1983.111ff.), for a different data set, that based on funerary inscriptions:

Generations	Humphreys	Davies
1	446	357
2	134*	44
3	17	16
4	4	5
5	1	1

Table 1: Table comparing the number of generations of a families recorded on Attic funerary monuments (Humphreys), and the degree of family continuity in the liturgical class at Athens (Davies).
(*Includes monuments recording parents and children, some of which might, on other criteria, count as a single generation.)

Most of these cases are based on epigraphic evidence or at least indirect inference from the sources. It is difficult to find direct historical attestation of fluidity in the rural population of Ancient Greece. There are reasons for this. In the first place accounts of rural life do not feature much in our authorities. Secondly the effects are long-term, over generations, and might have escaped the notice of ancient observers. In the third place ancestral pedigrees were a charter: in Greek, as in many traditional societies, the genealogical model was the means whereby the individual established his place in a free society. No one would advertise the aspects of fission or failure of lineage. Indeed both modern and ancient writers have viewed the population of the countryside as essentially unchanging:

> the early generations of Dorian migration to [sc. Melos] would no doubt have been crucial to the acquisition of land, and once a plot of land had been acquired by a family, ownership is likely to have remained fairly static until the late fifth century ...
>
> (Sparkes in Renfrew and Wagstaff 1976, 27)

No doubt it is unfair to place emphasis on such a passing comment, and one that the author goes on to qualify, but it indicates what might pass as uncontroversial. Thucydides seems to express a similar sentiment (2.16):

> ... from early times down to the present war most Athenians still lived in the country with their families and households, and were consequently not at all inclined to move now, especially as they had only just restored their establishments after the Persian invasion. Deep was their trouble and discontent at abandoning their houses and the hereditary temples of the ancient constitution ...
>
> (trans. Livingstone)

All the same, it is possible to see how, through mechanisms of change such as that indicated with the short span of the family, the basic pattern of rural settlement in Ancient Greece could be open to the transformations which are increasingly indicated by the archaeology of survey as well as by historical analysis. There are indeed parallel phenomena of movement and change, but of a more radical effect: colonisation, foreign service, and even political exile. Hesiod himself was the son of an immigrant, for his father had moved from Kyme to Askra in the eighth century. Presumably this sort of migration became more difficult as the political institutions of Greece became more fossilised and as population increased towards the climax of the Classical period. In the Archaic period, at least, as Davies has demonstrated for Athens (1978), new classes could be recruited to fill the ranks of the citizen body; whilst in Sparta there was a classic conflict of interest between maintaining the exclusive privileges of the few, and the effects of demographic decline on their manpower.

It might be helpful, by way of a counter case, to quote the example of north-west France in the medieval period. Of course the parallel cannot be precise, and in particular the differences in tenure, the alod and the benefice, feudal and pre-feudal relationships, the Church as landholder and patron, cannot be too strongly emphasised. There are, nevertheless, superficial similarities with Greece in the early Archaic period: it is a time of population growth, a period of aggressive colonisation, and an age of aristocratic ideology and power. There is a closer parallel in that the popular tradition in the transmission of property was indeed extreme egalitarian partible inheritance (Le Roy Ladurie 1976, esp. 52-61). But among the aristocracy there was a vital difference, a transformation which for

Normandy has been dated to the period c. 1020-1050. Bates (1982, 112f.; cf. also 118 and 134 referring to the work of Werner and Boussargues) suggests that the Norman aristocracy passed through a structural change: there was

> a tendency to organise the inheritance of the family property in favour of one son. The whole process was one which was basically a transformation of any one family from a large amorphous kin-group, which identified itself with no fixed residence and did not think in terms of ancestry transmitted in direct male line, into a lineage tenacious of its rights over generations. It had the effect of changing political relationships between such a family and the territorial prince.

Of Brittany, Jones (1981, 54) has commented

> within the duchy there are some particularly enduring tenurial arrangements, like the high proportion of large agglomerations formed in the eleventh and twelfth centuries, which survive in a recognisable form throughout the Middle Ages and beyond.

For whatever reason, though presumably in some sense an 'ideological' one, such a structural change is not to be recognised in Early Greece, and this must contribute towards the discontinuities in the political history of the early polis.

Synoecism

In investigating the term oikos, something has been shown of the potential advantages of the marriage of archaeology and history: neither discipline alone has the strength of the two combined. Perhaps a major contribution which archaeology can make is to encourage a formal description which is open to statistical treatment. In this case it would be of value to pursue the model of growth of the oikos in a more formal manner. Here however another important term in the Greek political vocabulary, *synoikismos*, will be examined in the light of its use by both historians and archaeologists. Certainly the latter have not been reticent in using the term and have probably over-extended its meaning by applying it to the prehistoric period. It is proposed here to examine some cases of the usage: prehistoric and historic. In fact it is hoped to show that the dialectic of archaeological and historic usage has led to conclusions almost the opposite of those expected.

In the classical sources the word can mean simply the collaboration of different groups in the founding of a city (e.g. Thucydides 3.92-93; cf. 1.24.2 and 6.5.1), but also means the foundation of a larger state by merging a number of independent communities (e.g. Thucydides 3.2; 2.15). The archaeologists have redefined this to imply the physical relocation of the population, or at least a political realignment which would result in a very different pattern of settlement, a radical redistribution of influence and population between the city and the country. Examples of just this have indeed been found.

(i) The Melos Survey proved that the move towards nucleation on the island started in the Early Cycladic (EC) III period, and by 2000 BC there was hardly any settlement other than at Phylakopi. While there are brilliant analyses in the Melos volume of the relationship between city and country during the Middle and Late Bronze Ages, the circumstances of the act or process of 'synoecism' remain unclear. The case, strongly reinforced in recent years by Barber and MacGillivray, for a serious discontinuity in EC III, makes for further complications. Moreover there is a parallel phenomenon on mainland Greece of nucleation during the transition from Early Helladic to Middle Helladic (the contemporary stages on the mainland of Greece). On the Laconia Survey we too have found evidence for this (cf. also Andel and Runnels 1987). But nucleation occurs in very different circumstances, circumstances of cultural impoverishment rather than advance.

> There seems to be a strong relationship between settlement
> nucleation and intervention and/or influence in the island by an
> external power.
>
> (Cherry in Renfrew and Wagstaff 1976, 254)

and further

> the factors ... may well lie in the social and political spheres and
> are not easily amenable to archaeological examination.   (258)

What we need is a history, and a history which I suspect only the precision of excavation can offer us.

(ii)   By way of a second example we can look to the end of the second millennium. Kilian has suggested that the spread of the settlement beyond the walls at Tiryns in the Late Helladic IIIC period (c. 1200-1100 BC) to form a settlement of 25 hectares reflects a synoecism (Kilian 1980, 1987). Indeed many years ago a similar proposal was suggested by Perrson (1931, 7). Likewise Benzi (1988) and MacDonald (1986) have both suggested that at the same time there was a concentration of population at Ialysos and an emigration from outlying areas on the island. The one case, based on the excavation of a site, and the other on cemetery evidence, would benefit from confirmation by field survey. Indeed Hope-Simpson's surveys have confirmed the picture of movements of population, though in Messenia with no suggestion of synoecism (MacDonald and Rupp 1972), while the survey of the Southern Argolid near to Tiryns has also produced evidence of a decline during LH IIIC (Runnels and van Andel 1987). The political situation could hardly be more different from the classic case, the disintegration rather than the formation of a state. Though there is a very broad context, witnessed for example by the foundation of new settlements such as that at Perati (Iakovidis 1969), signs of the radical re-planning of sites are seen at Lefkandi (Popham and Milburn 1971), and evidence of renewed activity at sites such as Asine.

(iii)   Next we turn to Attica. Thucydides (2.15) thought that Attica before the synoecism, although ruled by a king, was divided up into separate cities each with their own prytaneis and office-holders. Although Thucydides' context is the withdrawal of the Athenians behind their walls, what he stresses is not a movement of population from the other towns to Athens, which would have been apposite, but the constitutional unification: after the synoecism there was just one prytany and one body of archons at Athens. The synoecism of Attica was put in the Age of Heroes, and most archaeologists would be loath to try to bolster the prehistory of Mycenaean Attica by padding this myth into its fabric; though we have no reason to doubt that a part, at least, of Attica was united under the palace at Athens. Given the discontinuity of the Dark Age, historians have felt the need to affirm the reality of an Attic synoecism, but to place it at some stage in the proto-Geometric or Geometric period (Rhodes 1981, 76, *CAH* [2] III.3, 360-3, cf. also Diamant 1982 and Simms 1983). The model remains the same, that there was 'a centralisation of government' (loc. cit.) although the date and circumstances are different.

I would suggest that archaeology does not support this construction. Attica in the Dark Age has been discussed elsewhere in this volume by Morris, and formed the classic case in Snodgrass' *Archaeology and the Rise of the Greek State* (1977). If we follow the archaeology of Attica through the Dark Age we find the exact converse of the expected pattern of synoecism. From the end of the sub-Mycenaean cemetery on Salamis to the Late proto-Geometric period (say c. 1050-950 BC) finds are recovered from Athens and Athens alone. Then there is a gradual expansion into the Attic countryside. Ian Morris has taught us that we must be cautious and not make naive assumptions about the representative nature of Attic graves. Certainly I would agree with him that there is a population of Dark Age Attica which is archaeologically invisible. Nevertheless I think the pattern of expansion from Athens, rather than a centralisation into Athens, is real. In the first place the evidence comes not just from graves but also from sanctuary and settlement remains. Secondly there are areas elsewhere in Greece where the evidence is not so restricted to one site as in Attica: in the Argolid, for example, Early Dark Age material is found not only at Argos, but also at Mycenae, Tiryns, Nauplion and Asine; though even here the impression given is that as the Dark Age advanced there was an expansion from primary to secondary centres. In the third place, even when we grant that there is a population in Early Dark Age Attica which is archaeologically invisible, the concentration in Athens of that part which is visible must reflect a political reality. The notion of a central authority at Athens even in the tenth century BC has been made all the more plausible by the discovery of the mausoleum at Lefkandi (Popham 1982).

Insofar as an expansion into the countryside of Attica cannot be termed 'synoecism' in the classical sense, in the conditions of the period it need not be thought typical. Both Argos and Sparta increased their territories by the conquest of their independent neighbours; equally the Lelantine War cannot be dismissed as a mere boundary dispute. We can concede that the states of Chalkis, Eretria, Argos and Sparta existed when they fought these wars. Nevertheless if the city states were defined by their territorial boundaries and by their citizen body, then conquest must also have brought a new political establishment; and this new political accommodation must have followed rather than preceded the expansion of the territory. Attica may also have been exceptional in another, if connected respect. Many of the early poleis had a murky heroic ancestry: Corinth barely existed in the Bronze Age, Argos was outshone by Mycenae and Tiryns, Sparta, according to her own charter, had been repeopled by the descendants of Herakles. Athens on the other hand could claim an uninterrupted tradition back to Kekrops and before.

(iv) For the Classical period we can do no better than take the case of Megalopolis. For here we can turn to an archaeological survey directed specifically at investigating the synoecism. The final report is close to publication but for the moment we can quote a preliminary report on the current state:

> It is not yet possible to date settlements with sufficient precision to determine whether the foundation of the city of Megalopolis in 368 BC had an immediate effect on the rural population of the area. It is certain, however, that rural settlement continued well after the synoecism, the countryside was not emptied by it ...
> *Archaeological Reports* 1982-83, 28)

A not dissimilar conclusion was reached by the Hodkinsons in their discussion of Mantinea (Hodkinson and Hodkinson 1982).

Where do the written sources leave us? There undoubtedly was movement of population associated with synoecism, though perhaps from smaller town to the polis rather than from the rural villages and countryside (cf. Pausanias on Megalopolis 8.27.3 and Strabo 7.fr.21 on Thessalonike). There is no mention of redistribution of land. Thucydides at 1.58.2 uses *anoikizomai* for the gathering of the Chalkideans into Olynthos; the motive was defence, and it is not clear if it involved political unification (it is unclear whether Demosthenes' use of *synoikisthentes* at *De Falsa Legatione* (19) 263 indicates that a political realignment should be involved). At the same time the sources do not indicate that synoecism involved a constitutional revolution. Of course the joining of the citizens of, say, three separate poleis into one assembly, or abolishing the magistracies of three cities to become those of just one, or subsuming the councils of three into one body, must have had political consequences. Nevertheless the process of synoecism is not seen as revolutionary. Perhaps it is for this reason that, so far as I have been able to discover, the word *synoikizo* and its derivatives are not to be found anywhere in Aristotle's *Politics*.

In terms of the relation of city and country the prehistoric and early historic cases discussed above show that an influx of population can occur at times of disruption and insecurity. Indeed, ironically enough, the effect may be reminiscent of the influx into Athens at the time of the Peloponnesian War, though of course the circumstances were radically different. Synoecism in the classical sense, on the other hand, had less far-reaching effects in the distribution of the population. The pattern of settlement is sensitive to various forces; part of the mechanics of how it could respond has been suggested above in the discussion of the *oikos*, but political reform, in the sense that synoecism is political reform, is not a complete explanation; indeed nobody is likely to suggest that it is.

On a simplistic view, at least, the circumstances of their coming into being had far-reaching effects on the nature of the poleis of Athens and Sparta. The relationship between the demes of Attica and Athens in the Classical period has recently been investigated by Osborne (1984). Its origins must be traced back to the eighth century BC (Snodgrass 1977). The violent imperialism which saw the birth of the Spartan polis imposed a very different accommodation between the city of Sparta and its hinterland. This nexus of relationships will form a theme of the next section, but not least of our problems for Sparta is the lack of epigraphic, literary and forensic sources available for the study of classical Attica.

Hierarchy of settlement

This is something for which the Greeks had no word. It may help therefore to start here not with a word but with the archaeology. The Laconia Survey has examined some 70 km^2 of territory immediately adjacent to Sparta. At no point within the survey area is one more than about 12 km from Sparta - by way of comparison, for example, the survey area could fit quite comfortably into the main Athens basin. The accompanying map (fig.3) shows the distribution of sites

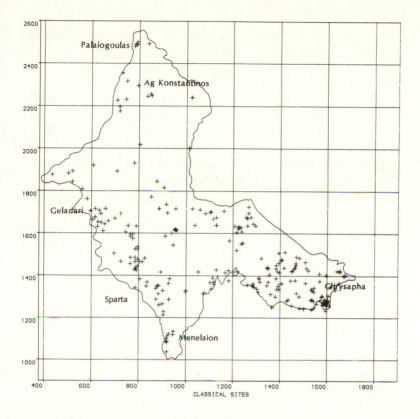

Figure 3: Map of sites of the Classical period (c.500 - 300 BC) discovered in the course of the Laconia Survey

identified as belonging to the Classical period. It must be stressed that the dating is provisional and subject to further confirmation in the light of the study of the pottery by Richard Catling. Equally it is not intended to imply that all these sites were occupied at the same time. It is quite clear that the whole area was intensively exploited in the Classical period, and this comes as no surprise to those who have seen the results of other intensive surveys. The vast majority of these are small agricultural sites and their distribution is more or less even over the territory except where nature intervenes; thus sites are relatively few in the northern half because the schist soil there is naturally poor and unstable; in the south central area sites are rare because of the highly dissected nature of the terrain. Against the largely geological pattern it is difficult to recognise any boundary effect due to the political geography of the region; perhaps at most a concentration close to Sparta possibly due to the city's suburbs spreading across the river.

Between Sparta and the many small rural sites, however, it is possible to distinguish intermediate ranks. At Palaiogoulas there is a small settlement with its own cemetery and sanctuary. This is probably to be identified with the ancient perioikic town of Sellasia (I am most grateful to Graham Shipley for showing me his unpublished discussion of the question).

At Chrysapha we have been able to map out another village site, similar in extent to Palaiogoulas, but whose ancient name and status is unknown to us. Closer to Sparta itself, just some 4 km away, lies the site of Yeladari, again a village site whose ancient name is not known. Then among the smaller agricultural sites we find a variation from quite extensive and apparently prosperous sites, like the Late Classical 'villa' to the south of Yeladari, to the humblest sites set in poor lands. We might also mention other types of site: sanctuaries such as the Menelaion and a newly discovered cult site set on the hills above the Chrysapha road; the great fortification at Ayios Konstantinos and the quarries by the Eurotas upstream from Sparta. At first the archaeologist might be tempted to reconstruct a simple hierarchy: Sparta at the top of a pyramid and the other sites ranged at various levels below.

If we are not misled by the literary sources, however, it is clear that a more complex multidimensional reality underlies the superficially simple pattern of a hierarchy; for there is a complicating factor of Sparta's peculiar institutions, and the relationship between Spartiates, Perioikoi and Helots. Of course the image of the five villages of Sparta, Thucydides' unsynoecised polis (1.10.2) , is a distortion, part of the Spartan mirage; it is, to say the least, disingenuous to suppose that the centre of the most powerful state of Classical Greece was nothing but a collection of humble villages. At the other extreme the boundaries of the polis of Sparta included, at its greatest extent, some 8,500 km^2 (Cartledge 1979, ch.1). We are confronted here with ambiguities of usage, for these boundaries are political only in a sense, and have as much to do with the defence of Laconia, as was shown more concretely at a later date when the fortifications were built to guard the main routes leaving Laconia (see

Pikoulas 1987 for this and the newly discovered fortress at Chartzeniko). The territory of Sparta defined in terms of Spartiate landholdings (cf. Cartledge 1979 and Hodkinson 1986) was considerably smaller, for included within the greater territory were the lands of the perioikic poleis. Yet the application of the term polis both to Sparta itself, and to settlements such as Sellasia, so much smaller in scale and power, seems hopelessly to strain the term. The usage was indeed vague in antiquity, but in cases like this one wonders if the usage was exploited to mask the realities of political power. Thus in trying to identify territory and site hierarchies on the ground, different definitions seem to apply in different contexts: political, military and economic.

Moreover it may be that there was also a 'ritual' territory, not perhaps explicitly defined as such by the Spartans themselves, but expressed in their calendar of festivals. An illustration of what I have in mind is the liminal rite carried out by the Spartan kings on their way to war at the sanctuary of Apollo at Thornax (a site which must lie within the survey area but which we unfortunately have been unable to identify). Although the major sanctuaries were located within Sparta (including Amyklai), the calendar of festivals took Spartans to Therapnai (the Menelaion), and it might be to the newly discovered sanctuary, adorned as it was with an Archaic temple similar to the old Menelaion. Something of the same import is suggested by the chilling story in Thucydides concerning the 2,000 helots who had distinguished themselves by their valour in the Peloponnesian War (4.80): they crowned themselves with wreaths (instead of the despised dogskin caps?) and made a round of the sanctuaries as a declaration of their freedom. They were later disposed of one by one.

Thus whilst the historical sources can divert the archaeologist from too simplistic a view of the human landscape in antiquity, they can equally present him with intractable problems of interpretation. Not infrequently the sources seem hopelessly ambiguous: it simply remains unknown whether the Laconian helots lived in villages or scattered on farms (cf. Cartledge 1979, 163f.). Whilst I would not rule out a solution to this problem on archaeological evidence there is a real difficulty: material evidence can indicate distinctions in prosperity, but does not tell us whether a given site was occupied by free men or slaves. The site at Yeladari seems to have been a village at this time, but we have no way from the finds (no inscriptions unfortunately), of saying whether its inhabitants were Perioikoi, Helots or even Spartiates.

Conclusion

The thread of argument of this paper has proved in the event to be knotted with difficulties. It has two strands: change in the pattern of settlement in the landscape and the reconciliation of archaeological and historical sources of evidence. The first strand presents us with problems of the mechanics: family and inheritance are important, but they need not be forces for stability. This is notoriously true of Sparta with the crisis of Oliganthropia, a shortfall of the privileged class, in the Classical period; the archaeological evidence suggests that a similar force operated in other states and at other periods, with different consequences. We are faced with problems of political reform and change: in the case of synoecism the conscious political act, the 'classical' reform, seems not to have altered radically the relationship between city and country. The 'archaeological' cases on the contrary are radical phenomena, but reflect violent upheaval and, at least in the case of the transformation of Attica during the Dark Age, longer term processes. Thirdly we need to identify the objects of change, and here the emphasis is on problems to be faced in the future. In the results of a survey such as the Laconia Survey we have a mass of data whose interpretation in relation to physical and human geography, and in terms of the economic, the social and the political is open to a tradition of analysis in the broad church of historical geography (e.g. Wagstaff 1987, Fowler 1972). If fruit is to come of intensive survey then we must hope that the crude generality of archaeology will be married to the refined distinction of history.

Acknowledgements

This paper has undergone several revisions since it was first delivered at the conference at Nottingham. I am deeply grateful to those who have helped in its painful progress. A particular debt is owed to the editors, who made a number of improvements which have been incorporated into the text. Anthony Snodgrass, Graham Shipley and my wife Lena have also read drafts at various stages, made useful suggestions and saved the text from errors. For the flaws which remain I must take responsibility.

The Laconia Survey is conducted under the aegis of the British School at Athens, and in collaboration with the Greek Ministry of Culture. We wish to thank Dr Spyropoulos, Ephor of Antiquities for Lakonia and Arkadia, and his staff for their help. We also wish to thank the following bodies for their financial support: Managing Committee of the British School at Athens, the Society of Antiquaries, the University of Nottingham Research Fund, the University of Amsterdam Faculty of Arts, the Allard Pierson Foundation, the Amsterdam University Society, Dutch Philological Research Fund, the Dutch Organisation for the Advance of Pure Research (Z.W.D.).

Bibliography

Andel, T.H. van and Russels, C. (1987), *Beyond the Acropolis: a Rural Greek Past*. Stanford.

Barber, R.L.H. and MacGillivray, J.A. (1984), *The Prehistorical Cyclades*. Edinburgh.

Bates, D. (1982), *Normandy Before 1066*. London.

Benzi, M., 'Rhodes in the LHIIIC period', in French and Wardle (1988), 253-62.

Bintliff, J.L. (1977), *Environment and Settlement in Prehistoric Greece*, British Archaeological Reports, International Series vol. 28. Oxford.

Bintliff, J.L. and Snodgrass, A.M. (1985), 'The Cambridge/Bradford Boeotian expedition; the first four years', *Journal of Field Archaeology* 12, 123-61.

Boardman, J. (1980), *The Greeks Overseas*. London.

Brann, E. (1962), *The Athenian Agora VIII. Late Geometric and Proto-Attic Pottery*. Princeton.

Camp, J.M. (1979), 'A drought in the late 8th century BC', *Hesperia* 48, 397-411.

Camp, J.M. (1985), *The Athenian Agora: Excavations in the Heart of Classical Athens*. London.

Cartledge, P. (1979), *Sparta and Lakonia*. London.

Catling, H.W. (1979), 'Knossos 1978', *Archaeological Reports* 25, 43-58.

Cherry, J.F. (1983), 'Frogs around the pond: perspectives on current archaeological survey projects in the Mediterranean region', in R. Keller and W. Rupp, *Archaeological Survey in the Mediterranean Region*, 375-416, British Archaeological Reports, International Series 155. Oxford.

Coldstream, J.N. (1960), 'A geometric well at Knossos', *Annual of the British School at Athens* 55, 159-71.

Coldstream, J.N. (forthcoming), *The North Cemetery at Knossos*.

Davies, J.K. (1971), *Athenian Propertied Families 600-300 BC*. Oxford.

Davies, J.K. (1978), 'Athenian citizenship: the descent group and its alternatives', *Classical Journal* 73, 105-21.

Davies, J.K. (1981), *Wealth and the Power of Wealth in Classical Athens*. New York.

Diamant, S. (1982), 'Theseus and the unification of Attica', in *Studies in Attic Epigraphy, History and Topography Presented to Eugene Vanderpool, Hesperia Supplement* 19, 38-50.

Donlan, W. (1985), 'The social groups of Dark Age Greece', *Classical Philology* 80, 293-308.

Fowler, P.J. (1972), *Archaeology and the Landscape*. London.

French, E.B. and Wardle, K. (1988), *Problems in Greek Prehistory*. Bristol.

Halstead, P. (1983), 'From determinism to uncertainty: social storage and the rise of the Minoan palace', in A. Sheridan and G. Bailey (eds.), *Economic Archaeology: Towards an Integration of Ecological and Social Approaches*, 187-213, British Archaeological Reports, International Series 96. Oxford.

Hodkinson, S. (1986), 'Land tenure and inheritance in classical Sparta', *Classical Quarterly* 36, 378-406.

Hodkinson, S. and Hodkinson H. (1981), 'Mantineia and the Mantinike: settlement and society in a Greek polis', *Annual of the British School at Athens* 76, 239-96.

Humphreys, S.C. (1983), *The Family, Women and Death* . London.

Iakovidis, S. (1969), *Perati, to Nekrotapheion*. Athens.

Jones, M.C.E. (1981), 'The Breton nobility and their masters from the civil war of 1341-64 to the late fifteenth century', in J.R.L. Highfield and R. Jeffs (eds.), *The Crown and Local Communities*. Gloucester.

Kilian, K. (1980), 'Zum Ende der mykenischen Epoche in der Argolis', *Jahrbuch des Römisch-Germanischen Zentralmuseums Mainz* 27, 166-95.

Kilian, K. (1988), 'Mycenaeans up to date, trends and changes in recent research', in French and Wardle (1988), 115-52.

Ladurie, E. Le Roy (1976), 'Family structures and inheritance customs in sixteenth century France', in J. Goody, J. Thirsk and E.P. Thompson (eds.), *Family and Inheritance: Rural Society in Western Europe 1200-1800*. Cambridge.

MacDonald, C. (1986), 'Problems in the twelfth century BC in the Dodecanese', *Annual of the British School at Athens* 81, 125-51.

McDonald, W.A., Coulson, W.D.E. and Rosser J. (1983), *Excavations at Nichoria in Southwest Greece 3, Dark Age and Byzantine Occupation*. Minneapolis.

McDonald, W.A. and Rapp, G.R. (1972), *The Minnesota Messenia Expedition. Reconstructing a Bronze Age Regional Environment*. Minneapolis.

Macready, S. and Thompson, F.H. (eds.) (1985), *Archaeological Field Survey in Britain and Abroad*. London.

Morris, I.M. (1987), *Burial and Ancient Society*. Cambridge.

Popham, M.R. and Milburn, E. (1971), 'The Late Helladic IIIC pottery of Xeropolis (Lefkandi): a summary', *Annual of the British School at Athens* 66, 333-52.

Popham, M.R., Touloupa, E. and Sackett, L.H. (1982), 'The hero of Lefkandi', *Antiquity* 56, 169-74.

Renfrew, C. and Wagstaff, J.M. (1976), *An Island Polity: the Archaeology of Exploitation on Melos*. Cambridge.

Rhodes, P.J. (1981), *A Commentary on the Aristotelian Athenaion Politeia*. Oxford.

Rihll, T.E. and Wilson, A.G. (1985), *Settlement Structures in Ancient Greece: Model-based Approaches to Analysis*, Working Paper 424, School of Geography, University of Leeds.

Runnels, C.N. and Andel, T.H. van (1987a), 'The evolution of settlement in the Southern Argolis and economic explanation', *Hesperia* 56, 303-34.

Simms, R.M. (1983), 'Eumolpus and the wars of Athens', *Greek, Roman and Byzantine Studies* 24, 197-208.

Snodgrass, A.M. (1977), *Archaeology and the Rise of the Greek State*. Cambridge.

Snodgrass, A.M. (1980), *Archaic Greece: the Age of Experiment.* London.

Snodgrass, A.M. (1983), 'Two demographic notes', 167-171 in R. Hägg (ed.), *The Greek Renaissance of the 8th Century BC.* Stockholm.

Wagstaff, J.M. (1987), *Landscape and Culture.* Oxford.

Wells, B. (1983), *Asine II.4.2-3. The proto-Geometric Period.* Stockholm.

Willetts (1967), *The Law Code of Gortyn.* Berlin.

Pride and prejudice, sense and subsistence: exchange and society in the Greek city

Robin Osborne

The question of the economic relationship between city and countryside has been frequently addressed by ancient historians. There has, moreover, been virtually universal agreement about what is the key question to ask. Thus Moses Finley, in his chapter on 'Town and Country' in *The Ancient Economy*, repeatedly asks 'How did an ancient city pay for its necessities?', and Geoffrey de Ste Croix in his section on 'Polis and chora' in *The Class Struggle in the Ancient Greek World* picks out as the prime feature to be noted that:

> A Greek (or Roman) city normally expected to feed itself from corn grown in its own chora (*territorium*) or at any rate grown nearby.[1]

But asking *this* question, and this question alone, has two undesirable consequences: it leads to the treatment of relationship between town and country in terms of a balance sheet;[2] and it effectively presupposes that town and country can be cleanly divided, despite the fact that in the Greek polis, at least, the actors themselves make no

---

[1] Finley (1973/1985) 131 (cf. 125, 139); de Ste Croix (1981) 11. A similar concern dominates Osborne (1987) 94ff.

[2] So Finley (1973/1985) 139, the structure of whose analysis is not as far as all that from that of Gomme (1937) which he criticises.

such clean division.[1] In this paper I want to approach the question of exchange between town and country from a very different angle, and I will argue that the economic relationship between town and country should be understood as much in terms of the need of wealthy landowners for cash as of the need of landless town residents for food.

The high priority put by Greek cities upon feeding their citizenry from the land is independent of the existence of the landless town resident and it has consequences which extend far beyond the question of the balance of trade, either within the city or between cities. The more securely a city could meet its own food needs from its own land the easier it was to maintain political independence. There seems therefore a direct correlation between the value put on growing at home the food needed for the city's subsistence, and the way that land was seen as the only proper investment, that land-ownership was, ideologically if not actually, tied to citizenship, and that all landowning was respectable, so that no 'class' divisions formed within the citizen body and no ideology of subordination developed.[2] Furthermore, the political implications of farming create a strong pressure for the landowner to dwell in the town, as the only place where citizen rights can be fully exercised, and to form the core of the citizen army by which both political independence and the fields are protected.

It is not simply that landowning was a socio-political act in the Greek city, but that the socio-political forces actually competed with the more purely economic forces. This is most graphically seen in the decision of active farmers to live in the town, away from the land that they own and work. But it is also the priority of the socio-political which makes for the complementarity of town and country-side which has been stressed as the peculiar feature of the Greek city (Humphreys 1978, 134). For where the town works as an enlarged village, which relates to the countryside as simply as a village to its fields, town and country are indivisible, and questions of feeding the town or of exchange between town and country simply do not arise.

This model of the city is consistent with two strongly contrasting means of land exploitation:

---

[1]   It is notable that de Ste Croix draws very heavily on the post-classical Greek world, with Jones (1940) providing his model city.

[2]   Thus, while English has various verbal ways of distinguishing small farmers from large landowners, Greek does not.

(i) systems of lordly surplus extraction by means of extra-economic compulsion (especially serfdom)

(ii) full peasant ownership of land.

The former is, broadly, the position at Sparta in the Classical period; the latter more or less the position in almost all other Greek cities. I have borrowed both categories from Professor Robert Brenner, who initiated a massive debate in *Past and Present* in the late 1970s and early 1980s with his claim that 'the original breakthrough in Europe to a system of more or less self-sustaining growth' was dependent upon the development of class relations through the breakdown of both the above situations - serfdom and peasant possession. Brenner's argument reinforces from a new direction the view that socio-political priorities in the Greek city competed with economic forces and impeded economic growth.

The model city is, however, something of a fictional construct. Cases of all landowners dwelling in the town were probably relatively rare, as perhaps were cities where land ownership was really the necessary and sufficient condition for citizenship. However, departures from the strict letter of the model may be of only trivial importance, for the real issue is whether cities acted *as if* the model situation were true. One example which might be argued to support the model is provided by the history of Mantineia. In 385 Sparta compelled the Mantineians to split up their town and go back to living in villages. Xenophon, recounting this, explicitly notes that those with property came to be pleased with the change because they were now living closer to their fields. Yet in fact the new situation did not create any new type of community functioning along lines and according to norms divergent from those of the model city, for as soon as the external pressure was removed the Mantineians reverted to a single city centre.[1]

But if the model seems to hold good for some Greek cities, how far does it hold good for that exceptional city, Athens, about which we know most and on which most studies of the economic relationship between city and countryside in ancient Greece have been centred? Certainly not all Athenians dwelt in the political centre -

[1] Xenophon, *Hellenika* 5.2.7, 6.5.3 with S. and H. Hodkinson (1981) 286-8.

scholars have probably consistently *over*-estimated the proportion doing so (Osborne 1985, 225 n.91) - but arguably the master-stroke of Kleisthenes was to divide the political centre, and by giving the villages of the countryside an integral and essential part in the political process to make it possible for all Athenians to live in *a* political centre. Athenians do seem to have continued to congregate together and not to have gone out and lived on their plots of land, and democracy probably could not have functioned had this not been so. Citizenship in Athens was not formally dependent on land-ownership: Lysias 34 makes it clear that some Athenians at least were aware of how enforcing such a link would alter the composition of the citizen body. But land ownership was dependent on citizenship. Moreover, some Athenians were quite as ready as other Greeks to make a big thing of the moral value of land-ownership: Xenophon (particularly in the *Oikonomikos*) provides the prime, but not the only, example. At the heart of the ideology of Athenian democracy was the contention that the Athenians were autochthonous, born from the very land, and this autochthony provided the fundamental support for the equality of all Athenians (and also for citizen exclusiveness).

Furthermore it is at the heart of Finley's claims that on the economic plane Athens was not in fact different in kind from other cities. Finley stresses that although the non-agricultural workforce was relatively large it did not produce anything that was significant in the economy of the city (except the silver, mined in the countryside) and the town remained a centre of consumption and not of production.

Seen from the point of view of the question of how ancient cities paid for their 'food, metals, slaves and other necessities' it is clear that the model city is one which is economically stagnant, for it has a very low demand for necessities which are not produced by the citizen himself. For Finley the Athenian exploitation of silver meant that even without meeting her own demands for food from her own territory Athens could meet her impressive import bill, and hence the Athenian countryside could stagnate just as much as other cities could. Once this viewpoint is adopted it becomes plausible to take literally the view implied by Dikaiopolis in Aristophanes' *Akharnians* 33-6 that traders were unknown outside the town (even in so large and properous a community as Akharnai), and to believe that the failure of archaeology or written records to give evidence of market places outside Athens, the Peiraieus and the mining region is significant. The countryside, it might seem, could maintain itself without any significant need to buy and sell on the market.

But is this claim really true? One way of examining it is to look at specific cases. For Athens a small number of men are relatively well known because they became involved in law courts in cases in which matters of property were involved. One such man is Phainippos, a figure of whom we would know nothing were it not for a single court case from which the opponent's speech is preserved as the 42nd oration in the Demosthenic corpus. The claim made in court is that Phainippos is richer than the speaker and therefore ought to undertake liturgical commitments in his stead. As a result the speech contains considerable detailed information about both the estate of Phainippos and the estate of the speaker, and even though we can be confident that this information is distorted, probably systematically distorted, it proves to be of exceptional interest when considered closely.

Kallippos' son Phainippos had inherited the properties of two families, his own paternal family and also his wife's, for he had been adopted as son by his father-in-law. His opponent alleges that both properties were so large that they had previously borne liturgic liabilities (21-3). As described in the speech the property consisted of a single landed estate, at Kytherros, a deme almost certainly in the Mesogaia area and which the most recent discussion (Traill 1986, 47-51) places in the Erasinos valley, south of Brauron. We do not know what Phainippos' paternal deme was, but his father-in-law was of Kolonai, not Kytherros.[1]

In an unprecedented, and notorious, measurement, Phainippos' opponent gives the circumference of the Kytherros estate as 'more than forty stades' (5), a measurement which, even if true, is consistent with the estate being of a wide range of areas (de Ste Croix 1966). More usefully the speaker described the nature of the agricultural exploitation and makes claims about the agricultural yield. Barley, vines and wood form the core of the estate's production: barley production is put at more than 1,000 *medimnoi* (which may imply that around 40 hectares were so cultivated), wine production at 800 *metretai*, and wood production is supposed to bring in 12 drachmas a day (7.20). The estate has two threshing floors (just possibly an indication that it combines two previously separate

---

[1] See generally Davies (1971) no.14734 and D22.

estates?), and a number of buildings used for storage of grain (7).

The only labour force mentioned by the speaker consists of six donkeys and two or more donkey-drivers who are referred to over the transport of wood, and the claim is made that these were employed year-round for this purpose. No other labour force, animal or human, is mentioned: given that the speaker wants to maximise, rather than minimise, the impression of the size and wealth of the estate there seem to be two possible reasons for this: either the six donkeys and their drivers were the only workforce and were employed on wood-cutting only in the season in which the speaker visited the estate, or else the permanent workforce otherwise employed by Phainippos was so small that it would have undermined the case being made. In favour of the former it might be noted that the speaker did visit the estate in Metageitnion (August), a month when, for example, the Eleusis accounts show that beasts of burden were free to be released from agricultural tasks in order to be used for the transport of marble; and close to the time at which Hesiod recommends that the farmer should devote his energies to woodcutting. Moreover it might be argued that the employment of such a force on woodcutting all the year round would imply a very large area devoted to woodland which it would be odd for the speaker not to make more of than he does.[1] In favour of the second suggestion, it might be noted that there probably was quite large scale use of hired labour in Attic agriculture to meet the peak period of labour demand.[2]

Phainippos' opponent is concerned to show the scale of Phainippos' resources, and he may omit from his description much that went on on the estate but was of trivial economic importance. It is simply impossible to tell whether Phainippos aimed to grow all the sorts of food his household needed on the estate or not: we certainly cannot assume that barley and wine were the only foodstuffs the estate produced. What is clear is that there is no way that his household (consisting, let us say, of twenty members), would

[1] The type of wood is not specified, but Meiggs (1982) 205-6 supposed it to have been firewood, in which case if this is more than casual exploitation Phainippos must have gone in for coppicing. There is plenty of evidence for coppicing in the Roman agronomists (see Meiggs 1982, 263, 266-9) but no explicit allusions in Greek authors.

[2] Cf. Osborne (1985) 142-6, Wood (1983, 1986) and, more generally, Wood (1988).

consume more than 10% of the claimed barley yield. The opponent puts into Phainippos' own mouth the admission that he had already sold part of the grain crop, and he further claims that Phainippos subsequently sold off more of the grain than was in store (6.8).

The speaker certainly exaggerates; and the barley price quoted (18 drachmas) is atypically high as a result of a particularly bad harvest in much of Attica. Nevertheless, even if we halve the figures given, Phainippos' estate must have yielded something approaching 5,000 drachmas of *cash* per annum. The opponent claims an income of 3,500 drachmas for wood (12 drachmas a day for the working year; if the wood was worked only in slack seasons the figure would be more like 1,000 drachmas), 18,000 drachmas for barley (1,000 *medimnoi* at 18 drachmas per *medimnos*; a price of 3-5 drachmas would be more realistic), and 9,600 drachmas for wine (800 *metretai* at 12 drachmas a *metretes*). This gives a total of about 31,000 drachmas (or about 15,000 on a reduced working year for wood and reduced price for barley).

What did Phainippos spend this cash on? The running costs of the estate cannot have been inconsiderable: even if we allow that subsistence food needs were met by home production, there remain donkeys and slaves to replace, hired labour to be paid, non-food necessities to purchase (clothes, tools, buildings and building maintenance), and so on. But it takes a massive stretch of the imagination to make these items reach even the conservative estimate of cash income I have posited. Yet, unless we are to believe that Phainippos is an utter liar, there is evidence in the speech that this cash income had been unable to cover his cash outlay. The speaker claims that, although there were no *horoi* marking debts visible on the estate when he visited it, Phainippos had since alleged that he had a whole series of debts: 6,000 drachmas owed to Pamphilos and Pheidoteles of Rhamnous; 4,000 drachmas to Aiantides of Phlya; and 1,400 drachmas to Aristomenes of Anagyrous (26-8). Only the last of these debts does the speaker claim to be able to show to have been repaid. For our purposes it is immaterial whether the debts were in fact outstanding at the time of the speech; what is important is the evidence they provide that in the recent past Phainippos' cash outlay had exceeded his cash income.

The speaker of [Demosthenes] 42 does not disclose the circumstances in which Phainippos contracted, or claimed to have contracted, these debts, for he wants the dikasts to believe them invented or no longer relevant. The best guide which we can get to the sort of reason why Phainippos might have contracted these debts is provided by our information about the circumstances in which other fourth-century Athenians have borrowed money. The evidence, from the orators and from the *horoi* themselves, was collected and analysed by Finley some 35 years ago in *Studies in Land and Credit*.[1] In summary, two common reasons for raising loans of a substantial size on the security of real estate are the raising of a dowry and the leasing of an orphan estate; loans to purchase plant or land, to pay for liturgical obligations, to pay for a family funeral, and to meet another man's temporary crisis are also known. Had Phainippos borrowed money to lease an orphan estate, or purchase plant or land, his opponent could not have been silent about it, for anything which increased the productive capacity of Phainippos' estate was grist to his mill in persuading the dikasts of Phainippos' wealth. Similarly, Phainippos cannot have borrowed money to perform a liturgy, for the opponent's very complaint is that Phainippos should be, but is not, performing a liturgy (22-3). Although no borrowing seems to be involved, Phainippos did claim that 1 talent of his property was not his to dispose of because it represented the dowry for the remarriage of his widowed mother.

It seems true that at least one of Phainippos' fathers had died quite recently, but although funerals could be expensive (a sum of 1,000 drachmas is involved in Demosthenes 40.52), the entire body of Phainippos' debt can hardly be put down to this. Again, although Apollodoros can claim to have bailed out his neighbour to the tune of 16 mnas (Demosthenes 53.12-13), and although the speaker certainly would not mention any philanthropic gestures on Phainippos' part, it is unlikely in the extreme that altruism lies behind Phainippos' debts. That we are left with no clear idea of what was behind Phainippos' borrowing is itself important: it is a sign of how little we understand of the major demands for cash that a wealthy Athenian might face. Further to speculate on the origins of Phainippos' need for cash in large quantities would be futile; but there is much to be gained from the scrutiny of the way in which Phainippos ran the estate in the light of his manifest need to generate cash.

Phainippos' opponent describes his estate as an *eskhatia*. This

[1]   Finley (1951/1985); for a thoroughgoing examination of credit at Athens see Millett (forthcoming).

almost certainly implies that it was brought into cultivation
relatively late, and probably implies that the land was to some extent
marginal (Lewis 1973, 210-12). The grain crop is sometimes referred
to simply as *sitos*, but when specification is given it is always that
the crop is barley. The Eleusis 'First-fruits' account, of very similar
date to this speech, suggests that much more barley was grown in
Attica than wheat (Garnsey 1985; 1988, 102). Barley was certainly
eaten by men as well as by animals, but there is some sign of a
preference for wheat (Gallo 1985; Garnsey 1988, 99 n.27).
Phainippos' decision to grow barley rather than wheat may reflect the
marginality of his estate: barley is more tolerant of drought than is
wheat. But the decision must also be seen in the light of the presence
of vines on the estate. That Phainippos had a productive vineyard
implies that at least part of the estate had an adequate water supply,
and yet Phainippos does not use that well-watered land for wheat.
Growing barley may well have given a consistent yield of a not very
profitable crop on the less good land of the estate; growing vines
gave a cash crop that was regularly in high demand, and which could
be stored for relatively long periods to be disposed of when need arose
or when market conditions were particularly favourable. The estate
was bound to produce more, perhaps much more, than the subsistence
needs of the household, and it seems that Phainippos directed his
farming activities to low risk enterprises on the one hand, and high
cash yielding enterprises on the other.

That Phainippos had one eye on the market seems to be further
confirmed by his exploitation of the woodland. If the suggestion that
exploitation of woodland was seasonal rather than permanent is
correct, then it illustrates nicely the need of the farmer who employs
permanent rather than just casual labour to fill the slack periods of
the agricultural year productively. Full employment is much more of
a priority for the owner of draught animals and slaves than for the
peasant who has neither. But the decision to exploit wood is also
interesting. The wood seems to be of no intrinsic use for the estate, it
is being carted away and sold (perhaps in Athens, as John Davies
suggests (1971, 553), or perhaps in the mining region?). Phainippos'
opponent expresses the yield in term of drachmas a day, and although
it is in his interest to allege a cash income it would be perverse not
to accept that woodcutting on the scale alleged must have generated
some cash return. Hamish Forbes has recently stressed that the
exploitation of woodland resources has traditionally been one of the

main sources of cash for small farmers in Greece:[1] Phainippos may
have had a larger cash need than most of his neighbours, but this way
of meeting the need may have been quite widely employed.

In sum, it seems reasonable to claim, on the basis of his
opponent's allegations, that Phainippos had a very considerable need
for cash and that he organised the exploitation of his estate in such a
way as to bring in as steady a cash income as possible. He sells off
his barley little by little from shortly after the harvest, apparently
keener to get cash in hand than to gamble on the future movement of
prices. His opponent alleges that he has broken the seals put on the
grain stores and has continued to sell grain, and also that he has
continued to sell wood (8-9): if this is true it looks as if Phainippos
was not prepared to let a vexatious court case stand in the way of his
established marketing practices.

It must be admitted that the information that we have about
Phainippos is exceptional; but was he atypical in his needs and
practices? A glance at the situation of his opponent, only partially
revealed, suggests that many Athenian rich may have been in similar
circumstances and faced similar demands. The speaker in
Demosthenes 42 claims that he himself was left 4,500 drachmas by
his father, as was his brother, and that it is difficult to live off so
little. He admits that he increased his fortune by activities in the
mining region, claiming that he made this money by working and
labouring with his own body (whatever that may mean). But he then
'shared a common misfortune with others labouring in the mines',
and lost some money 'privately' by incurring great fines, and then
finally had to pay a fine of 3 talents to the city - 'a talent per share' -
because he had an interest in a mine which was confiscated (3, 20,
22, 29).

Scholars who have discussed this speech have frequently followed
the lead of the speaker and suspected Phainippos of some sort of
cover-up; but it was not in his opponent's interest, either, to reveal
all about himself. The picture which he draws of turning a moderate
estate into one of the largest in Athens (he was one of the 300
established by Demosthenes' Naval Law of 340) through his own
labour in the mines is one designed to win sympathy, from dikasts

---

[1]   Forbes (unpublished). I am very grateful to Dr Forbes for letting me
read this stimulating paper. See also Jolas and Zonabend (1973/1978).
Phainippos seems to have no pastoral interests.

and modern readers alike. That picture cannot have been obviously false, but since money invested in the mines was not easily visible we cannot be confident that the 4,500 drachmas which his father left to him was the totality of the legacy: it is not beyond the bounds of possibility that that was the value of the landed estate which he was left, and that there were already established mining interests on top of that. Certainly the speaker must have been able to pay off his mining fines in order to bring this case at all, and that means that he has been able to produce cash to settle a number of fines including one amounting to perhaps 3 talents.[1]

However sceptical we may be of the details, we are certainly faced here with a man who has met major demands for cash and has been left still in a position where he is not self-evidently incapable of bearing a trierarchy. The demands to which he admits are not at all of the same sort as those faced by Phainippos, but they are of a very similar scale. Both these rich men could represent themselves as having to meet very heavy demands for cash and expect that the dikasts, who might be unfamiliar with the situation of such very rich men, but who were likely to be suspicious, would believe them. Yet in the very nature of the case neither of them is counting public demand for cash in the form of liturgies or *eisphorai* into his obligations and expenditure.

What we know of *eisphorai* and liturgies suggests that the demands which these imposed upon the rich were at least as great as the private demands. *Eisphorai* were periodic levies on the rich, occasional in the fifth century, more systematic and regular in the fourth. Our information is not such that we can accurately assess the impact of these levies on individual households in either century, but the random selection of preserved figures gives some impression of the scale of the demand. The first *eisphora* of the Peloponnesian War is said to have been intended to raise 200 talents (Thucydides 3.19) - far more than the tribute paid by any ally. During the period from 411/10 to 403/2 one wealthy man (Lysias 21.3) paid out 3,000 and 4,000 dr. in two *eisphorai*. In the fourth century an assessment of the total capital value of property holdings in Attica was made and *eisphora* were then raised at 0.5%, 1% or 2% of capital in the belief

---

[1] It may have been possible, depending on the precise arrangements for sharing the mine, for Phainippos' opponent to represent his share of the fine as larger than it was in fact.

that such levies would yield 30, 60 and 120 talents respectively.[1] It seems likely that at the same time that this assessment of property was made those liable to pay the levy were organised into symmories and that, then or shortly afterwards, the richest members of each symmory were responsible for advancing the whole sum due from the symmory and for recovering the sums due from the other members of the symmory. The number of those liable to pay the *eisphora* is much disputed and is closely bound up with the question of whether or not the same symmories were employed for raising *eisphora* and for the performance of liturgies.[2] No modern scholar, however, seems to want to maintain that *less* than 1200 Athenian property holders were liable to pay the *eisphora*: i.e. just less than 5% of Athenians probably had to contribute to these levies. The impact that the *eisphora* made on the fortunes of these rich men obviously depended in part on the frequency with which the levies were made. The amounts demanded from an individual on each occasion were not large but they would still make a substantial hole in cash holdings: if we accept Phainippos' own account of his debts and assume that they will not have amounted to more than half the total value of the estate then for him *eisphora* will have meant payment in the order of 150 to 600 drachmas a time (cf. Davies 1971, 554).

In the case of liturgies our information for cost come almost exclusively from litigious contexts, and are therefore subject to forensic inflation. However, a conservative estimate of the amount paid out on festival liturgies in Athens suggests that in a normal year around 100,000 drachmas may have been expended by around 100 citizens, and that in every fourth year, when the major Panathenaic celebration fell, this expenditure rose to something over 120,000 drachmas with about 20 more men to share it (Davies 1967; 1971, xxi-11). But this expenditure on festivals is almost negligible compared to the cost of maintaining the Athenian fleet. Even on a fairly conservative reckoning of 3,000 drachmas for a trierarchy (and some individuals and groups certainly spent more), the cost of maintaining 120 ships at sea (as recorded for 356) would have been

[1] Demosthenes 14.27, cf. 27.7. The ancient testimonia on the fourth - century reform of Athenian finances are usefully collected and translated in Harding (1985) no.39.

[2] See most recently Rhodes (1982, 1985) and MacDowell (1986). The debate badly needs to be put in a wider context.

some 60 talents (360,000 drachmas), and the cost of 170 ships at sea (as recorded in 322) 85 talents (510,000 drachmas).[1]

For liturgies alone, therefore, the richest individual Athenians, probably numbering no more than 1,000 (Demosthenes 14.16-19), will have had to find up to 100 talents a year of spare cash. No individual could be called upon more frequently than one year in two to bear a festal liturgy, and no more frequently than one year in three to bear a trierarchy, but the sums which they had to find were only more lumpy, not in the end smaller, for that. Some rich men certainly mortgaged their land to raise the cash for a trierarchy: two cases of this are known in the fourth century, and it may not have been uncommon.[2] Property was only mortgaged to other citizens, and thus even if the practice was widespread the amount of cash that had to be extorted from the wealthier section of the citizen body is unaffected. Moreover mortgaging was only in the end helpful for the individual if he either could pay off the sum mortgaged before next being called upon to bear a liturgy or was so reduced in means by the mortgage that he would not in future be liable, at least for the trierarchy.

In sum, large numbers of wealthy Athenians needed large amounts of cash, and needed them not just occasionally but regularly. *Horoi* illustrate some of the more publicly proclaimed reasons for raising cash in large sums; Phainippos' financial position suggests that there were also other private reasons which might be less publicly proclaimed; Phainippos' opponent's fines indicate the way in which the Athenian fondness for litigation could also take its financial toll; *eisphora* and liturgies illustrate, but probably do not exhaust, the massive public demand, for as well as these payments which were legally unavoidable it remained true in fourth-century Athens that wealth obliged the holder to contribute philanthropically to both local

---

[1] On the cost of being trierarch see Davies (1971); 120 ships at sea in 356: Diodoros 16.21.1; 170 ships at sea in 322: Diodoros 18.15.8; for further figures see Davies (1981) 20-2. The number of ships possessed by the Athenians was far in excess of the number that appear ever to have been manned in a single year: 283 in 357-6 (*IG* ii^2 1611 3-9), 412 in 325/4 (*IG* ii^2 1629 783-812). The naval lists regularly give both the total number of ships (at sea and in the dockyards) and also separately the number of ships at sea.

[2] Demosthenes 28.17-18 with 21.78-80, and Demosthenes 50.13.61. See Finley (1951/1985) 84 and no. 56.

community and polis as a whole. All of this suggests that a picture of Athens which shows exchange in the society purely in terms of the city's need to obtain food and other necessities misses an important dimension: the country also needed cash from the market.

How, then, was cash generated to meet these demands? The parties to the Phainippos case illustrate two traditional ways of raising cash: Phainippos himself relies on relatively unsophisticated agricultural practices; his opponent reaps most of his money from mining silver. But the demand for cash may have led to the development of agricultural and business practices less traditional than these. Various lease documents from the fourth century point to an apparently booming demand for public land to lease, and rich men eagerly snap up even small plots of such land (Osborne 1985, 54-9). Such men clearly do not require such plots in order to meet their own food needs. Pride and the high social value of landowning certainly play some part in such leases, but a desire for an additional source of income, exempt in some cases from liability to the *eisphora* (see Osborne 1987, 42-3) may well have influenced such men and encouraged such leasing. Private leasing of land also went on on a scale rather greater than has been appreciated in the past (Osborne 1988). Here the advantages to the lessor must be very largely economic, and while the lessee may have non-economic motives this is increasingly unlikely when leases are for short terms. Potential economic advantages for the lessee might include the possibility of making more efficient use of a labour force through economies of scale, possibilities of diversification, or simply the gamble on making a quick profit without having to face the consequences of agricultural malpractice.

The administration of city taxes also offered some opportunities for passing on the demand for cash to others, some of them outside the citizen body. Alarmingly, a high proportion of our knowledge of such taxes comes from chance mentions in inscriptions, and it is impossible to quantify even the number of taxes, let alone to attempt to calculate what they raised or what was in it for the tax farmer. Typical of the sources of our knowledge is the document recording the selling off of the property of one Meixidemos of the deme of Myrrhinous after he had been unable to pay off a debt of more than half a talent to the public treasury. He had incurred this debt by going surety for a number of individuals who had contracted to raise various taxes but had never produced the cash. Either Meixedemos' friends were criminally exploiting him, or they did not find the activity of raising taxes as easy or as profitable as they had expected, but their activities show something of the theoretical possibilities for profiting from undertaking public services of this kind. That some of the taxes involved very large sums and could yield very considerable profit to those who farmed them is strongly suggested by the story told by Andokides about the bidding and counterbidding for the privilege of exacting the 2% tax on imports and exports, in which sums of 30 and 36 talents are involved (Andokides 1.133f.).

Leases and taxes, like mortgages, do not create wealth, they simply redistribute it, leases among the citizen body, taxes among a slightly wider circle. For the Athenian rich to meet their private and public demands for cash in large quantities something other than cash had to be turned into cash somewhere along the line. War itself brought in large amounts of booty (cf. Austin 1986) which could be converted into Athenian 'owls', but it hardly brought it in regularly enough for the rich in general to rely upon it. In the end we must contemplate the possibility that one or both of the following propositions are true:

1) that manufacture did in fact play a significant part in the creation of wealth at Athens;

2) that agriculture itself was, for substantial landowners at least, highly profitable, and if highly profitable then, given that Athenians did not go in for protectionism, also highly productive.

Both of these propositions go against firmly held modern convictions. Yet only by exalting the silver mines to a massively predominant place in the Athenian economy can both propositions be rendered unnecessary. That this is unjustified is indicated by the survival of Athens during the first third of the fourth century, when very little seems to have been done in the mines, and by the evidence for who grew wealthy from mining activities. Phainippos himself, whose mining connections consist at most in the mines providing a market for his wood, witnesses to the possibilities of creating wealth and producing cash at Athens without dabbling in silver.

Finley's arguments against ascribing a major economic importance to manufacture in any Greek polis, even Athens, remain strong. But could agriculture have produced a cash income on the scale demanded? One crude way of assessing this is to convert the cash demand into barley production. Even if we assume a highish barley price of 5 drachmas a *medimnos*, 120,000 *medimnoi* have to be *sold* in order to raise the 100 talents needed, in some years at least, to meet *public* demand. 120,000 *medimnoi* (almost 5 million kg) would feed almost 25,000 people for a year. Given that, if Phainippos is at all typical, the rich will have been spending as much on private as on public outlay we should be thinking of, say, 10 million kg of barley (or equivalent) needing to be *sold* by rich Athenian farmers every year to supply the cash they required. Using the assumptions employed by Peter Garnsey (1985) and supposing that one quarter of Attica was in cereal production, this would mean that something over a quarter of the grain produced in Attica would have to be marketed. Perikles, in the anecdote related by Plutarch (*Perikles* 16), may be unusual in selling *all* the produce of his land immediately after the harvests, but if the cash demands of the Athenian rich were met largely from agriculture then it seems inevitable that they were committed very heavily indeed to market transactions.

Even if it was possible for agriculture to generate a sufficient supply of agricultural produce to raise the cash, is it possible to generate sufficient demand for such produce? There will have been some demand for agricultural produce in the countryside itself, both from those whose land was insufficiently productive to meet their needs and from those who concentrated on producing only one or two crops from their land. That heavy specialisation was at all widespread seems unlikely however: whenever the produce of an estate is described (as in the Attic stelai, or in Demosthenes 42) or prescribed (as in some lease documents) a variety of crops can be seen to be grown, and this is exactly what we would expect in a situation where most estates consisted of discrete plots of land enjoying different ecological conditions and suited to different use. The two primary markets for agricultural produce within Attica must have been the town, and, at least for the middle half of the fourth century, the mining region, where perhaps 10,000 or more slaves could be employed (see Conophago 1980, 341-54 for speculations about numbers). That the mines did create an extraordinary demand seems to be indicated by the exceptional settlement pattern of the Sounion region, and the density of purely classical, particularly fourth-century, agricultural activity in the Kharaka valley, west of Sounion, which has been revealed by the recent German survey.[1] Barley might be regarded as food particularly suitable for slaves, and if Phainippos were sending his wood to the mines then that might be in virtue of connections established through marketing his barley there also (and one might further speculate that his selling in the mining region may have been what brought him to the notice of his opponent, himself heavily involved with mining). For all that, however, the bulk of the demand must have come from the town.

How, then, did the town pay? In some considerable degree the town may have paid because, directly or indirectly, it was in receipt of much of the money that the rich were producing in *eisphorai* and liturgical contributions. The beneficiaries of liturgical activity must have been widely spread, for there was probably no area of public life that residents of the town monopolised, but it seems undeniable, even if very hard to demonstrate, that town residents took more than their fair share of and in public activities. Private services and craft activities will have played a further part in enabling the town to pay, and will have contributed to a small degree by bringing in cash from outside the city.

All these considerations point to a very considerable volume and complexity of exchange within the city of Athens. It is difficult to believe that this can have been achieved without a high degree of monetization. The ability of the wealthy to meet public and private demand seems to have depended on a high degree of liquidity, not just in their personal economies but in the economy of the city as a whole, and a rapidity of exchange transactions which a partially monetized economy could hardly have achieved. But it also depended on a high level of general prosperity, for it was only a relatively prosperous citizen that could maintain the buoyant markets upon which the rich depended. In a tight circle the expenditures by which the rich justified and maintained their social, and indeed political, dominance required the public payment of magistrates, dikasts and those who attended the assembly which maintained democracy; while in turn those not liable for liturgies or *eisphorai* depended upon the rich being able to bear such burdens in order to free the funds to pay themselves for their democratic acitivities by which they kept the edge on their prosperity.

---

[1] Osborne (1985) 29-36 plus Lohmann (1985) 71-96, whose findings have to be considered in the context of the history of the silver mines.

Athens in the fourth century clearly put her own wealthy citizens under the same sort and scale of pressure to find cash as her exaction of tribute in the fifth century put the wealthy in the allied states of the empire. There is, however, one major difference: in the fourth century in Athens public demand was demand for cash which, on the whole, stayed within the system and was not drained off outside Attica. In the empire the tribute demanded by Athens was removed to Athens itself, and very little probably found its way back to most allied cities, even indirectly. The relatively low level of tribute demanded of the allies, at least until the Peloponnesian war, has to be seen in that light (cf. Renfrew 1982).

The claim being made here, that the rich Athenian citizens were heavily involved in the market in order to meet the huge demands for cash which they faced, contrasts markedly with the picture painted by Finley (1973/1985, 108), who maintained that large landowners had 'a "peasant-like" passion for self-sufficiency' and that they did not have a 'qualitatively different approach to the problems and possibilities of farming' from that of the small farmer. Finley's statements amount to a denial that the very different situation of the large landowner, who employs labour, whether slave or free, rather than depending on his own and his family's work, led to a different conception of what estate management was about. Yet it was certainly not true of the wealthy Athenian, as has been claimed of the subsistence peasant, that 'savings are kept in the production-consumption unit. They are not thrown into circulation', nor that 'increasing the rate or the absolute volume of surplus means increasing self-exploitation'.

Why then did Finley come to believe so strongly in a 'peasant-like' mentality among the rich? There can be no simple explanation for what is a very complex picture, more subtle than my selective quotation has allowed, but four factors deserve to be picked out. The first of these is the influence of the classic article by Mickwitz, called 'Economic rationalism in Greco-Roman agriculture', published in 1937. On the basis largely of Egyptian papyri of estate accounts and Roman agronomists' attempts to calculate profitability Mickwitz argued that book-keeping skills and the conceptions vital to gaining a proper view of profitability, and hence enabling sensible choices to be made between strategies in agriculture, were never developed in antiquity. He suggested that because farmers followed methods of public accounting, which were aimed at eliminating fraud not at determining profitability, and did not develop proper commercial accounting, it was impossible for economic rationality to develop.

That adequate commercial book-keeping methods were not developed is indisputable, but to claim that in the absence of such book-keeping methods it was impossible for farmers (or indeed merchants) to behave in a way that was economically rational is to propose an unrealistically narrow definition of rational economic behaviour. As Mickwitz himself points out, commercial book-keeping methods were not developed in Western Europe at all until the agricultural revolution of the late eighteenth century. This brings us back into Brenner country (Aston and Philpin, 1985). Robert Brenner has argued that the breakthrough to sustained economic growth only occurred when the producers were forced, in order to maintain themselves, to buy and sell on the market. I have argued that in Classical Athens the wealthy Athenian landowner was forced into the market. Just as the limited scale of this alteration of the system of land exploitation did not lead to sustained economic growth, so also it can be argued that it did not lead to a situation where the application of commercial book-keeping practices would have made economic sense.

The number of Athenians who faced major public demands for cash was probably in the region of 1,000; a somewhat larger number will have been on the margins of those demands and will have shared the private needs for cash. But, although we are very ill informed about the distribution of wealth through the Athenian citizen body,[1] it seems unlikely that more than say 10% of the citizens were subject to such pressures. The market into which they were forced in order to meet these demands was a purely local one, in an economy that was self-contained to a very high degree. In an economy on so small a scale, in an environment so subject to violent and unpredictable variations, economic modelling of supply and demand becomes a fool's game. The assumptions necessary in order to calculate profitability simply could not be made unless an extremely long-term view were taken, and even the richest could not afford to take such a view. Moreover economic stability was not threatened simply by environmentally determined fluctuations in food supply, but also by political factors: classical Greek society was, by modern standards

---

[1]   Davies (1981) 34-7 with Rhodes (1982, 1985) 5.

extremely unstable both socially and politically, and thepolis was threatened by instability in other poleis as well as by instability at home. Thus totally irregular factors, which were strictly non-economic, threatened even the very long term view.

In a famous passage, Xenophon presupposes that all markets are limited except for the market for silver (*Poroi* 4.4-6). Short-sighted as such a remark may seem to us, it is actually a perception of the nature and conditions of trade in the fourth-century Greek world. It was thus for perfectly good reasons that ancient Athenian landowners failed to act in a way which Mickwitz would describe as 'economically rational': natural and social factors combined to ensure that the economy could not sensibly or meaningfully be treated as independent.

The second factor shaping Finley's view of the wealthy Athenian as acting simply like a wealthy peasant is his own study of the *horoi*. In his classic analysis Finley showed that the loans on real security which the *horoi* marked were all loans taken to finance conspicuous consumption, not for productive investment; they were loans taken for social reasons rather than for purely economic ones. While the observation is undoubtedly correct, the explanation is perhaps more complex than Finley allowed, for the overtones of economic transactions were not simply social but also political.

This can be seen clearly not just in the case of Phainippos, who has served here as the model of the landowner responding to public and private cash demands, but also in those who pursued more innovative economic strategies. In the case of Phainippos it is not just that his market is limited to the city, the socio-political unit, and hence that his income is intimately connected with social and political events; it is also that his private and public obligations to produce cash in large quantities are themselves a product of the society and of its political organisation. In Athens, where the local community is itself a political community, and where the high social value of landowning is closely linked to political identity and to financial contributions (landed wealth is visible and hence 'good'), the economics of the exploitation of that land could not but be bound up with social and political factors.

Two fourth-century figures show that there were some who did respond to the pressures by fundamentally altering their economic base. One of these is Demosthenes' father, whose considerable wealth was not tied up in land at all, but a more interesting case is offered by

Timarkhos. For while we do not know the origin of Demosthenes' father's wealth or the extent to which it was built up by non-agricultural activities, we do know, admittedly from a hostile source, that Timarkhos made a positive decision to sell off his land. Aiskhines devotes a considerable section of his speech against Timarkhos (Aiskhines 1.94-105) to the way in which Timarkhos has (mis)managed his property, complaining frequently that Timarkhos has sold off both land and investments in the mines and has hence rendered invisible property from which another man would have borne liturgies. Aiskhines' peroration at the conclusion of this section well reveals the social and political impropriety of what could be represented as economic irresponsibility:

> Timarkhos has nothing left - no house, no multiple dwelling, no land, no slaves, no money out on loan, nothing of the sort of resources from which law-abiding men live. He has replaced his ancestral property with abuse, vexatious litigation, cockiness, a life of luxury, cowardliness, shamelessness, not knowing to blush at what is base. Those are the qualities that go to make him into the worst and most unprofitable of citizens.

The third factor which went to make up Finley's view was his observation of the moralising framework in which ancient authors put their comments on matters economic. Notably, only Aristotle matches Cicero and Xenophon for frequency of citations in *The Ancient Economy*. But again it is one thing to note the impossibility of disembedding the economic from values that are socially and politically conditioned, but it is quite another to conclude that the rich actually acted in ways indistinguishable from subsistence farmers.

That Finley could write in such a way was further conditioned by a fourth factor: his distrust for statistics. Such a distrust is in many ways proper, but although precision is almost never possible in quantifications, even with regard to Athens, let alone other parts of the Greek world, broad orders of magnitude are not always beyond recovery. Finley's own work in *Studies in Land and Credit* drew some of its great value from *not* eschewing the statistical, and my paper has attempted to establish a framework of understanding on the basis of some rough and ready, but conservative calculations.

That large Athenian landowners should not look to us at all like modern farmers should cause no surprise; nor should it cause us to regard them as peasants writ large. Men like Phainippos faced demands for cash different not just in quantity but in kind from the demands faced by the peasant. Even in the brief description which we have of his running of his estate we can, I have argued, see traces of him pursuing a cash-oriented farming strategy. That he could calculate the profitability of his barley and wine and compare them in terms of tables and figures is inconceivable (and I defy anyone to do it for him!) but that does not mean that he farmed at random or without any knowledge of the likely results. Phainippos' farming policy certainly was not centred on self-sufficiency, and the account which we are given gives no warrant for ascribing to him a 'satisficer' rather than a 'maximiser' mentality.

It is basic to Finley's view of the Greek city that the economic relationship between town and country turned on the demand of the town for food. The town created a demand for food which the country as a whole, or simply the immediate hinterland of the town, met. In what I have said I have tried to move the emphasis by stressing that the social and political obligations of the wealthy created a need for cash which demanded that they enter the market. The goods which they supplied to the market may have made possible and indeed encouraged the growth of the town as a population centre, but it was occasioned by the existence of the town as a political centre, something which is, conceptually at least, quite a different thing. The public spending of the polis, and particularly of the democratic polis, can be seen to have stimulated both town and country. Wealthy landowners became dependent on selling in town markets in order to preserve their wealth *and* their political status: if they did not enter the market on a large scale they could only meet their political obligations by jeopardising their wealth. To understand the economic relationship between town and country in classical Athens we must look at the production of the countryside as well as at the consumption of the town.

Two questions arise from all this: was fourth-century Athens and the behaviour of fourth-century Athenians different from fifth-century? and was Athens unique? The sorts of evidence deployed here on fourth-century Athens are available neither for fifth-century Athens nor for other parts of Greece. Certainly the access to the resources of the empire, for individual Athenians as well as for the polis as a whole, must have made a considerable difference to the demands placed on wealthy Athenian citizens and upon their ability to meet those demands. Nevertheless the liturgy system was not an invention of the fourth century; trierarchies already existed in the fifth century (even though the responsibilities and, probably, the costs were rather different),[1] and the social pressures towards private expenditure may well have been greater rather than less. Even though many Athenians gained revenue from land held outside Attica during the empire that will have made entry into the market more, rather than less, essential and to a greater rather than a smaller number of Athenian citizens.

With other Greek poleis the argument must proceed in different ways in different cases according to the nature of the evidence available. In conclusion here I want to point to one remarkable piece of evidence from the island of Tenos, dated to around 300 BC. A unique *stele*, now in the British Museum, lists transactions involving real estate registered with the *astynomoi* over a period of less than two years.[2] The transactions are described as 'sales', but it is clear that some at least are credit transactions rather than proper sales. The inscription provides a wealth of prosopographical and topographical data, but my concern here is with two features only: the number of individuals involved in the transactions, and the amount of cash that is moving about. The 47 transactions on the *stele* involve at least 45 different individuals making 'purchases', and although many of those who make purchases do also appear 'selling' or acting as guarantors it is clear that the rich amongst whom wealth circulated on Tenos were not simply a tiny clique. Some of the sums paid in the transactions are lost but the total recorded as passing from one pocket to another is in excess of 70,000 drachmas, and this in less than two years. The smallest amount exchanged is 100 drachmas, the largest 8,000 drachmas. It seems impossible to conclude other than that there was considerable liquidity in the economy of Hellenistic Tenos, a situation which is barely conceivable unless these wealthy landowners were involved in marketing agricultural produce in a big way. While we have no idea why the rich of Tenos were mortgaging

---

[1]   Xenophon, *Constitution of Athens* 3.4 alleges that there were 400 trierarchs in the middle of the fifth century. Certainly it seems that a trierarch was appointed for every trireme in the ship-sheds (Thucydides 2.24.2). In the fourth century trierarchs were only appointed once it had been decided to send ships out: *IG* ii^2 1629 180-271, Demosthenes 4.36.

[2]   *IG* xii.5.872; Dareste, Haussoullier and Reinach (1891) 64-106.

or selling property at such a rate in these years, their activity does suggest that the demands for cash found in the Athens of the fourth century were by no means unique to it.

The manifest need of the Athenian wealthy for cash, and the evidence that the wealthy on Tenos also had, and probably had to have, large amounts of cash at their disposal, serve to confirm the socio-political aspects of landowning, the prominence of which was emphasised at the beginning of this paper. But those social and political overtones did not require the adoption of an allegedly 'peasant' mentality, indeed they rather required heavy involvement in the market. That to all intents and purposes even Athens was not bound into any 'system of markets' (Finley 1973/1985, 22) does have implications for economic development, but that does not mean that the Athenian economy was dormant, or that economic activity within the city was at a low level. The scale of economic activity in fourth-century Athens was large, the amount and rate of exchange, both there and on Tenos, not to be sneezed at, and it was political demand, at least in the case of Athens, that played a major part in securing that that was so. With reference to the Roman empire Keith Hopkins (1983) has written:

> Increased monetization suggests increased trade: more transactions by producers selling food, goods, and metal to unspecified customers, with money as the medium of exchange. A Rabbi Isaac in the second century AD advised: 'A man should always divide his money: one third in land, one third in trade, and keep one third in hand' (Bava Mezia 42a). It was advice whichnot many could follow, but in the beginning of the ancient economy, such advice would have been meaningless.

If the beginning of the ancient economy is taken to include fourth-century Athens then the advice would have been far from meaningless: many Athenian wealthy, and even not so wealthy, men needed to divide their money in just that way; and the same is far from ruled out for other Greek poleis and other periods.

Acknowledgements

I am grateful to the participants at the Nottingham conference and to John Salmon, David Lewis and Stephen Hodkinson for comments on an earlier version of this paper.

Bibliography

Aston, T.H. and Philpin, C.H.E. (eds.) (1985), *The Brenner Debate: Agrarian Class Structure and Economic Development in Pre-industrial Europe*. Cambridge.

Austin, M.M. (1986), 'Hellenistic kings, war and the economy', in *Classical Quarterly* n.s. 36, 450-66.

Conophagos, C. (1980), *Le Laurium antique*. Athens.

Dareste, R., Haussoullier, B. and Reinach, Th. (1891), *Recueil des inscriptions juridiques grecques* I. Paris.

Davies, J.K. (1967), 'Demosthenes on liturgies: a note', *Journal of Hellenic Studies* 87, 33-40.

Davies, J.K. (1971), *Athenian Propertied Families 600-300 BC*. Oxford.

Davies, J.K. (1981), *Wealth and the Power of Wealth in Classical Athens*. New York.

Finley, M.I. (1951/1985), *Studies in Land and Credit in Ancient Athens, 500-200 BC*, reprinted with introduction by P.C. Millett (1985). New York.

Finley, M.I. (1973/1985), *The Ancient Economy* (revised edn. 1985). London.

Forbes, H. (unpublished), 'The struggle for cash: the integrated exploitation of the cultivated and non-cultivated landscapes in the southern Argolis, Peloponnesus, Greece'.

Gallo, L. (1985), 'Alimentazione e classi sociali: una nota su orzo e frumento in Grecia', *OPUS* 2, 449-72.

Garnsey, P.D.A. (1985), 'Grain for Athens', in P.A. Cartledge and F.D. Harvey (eds.), *Crux. Essays Presented to G.E.M. de Ste Croix*, 62-75. London.

Garnsey, P.D.A. (1988), *Famine and Food Supply in the Graeco-Roman World. Responses to Risk and Crisis*. Cambridge.

Gomme, A.W. (1937), *Essays in Greek History and Literature*. Oxford.

Gudeman, S. (1978), *The Demise of a Rural Economy*. London.

Harding, P. (1985), *Translated Documents of Greece and Rome 2. From the End of the Peloponnesian War to the Battle of Ipsus*. Cambridge.

Hodkinson, S. and Hodkinson, H. (1981), 'Mantineia and the Mantinike. Settlement and society in a Greek polis', *Annual of the British School at Athens* 76, 239-96.

Hopkins, M.K. (1983), 'Introduction' in P. Garnsey, K. Hopkins and C.R. Whittaker (eds.), *Trade in the Ancient Economy*. London.

Humphreys, S.C. (1978), *Anthropology and the Greeks*. London.

Jolas, T., Zonabend, F. (1973/1978), 'Gens du finage: gens du bois', *Annales ESC* 28 (1973), 285-305, reprinted and translated in R. Forster and O. Ranum (eds.), *Rural Society in France* (1978) 126-51.

Jones, A.H.M. (1940), *The Greek City from Alexander to Justinian*. Oxford.

Lewis, D.M. (1973), 'The Athenian *rationes centesimarum*', in M.I. Finley (ed.), *Problèmes de la terre en Grèce ancienne* , 181-212. Paris.

Lohmann, H. (1985), 'Landleben im klassischen Attika. Ergebnisse und Probleme einer archäologischen Landesaufnahme des Demos Atene', *Jahrbuch Ruhr-Universität Bochum* (1985) 71-96.

MacDowell, D.M. (1986), 'The law of Periandros about symmories', *Classical Quarterly* n.s. 36, 438-49.

Meiggs, R. (1982), *Trees and Timber in the Ancient Mediterranean World*. Oxford.

Mickwitz, G. (1937), 'Economic rationalism in Greco-Roman agriculture', *English Historical Review* , 577-89.

Millett, P.C. (forthcoming), *Lending and Borrowing in Ancient Athens*. Cambridge.

Osborne, R.G. (1985), *Demos. The Discovery of Classical Attika*. Cambridge.

Osborne, R.G. (1987), *Classical Landscape with Figures. The Ancient Greek City and its Countryside*. London.

Osborne, R.G. (1988), 'Social and economic implications of the leasing of land and property in classical and hellenistic Greece', *Chiron* 18, 225-70.

Renfrew, A.C. (1982), 'Polity and power: interaction, intensification and exploitations', in A.C. Renfrew and J.M. Wagstaff (eds.), *An Island Polity. The Archaeology of Exploitation in Melos,* 264-90. Cambridge.

Rhodes, P.J. (1982, 1985), 'Problems in Athenian *Eisphora* and liturgies', *American Journal of Ancient History* 7, 1-19.

Ste Croix, G.E.M. de (1966), 'The estate of Phainippus (Ps-Dem.xlii)', in E. Badian (ed.), *Ancient Society and Institutions: Studies Presented to Victor Ehrenberg*, 109-14. Oxford.

Ste Croix, G.E.M. de (1981), *The Class Struggle in the Ancient Greek World.* London.

Traill, J.S. (1986), *Demos and Trittys. Epigraphical and Topographical Studies in the Organisation of Attica.* Toronto.

Wood, E.M. (1983, 1986), 'Agricultural slavery in classical Athens', in *American Journal of Ancient History* 8, 1-47.

Wood, E.M. (1988), *Peasant-citizen and Slave. The Foundations of Athenian Democracy.* London.

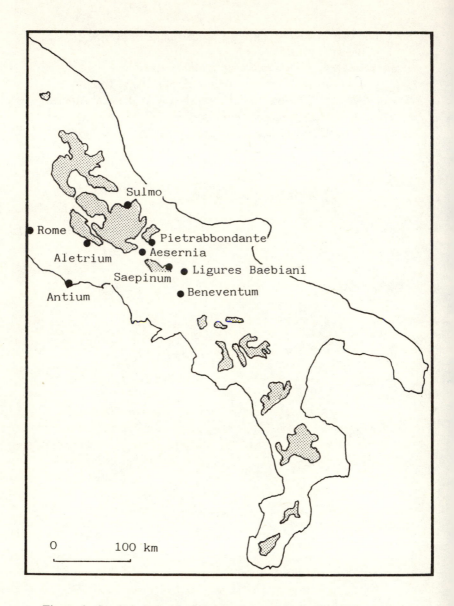

Figure 1: Southern Italy (shaded areas represent land over 1000m)

∞ **6** ∞

Settlement, city and elite in Samnium and Lycia

John R. Patterson

Introduction

This paper is a study of the phenomenon we call 'Romanisation' - the effects that Roman rule had on the economies and societies of the ancient Mediterranean. It focuses especially on the mountainous regions of the Empire, and concentrates on two areas in particular, Samnium in the Italian Appennines and Lycia, in the south-west corner of Turkey; its main theme is the developments which characterise these areas in the first two centuries AD, but there are implications of more general interest, too.

In recent years I have been involved in archaeological fieldwork in both Samnium and Lycia. In the case of Samnium, I took part in the San Vincenzo project directed by Richard Hodges of Sheffield University (see Hodges and Mitchell 1985). It involved a multi-period field-survey of the upper Volturno valley, which in the early mediaeval era formed the lands of the abbey of San Vincenzo; I also undertook field-survey in the territory of the Ligures Baebiani, under my own auspices (Patterson 1988). In Turkey, I took part in the Balboura Project directed by J.J. Coulton (Coulton 1987b) which has been investigating the ancient city of Balboura in northern Lycia; in fact, this paper owes its origin to attempts to devise models for settlement patterns and urban change in Lycia, derived from the situations identified in Samnium. The comparison is by no means an artificial one: firstly, despite their very different political histories, Samnium and Lycia have much in common. Both areas are composed of rough mountains and small, fertile, plains; in general they are poorly served by ancient routes, largely because of the difficulty of the terrain - and economically speaking, too, they are very much 'off the beaten track'. Clearly there is scope here for productive comparison and contrast.

There is also, however, a more general problem of methodology to be faced. Economic and social changes in Italy as a consequence of Roman rule have always had a high place on the historian's agenda; partly because the conquest of Italy was a vital precursor of Rome's subsequent overseas expansion, and of the thoroughly attested and discussed political struggles which led to the fall of the Republic. Besides, the existence of ancient agricultural treatises like those of Cato and Varro set out clearly the terms of the debate - foreign slaves or indigenous tenants? Large estates or small peasant holdings? Similarly, the development of field-survey techniques in Italy (and indeed Greece) provides us with comparisons and possible models when we undertake new projects in previously unexplored parts of those countries. When we look at the history of landholding and agriculture in Asia Minor in the Roman period, however, we have no such starting points, and have to derive models from elsewhere in the ancient world, which we can then test by means of archaeological field-survey, excavation, and detailed analysis of the epigraphic record.

A third general point concerns the importance of towns in my model. In recent years the development of archaeological field-survey, and its undoubted attractions for the archaeologist by contrast with excavation (see Snodgrass 1982), and the increased interest among archaeologically minded historians in the ancient countryside, have led to something of a neglect of the archaeology of towns, which were seen largely in terms of their monumental architecture, and as irrelevant for the problems of peasant society and the peasant economy. It seems to me vital to investigate the towns of the ancient world as thoroughly as their territories, and it is welcome in this connection that the technique of field-survey is increasingly being employed for the study of urban and village settlements as well as for the isolated farmsteads of the countryside (e.g. Bintliff and Snodgrass 1985).

This paper considers three important facets of town-country relations - public building in the towns, settlement change in the countryside, and the mobility shown by those members of the elites who acquired their wealth in the countryside, but spent it principally in the towns. The first half looks at Samnium, the second considers

Lycia and assesses how far the pattern found in Samnium is reflected there - to see whether there is a structural link between these three elements, or whether their association is purely coincidental. The concluding section considers some more general implications.

Two things have to be emphasised at the outset: that even bearing in mind its comparatively out-of-the-way position, much more archaeological fieldwork and in particular excavation has taken place in Samnium than in Lycia: the Balboura project itself is at a comparatively early stage. So naturally many of the conclusions take the form of hypotheses to be tested. This is especially true of the discussion of settlement in Lycia as much more field-survey needs to be done around the urban centre of Balboura and in the territory of the town: this is planned for the coming years. My aim is to provide a working hypothesis which fieldwork can then support or disprove.

Samnium

Samnium, strictly defined, is that part of the central Appenines occupied in antiquity by the Pentri and Frentani. However, many of the adjacent areas share a similar economic and political history and must also be taken into consideration. The Samnites played a major part in the early history of Roman expansion in Italy, as Rome's chief opponents for nearly a century; after the Romans had finally taken control of Samnite territory, they founded colonies at Beneventum (268 BC) and Aesernia (263 BC) to consolidate their control. However, the Samnites were again in the forefront of opposition to Rome during the Social War, when Aesernia became for a time the headquarters of the rebels. The area is generally characterised by geographical remoteness and cultural identity (Salmon 1967).

Public building

Before looking in detail at the history of public building in Samnium, it is important to set this in context by examining public building elsewhere in Italy during the Republican period. To do this thoroughly would be a vast undertaking, so I have chosen to look at two particular types of building as indicators of more general patterns, namely baths and aqueducts. Bathing was an essential part of Roman social life, and so serves as a valuable indicator of 'Romanisation' - as Tacitus saw, when he commented that the Britons under Agricola 'gave way to the enticements of vice - porticoes, baths and elegant dinners' (*Agricola* 21.2). Similarly, the building of aqueducts is only feasible when town and territory are integrally associated, and the political situation sufficiently stable for towns to rely on water-supplies originating from outside their walls, as Coulton observes (1987a, 73). It is also important to look at the two types of building together: although towns generally tended to have only one aqueduct, this was liable to cost a substantial sum of money, while on the other hand they might acquire quite a large number of less expensive bath-houses, built with municipal finances or by individual benefactors. So if we look both at bath-houses *and* aqueducts, we should build up a reasonably accurate picture of the situation overall.

The first trend to be noticed is the occasional involvement of officials of the state in building projects in Roman colonies in Italy. For instance, at Antium, on the Tyrrhenian coast south of Ostia, Gaius Lucretius Gallus built an aqueduct 'ex manubiis' in 170 BC (Livy 43.4.6). We know both that he had an estate in the Antium area (Livy 43.4.6-7), and that his campaigns in the East were particularly rapacious (Shatzman 1975, 254; Crawford 1977, 51), but the benefaction is still carried out on the model of traditional spending of wealth acquired as booty - on temples, roads and other public facilities, to benefit the Roman populace and bring glory on the builder and distinction on his family for posterity. Equally, when an aqueduct was built at Potentia four years later (Livy 41.27.11), the censors Fulvius Flaccus and Postumius Albinus were acting as representatives of Rome in a newly founded colony - in which the Fulvian *gens* had already been involved (Livy 39.44.10). These two examples demonstrate the extent to which Roman public building in Italy became an extension of similar activity in the city of Rome itself - Torelli (1983, 244) points out the importance of the Potentia example as an illustration of the increasing interest in Italy of the Roman senatorial elite. Both projects involve the expenditure of income derived from Rome's imperial expansion in the east. But with this wealth came also the opportunity for men like L. Betilienus Varus of Aletrium to provide their cities with a whole host of amenities - in the case of Betilienus, roads, a portico, a sports field for athletic contests, a sundial, a market-building, a basilica and treasury, a plunge-pool for the baths and a water-supply (*CIL* X 5807 = *ILS* 5348). He seems to have been involved in the oil-trade from Brundisium - another illustration of the way the profits of empire were being spent (Zevi 1976, 88). Benefactions on this scale were still exceptional, but we do find towns also using their own funds to provide facilities during the last two centuries of the Republic, as at Pompeii, where the Forum baths were built and the Stabian baths extended using public funds (Eschebach 1973; 1979; Castren 1975, 87-8).

What is common about these examples is the fact that they are all taken from Latium and Campania - either Roman colonies, or towns in the most prosperous part of southern Italy. The situation in Samnium and in the central Appennines by contrast is generally very different. In Samnium we find very little in the way of urban public building in this period - or indeed of towns, for that matter, as the characteristic unit of settlement in Samnium seems to have been the village. Even the Latin colonies at Beneventum and Aesernia show little trace of enthusiasm for benefaction and public building (Torelli 1983, 247). Instead, the money derived from Roman imperial expansion seems in Samnium to have been spent in the main on the building and improvement of the rural sanctuaries which also characterised the area. The best-known example is the monumental complex at Pietrabbondante, where one temple was built in the early second century BC, to be followed by another, with associated theatre, which was constructed later in the same century, replacing an earlier sanctuary-complex. Responsible for this new building was the Staius family - just as the Papius family built the sanctuary at Schiavi d'Abruzzo. It is possible that the wealthy families of Samnium also spent their wealth on improving the villages, the *pagi* and *vici*, to which Livy refers (9.13.6) - and the evidence of recent research at Monte Vairano show the high level of material culture in one of these sites (De Benedittis 1980). Most, however, of the epigraphic evidence surviving implies that the local administrations were responsible for those public buildings that were to be found in these places (La Regina 1968).

In the imperial period the situation changed dramatically. All over Italy there was a resurgence of building under the principate of Augustus, and especially in the colonies founded by the *princeps* and by the triumvirs. Towns like Venafrum, Brixia, Capua and Bononia are given aqueducts at this stage (Keppie 1983, 114-23). But in addition to this general development, we can from the last years of the Republic, and especially in the first years of the Principate, identify an increased level of public building in Samnium - not so much now in the *pagi* and *vici*, but in the towns which had been designated as administrative centres by Augustus (La Regina 1970). This renewed activity is characteristically directed towards the construction of 'Roman' style buildings, as the indigenous sanctuaries are abandoned or become attached to the new *municipia*; we find baths and aqueducts being provided by municipal funds or through the generosity of private benefactors. But as time goes on, we find private finance predominating in the building and repair of these monuments - firstly in the lowland areas of Italy, and eventually in the Appennines too. Thereafter private benefaction seems to be paramount: the baths and aqueducts continue to be repaired into the third century AD.

So I think some interesting general conclusions can be drawn by looking at the building of aqueducts and baths in Roman Italy. Firstly, there are quite striking differences in the sequence of building between different regions of Italy, notably Samnium on the one hand and Latium and Campania on the other. Public building in towns begins at an earlier stage on the coastal plains, by comparison with the Appennine interior. Secondly, it is essential to see the connection of political change at Rome - for example the enfranchisement of the allies, and the 'triumph of Italy over Rome' as Syme defined the accession to power of Augustus (1939, 453) - with both the development of public building, and the changes in elite mobility to be discussed in the next section.

Elite mobility

At this point, the second element in the equation - elite mobility - becomes particularly relevant; its importance in contributing to the pattern of public building has already been suggested. By the term 'elite mobility' I refer not to the replacement of a traditional elite by the upwardly mobile, but to a transferral of activities by existing elites to a new (and more prestigious) location. The most easily identifiable example of this type of mobility is entry to the Roman Senate by members of local elites in Italy, but other examples of the phenomenon can be noted too. For instance, in the first century BC and especially under the principate of Augustus, we can see elite members tranferring their attentions from the *vici* and *pagi* to the newly developing *municipia* within Samnium. A pair of inscriptions illustrates this nicely: L. Gavidius Afer, an *aedile* of the *pagus* of Betifulum in the territory of Sulmo, is commemorated on one inscription (Piccirilli 1931, 460); the other records the career of C. Gavidius Praesens, who is described as 'the first councillor from Betifulum' (*CIL* IX 3088 = *ILS* 6531). So we can see the Gavidii moving their attentions from the village of Betifulum to the *municipium* of Sulmo. The next stage is illustrated by the career of Q. Varius Geminus of Superaequum, who became a senator and served as legate of Augustus and curator of temples and monuments in the city of Rome: he is described on an honorific monument as 'the first senator from the Paelignian people' (*CIL* IX 3305 = *ILS* 932).

Prosopographical studies, in particular the work of Wiseman (1971) and Torelli (1982), have illustrated the importance of regional variation within the central Appennines in influencing patterns of mobility among local elites; for instance, Wiseman demonstrates that the Marsi were far in advance of their Sabellian neighbours in gaining senatorial rank at Rome, and tentatively explains this by showing how important physical proximity to Rome or to routes travelled by Romans was in allowing access to political honours (1971, 28ff.). However, I think it is valid to draw a distinction between the late Republic and the early Empire - the period discussed by Wiseman - and the subsequent developments of the first and second centuries AD. In the first period, the advancement of Samnites to the Senate can be specifically linked with certain political developments or individual acts of patronage - hence for example, the case of the first known Samnite senator, Statius, who seems to have owed his success to his support of Sulla (Wiseman 1971, 263), the advancement of other Samnites in the course of the Civil Wars (Wiseman 1971, 249; Torelli 1982, 172), and the specific assistance given by the emperor Claudius (well known for his generosity in encouraging provincials to join the Senate: *ILS* 212, Tacitus, *Annals* 11. 23f.) to the Samnite elites (Torelli 1982, 172). The second period is characterised by less dramatic but more substantial Samnite advancement. In this period we can see families like the Neratii, from Saepinum, gaining the highest offices: L. Neratius Marcellus, for example, was consul in 95

AD and subsequently governor of Britain (Birley 1981, 87ff.; Gaggiotti 1982). It is disputed whether the Neratii were of Samnite origin or descended from settlers (Gaggiotti, 1983, 141) - but we know of a C. Neratius who was apparently a magistrate in the town in the time of Augustus (*Année Épigraphique* 1927, 118). Perhaps most significant is the fact that his family still owned substantial properties in the territory of the neighbouring city of Ligures Baebiani in the time of Trajan (Champlin 1981, 256-8).

So this account of mobility among the Samnite elites can be summarised as follows. A few individuals of Samnite stock - largely because of individual patronage - gained access to the Senate in the late Republic and the early Empire, but the greatest influx from Samnium came in the late first and second centuries AD. This development can be seen as a symptom of the increasing wealth, influence, and urban orientation of the elites of Samnium, from the time of Augustus onwards, which is also manifested in the growth of public building illustrated in the previous section.

Settlement patterns

Here the evidence is primarily archaeological, but occasional pieces of epigraphic evidence do help, notably the alimentary tables from Ligures Baebiani (in Samnium) and Veleia. Here too regional variation is of vital importance; again I focus my attention on Samnium, and summarise the main conclusions of a synoptic study of the problems of settlement change in central Italy (Patterson 1987).

The most extensive field-survey in Samnium was that carried out by Graeme Barker in the Biferno valley area: it revealed that between the late first century BC and the early second century AD, a half to two-thirds of the sites occupied disappeared (Barker, Lloyd and Webley 1978; Lloyd and Barker 1981). The same pattern seems to be true of the upper Volturno valley (Patterson 1985) and also in the territory of the Ligures Baebiani (Patterson 1988), though with some local variation in each case.

In order to understand the implications of this fall in the number of occupied sites, it is essential to compare the evidence of the Trajanic alimentary table from Ligures Baebiani. The *alimenta* were set up by the emperor Trajan early in the second century AD to provide food for children in the towns of Italy, and the arrangements for the organisation of two of these schemes are preserved in the form of bronze tablets. These list the farms (or *fundi*) hypothecated to the schemes by the local landowners, who received a lump-sum loan from the emperor but were then obliged to pay a given proportion of the loan every year into the fund for the maintenance of poor children. The bronze tablets record the estates contributed to the scheme, and the names of these *fundi* imply that several estates had in many cases been joined together to create larger units. Now clearly the dates at which the *fundi* had their names fixed is vital for the interpretation of this piece of evidence - giving a *terminus post quem* for the amalgamation of the estates. I would suggest that the *fundi* were officially codified during the principate of Augustus (Patterson 1987, 141-2). If this is correct then much of the amalgamation of estates must have taken place between the time of Augustus and the time of Trajan, when the alimentary table was compiled (Champlin 1981, 245-6 for an alternative interpretation).

So the evidence of the alimentary scheme complements that provided by archaeological field-survey: the decline in the number of sites identified through survey is explained by reference to the increasing agglomeration of rural estates. The problem then arises of what this change actually meant in practice for the country people who owned or occupied these estates. Various possibilities could exist: that the peasants remained on the land as tenants of the larger proprietors, living in poor and squalid circumstances; or that they left the land to become bandits (a scourge in many parts of Italy even under the supposed rural peace of the empire (Shaw 1984) and particularly characteristic of the central Appennines); or departed from the land altogether, to go to the city of Rome (which was continually sucking in manpower) or the other cities of Italy. This last possibility is discussed in greater detail below - but essentially, the situation in Samnium seems to be characterised by a gradual increase in the size of landed estates during the first century AD.

Drafting the model

At this point the different components of the model can be interrelated. During the first two centuries AD, dramatic changes took place in Samnium. The interests of the local elites transferred themselves from the traditional *vici* to the newly constituted *municipia*, and eventually some individuals became senators themselves. But in the intervening period, between the growth of towns in Samnium and the large-scale penetration of the Senate by the Samnite elites, there was a period of dramatic elite competition within the towns of Samnium, as local dignitaries competed amongst themselves for prestige: it was in this period that the Samnite towns gained many of their public buildings. Thereafter the elite members who succeeded in reaching the Senate were in a strong position when it came to attracting imperial patronage to their home towns; their own day-to-day contributions to local finances may have been substantially reduced (Torelli 1982, 176) - although the continuing importance of construction and restoration of buildings shows that this did not result in a total neglect of the towns.

So there seems to be a strong link between elite mobility and public building: elite mobility is essentially the product of local competition in the Roman system, and public building was one of the ways in which members of elites could compete for *gloria*. But these changes were closely linked to rural development too. In order to enter the Senate the members of the Samnite elites had to possess the million sesterces which was the senatorial property qualification. By comparison, the sum of 100,000 HS is often attested as the qualifying sum for membership of the municipal council in many towns in Italy - and even smaller figures are also known (Duncan-Jones 1982, 243). Clearly increased wealth must have played a part in their advancement, and it is here that we can identify a close link with rural change. Throughout the first century AD, the estates of the Samnite elites became larger and larger as they took over the properties of the poor and of lesser members of the elites - by inheritance or purchase, if not by the violent means attested in the time of the Gracchi and in the first century BC (Brunt 1971, 551-7). And it is this amalgamation of landholdings that we can see reflected in the results of archaeological field-survey and the data provided by the Ligures Baebiani Table. This is not to deny that even before Augustus some large estates existed in Samnium, owned by indigenous wealthy families, as John Lloyd convincingly argues in a forthcoming paper; rather that the scale of large properties increased in size under the Empire, enabling their owners to compete in wealth on a pan-Italian basis. In a region of Italy comparatively poor in agricultural terms, it was a long process to acquire enough wealth for the senatorial qualification (Wiseman 1971, 26).

It can be argued, furthermore, that one effect of this increased agglomeration of estates was a drift to the cities on the part of the rural poor: that the economies of scale practised on the larger rural estates, and the increased productivity extracted from rural labourers by landholders, meant that the estates could be worked with a lower input of labour than before. The dispossessed rural dwellers moved to the towns, where they were given occasional employment in public building schemes financed by the increasingly wealthy elites, and benefited from the occasional feasts and distributions of *crustulum* and *mulsum* organised by local aristocrats. Eventually, their children were supported by the alimentary schemes set up by Trajan and other emperors (Patterson 1987, 144-6). This further hypothesis is, however, as yet difficult to prove, given that the traditional focus of much urban archaeology in Italy has been on the monumental centres of towns, rather than the shanties on their periphery which would have housed such a displaced population. It also raises the question of possible fluctuations in population in this period. But the general line of development is clear - urban building, elite competition and increased estate sizes were all closely and inextricably linked in Roman Samnium.

Lycia

What relevance does all this have to the situation in Asia Minor, and more specifically the town of Balboura and its territory?

First of all, Balboura itself: its early history is rather obscure, but its origins as a polis seem to have been in the late third or early second century BC. It belonged to a tetrapolis composed of four towns - Cibyra, Bubon and Oenoanda, as well as Balboura - which was then divided between Lycia and Asia by the Roman general L. Licinius Murena in 84 BC (Bean 1978, 166-70). Lycia as a whole was under the rule of the Ptolemies after the third century BC, but was conquered by Antiochus III in 197 BC; after Antiochus' defeat by the Romans it was regarded as enemy territory and given to the Rhodians. The constant protests at Rhodian rule by the Lycians, however, led to their independence and self-government under the *Koinon* (Federation) of the Lycians. Lycian freedom came to an abrupt end in the reign of Claudius, who annexed the area and attached

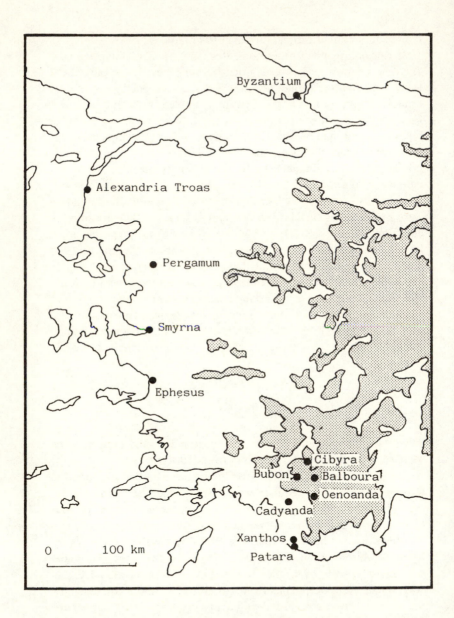

Figure 2: Western Asia Minor (shaded areas represent land over 1000m)

it to neighbouring Pamphylia as a province under the control of a governor, Q. Veranius (Gordon 1953, 243ff.). It seems to have been freed again by Nero, but was then definitively taken under Roman control by Vespasian (Keil 1936; Magie 1950, 529-30).

Most of the archaeological research which has taken place in Lycia has been concentrated on the urban centres, so the information we have on rural settlement is rather meagre. However, we do know that in addition to the poleis there were also numerous villages, *komai* (Coulton 1982, 123), and estate centres, *monagriai*, scattered around the territory - these are attested by an inscription giving details of contributions to a festival at Oenoanda (Wörrle 1988). So in upland Lycia as well as in Samnium, small villages formed an important part of the settlement system. In both cases this is likely to have been related to the pattern of the landscape, which was made up of numerous small plains surrounded by mountains, most easily exploited by means of small nucleated settlements. Pastoralism may also have been important here as it certainly was in Roman Samnium (Gabba and Pasquinucci 1979, 79-182). So the basic arrangement of settlement - a few towns, and many scattered villages - recalls Samnium as much as the landscape does.

Public building

Just as in Italy, urban building varies in date and rhythm between various different parts of Asia Minor. The first aqueduct we know of in Asia Minor was that at Ephesus, dating to the reign of Augustus (Coulton 1987a, 73). Dio of Prusa, speaking in the late first century AD, cites four cities as shining examples of public building and its virtues: Smyrna, Ephesus, Tarsus and Antioch (*Orations* 40.11). Apparently Dio's opponents on the council of Prusa objected to his attempts to bring their own city into the same league as these (*Orations* 47.12ff.), which were not only large and wealthy cities with close imperial patronage, but were also on the sea and thus ideally placed to gather the benefits of the *Pax Romana* in terms of trade and commerce. In the mid-second century AD Herodes Atticus built an aqueduct for the city of Alexandria Troas - the account Philostratus gives us implies that it was scandalous that such a city should have lacked a water-supply at that time - presumably making a comparison with other wealthy coastal cities (*Lives of the Sophists* 548).

Our knowledge of the sequence and rhythm of public building in Lycia in particular has been greatly increased by the work carried out at Oenoanda by J.J. Coulton and the late Alan Hall (Coulton 1983; Stenton and Coulton 1986). Their study of surviving monuments has confirmed the general impression given by the epigraphic record (Broughton 1938, 779-84), namely that the main period of substantial Roman urban public building in Lycia essentially starts in the Flavian period, to which the aqueducts at Oenoanda and Balboura belong, as well as the one at Patara on the coast (Coulton 1983, 9; Stenton and Coulton 1986, 43-4; 56-8). The building of these aqueducts is apparently associated with the construction of bath-houses in these cities (Coulton 1987a, 82), but given that one of the two aqueducts supplying Balboura is specifically dedicated to Vespasian, Titus and Domitian, it is also possible that one element in the impetus that led to the provision of the water-supply was the atmosphere of change that followed the reorganisation of the area under Vespasian. The imposition of the Roman peace would, as Coulton notes (1987a), have created the conditions which would allow the safe provision of external water-supplies. Besides, Vespasian seems to have intervened personally to build certain monuments: he organised the building of bath-houses at Patara and Cadyanda out of diverted public funds (Mitchell 1987, 21).

Public building on a lavish scale continued in Lycia into the third century, with its apogee in the latter half of the second century AD. Most of the datable inscriptions from Balboura (now being studied by Nicholas Milner) were set up in the second century, and many of the monuments too - for example, the exedra of Meleager, who was also responsible for instituting a festival in the town, approved by Antoninus Pius in 158 AD (Coulton 1987b, 207). The agora-complex, and many other buildings at Oenoanda, likewise date to the second century (Coulton 1983; Coulton 1986). Since the two cities seem to be characteristic of the rest of Lycia in this respect, we can see the widespread enthusiasm for public building which characterises Samnium in the Augustan period appearing in Lycia some seventy years later - after its establishment as a Roman province.

One major difference which has to be emphasised, however, is that the polis system already existed in Lycia, whereas, with the exception of the colonies founded by Rome, and a few quasi-urban centres like

Monte Vairano, there were no towns in Samnium. It is striking in the case of Balboura, however, that the baths and other buildings of the imperial period were built on or just above the plain overlooked by the city, whereas the Hellenistic city was built on an inaccessible hill, where monumental building only recurred with the insecurity of the late Empire. For all practical purposes, the 'new' town of Balboura, on the plain, was just as much a departure from traditional practices as the Roman towns of Samnium were from the traditional Samnite hillforts.

So in Lycia as well as Samnium, the years following the effective imposition of Roman control in a marginal, mountainous area were characterised by a dramatic growth in the extent and scale of public building.

Elite mobility

The extension of the Roman citizenship, and as a consequence the extension of membership of the senatorial order, to citizens of the Empire, was one of the most striking aspects of the Roman imperial system; and the increasing predominance of provincials in the Senate is one of the most striking features of Roman public life in the second century AD. Hammond (1957) calculates that while 17% of identifiable senators originated in Greece and Asia Minor in the latter part of the first century AD, by the end of the second century the figure had risen to 58%: a dramatic increase.

Just as with the advancement of Samnites, we can see regional variation playing a part in the extent to which members of the local elites in the towns of Asia Minor entered the Senate. Inhabitants of the Caesarian and Augustan colonies seem to have been in the forefront of entry to the Senate in the first half of the first century AD, with a few notable exceptions, like Q. Pompeius Macer of Mytilene, praetor in AD 15, whose grandfather had been a close associate of Pompey (Strabo 13, 618). From the Flavian era onward, though, Greek-speaking senators of eastern origin began to play an increasingly visible role; at first, those honoured are generally members of native royal houses, or originate from great cities like Ephesus, Pergamum or Ancyra; but subsequently senatorial rank is acquired by members of local elites from all over Asia Minor (Walton 1929; Levick 1967; Halfmann 1982). However, only at the end of the

first century AD do we know of a Lycian entering the Senate: M.
Arruntius Claudianus of Xanthos, patron and benefactor of that city,
who was honoured for his generosity and his achievements by the
Xanthians and the Federation of the Lycians (which was still
functioning within the Roman province). His full name has only
recently been identified, from an inscription found at the Letoon
sanctuary at Xanthos (Balland 1981, 143-71). As capital of Lycia and
seat of the Federation, it was not surprising that Xanthos produced
the first Lycian to enter the Senate: though it has to be borne in mind
that there were close family ties between the elites of the different
Lycian cities. More Lycian senators are known from the second
century; an inscription recording the family tree of the Licinius
family, mentioning several senators and giving a detailed body of
information on Lycian high society, was found at   (*IGRR* III 500).
Ti. Claudius Agrippinus, for instance, became a member of the Arval
Brethren in   AD 155, and consul too, though the date of this honour
is not clear; his son, Ti. Claudius Dryantianus Antoninus, likewise a
senator, was alleged to have plotted against Marcus Aurelius in AD
175 (Jameson 1966, 125-6; Jameson 1973, 283-6; Halfmann 1982,
639-41). Here again the coastal families take the lead - the Claudii
Dryantiani (of Patara) gain access to the Senate, and are linked to the
Licinii of Oenoanda by marriage.

So the parallel with Samnium is again clear: the province of Lycia
providing entrants to the Senate several decades after the more
developed coastal cities, and several decades after the 'take-off' in
urban development which was symptomatic of increased elite
competition. It is important to emphasise, though, that not all the
benefactors themselves reached the Senate: one of the best known
benefactors to the Lycian cities, Opramoas of Rhodiapolis (see
Coulton 1987c), was not himself a senator, though he was proud of
his family relationships with senators. His niece married one - Ti.
Claudius Agrippinus.

Applying the model

The third element I considered in my discussion of Samnium was
rural settlement change, but this is clearly difficult in the case of
Lycia, in the absence (as yet) of detailed archaeological evidence from
the territories of Balboura or of Oenoanda. The Samnite parallels

would suggest that the villages would decline as centres of elite activity, that the number of scattered farms would decrease, and the town of Balboura would expand - as a place of residence for displaced country-dwellers as well as a centre of elite activity. There are some indications that there were large private estates in the vicinity of Balboura, from rather scanty epigraphic evidence - we know of a number of cases where benefactors made over estates to cities in lieu of cash gifts (Broughton 1938, 669). At Cibyra, the next city to the north of Balboura, we know of the confiscation by the city of an estate with 107 slaves (*IGRR* IV 914; Robert 1937, 377). But this kind of information gives us no chronological dynamic at all. By contrast, the development of a new monumental centre provides a striking parallel to the Samnite situation, and there is also some evidence which seems to confirm, albeit provisionally, the second part of the hypothesis too. In 1986 and 1987, I conducted a preliminary survey of the 'lower city' which apparently consisted of an area of habitation around the urban monuments of imperial date at Balboura, and now survives only in the form of a pottery scatter. Unfortunately, analysis of the pottery collected during these two seasons has been delayed; but first indications seem to suggest that by far the largest proportion of this pottery was of imperial date. This, I would argue, demonstrates that in fact the city of Balboura *did* grow - though exactly at what stage this growth took place is as yet far from clear. I prefer this analysis to the alternative view of the data, that rather than actually increasing in size, the city just moved from a hilltop location to one surrounding the new monumental centre: it seems to me that the economic upheaval involved in the building of an entirely new monumental complex must have had significant effects on the settlement structure of the city and its immediate surroundings, even if this was only a consequence of the new year-round water-supply now piped into the city through the two aqueducts. I should stress again the provisional nature of this working hypothesis, which will receive further examination during forthcoming seasons of work at Balboura.

One obvious distinction between Samnium and Lycia is that the latter was a province, while the former was in Italy: the Lycians had to pay tax. The case of Lycia seems to be a classic example of the link between tax, trade and urban development outlined by Hopkins (1978; 1980); Lycia had paid tax (in cash) under the rule of the Ptolemies (P. Tebtunis 8), but was presumably free of taxation during its period of freedom. The annexation of the area under Claudius and subsequently Vespasian, and the energetic collection of taxes by the latter (Suetonius, *Vespasian* 16, 1) must have had important consequences for the local urban economies, exacerbating the general tendencies paralleled by the situation in Samnium, where tax-collection was not a significant factor.

Conclusions

The parallels shown between the hill-country of south-west Turkey and that of central Italy tend, I would argue, to suggest that there are structural links between elite mobility, increased public building, and increased private wealth leading to settlement change. These phenomena can be identified in Samnium from the Augustan principate, and in Lycia from the time of Vespasian. Some seventy years elapse in both cases before a significant number of local dignitaries reach senatorial rank, but in each case the process is the same. The first conclusion to be drawn, then, is that the comparison of two apparently different areas, at opposite ends of the Mediterranean, can be an illuminating way of devising new models for areas which have in the past been comparatively little studied from this sort of perspective.

If we accept the structural links between settlement change, elite mobility and urban public building, this does not commit us to dismissing the importance of external political, social and economic factors in the history of a particular area. External influences can be identified at a number of stages in the developments outlined here. The growth of estates, the advancement of the Samnite elites to the senate, and urban development in this part of Italy, seem to have been fairly sluggish until Augustan initiatives picked out certain settlements as administrative centres, and equipped others with the paraphernalia of civilised living. Similarly, the effective transformation of Lycia from client state to province under Vespasian had many significant effects: a general climate of change, the employment of the 'pump-priming' technique to encourage competitive benefaction and urbanisation, for example by his building programmes at Patara and Cadyanda, the exploitation of the *Pax Augusta* by cities which were now able to build outside their walls, without fear of the bandits for which Lycia had long been infamous - it is ironic that banditry became a renewed problem in the area in the third century AD, perhaps as a consequence of estate growth and rural impoverishment. Lastly, but perhaps most significantly, the imposition of taxation, which as an exaction in cash had major implications for the local economy.

Elite mobility, urbanisation, and settlement change were, then, three identifying features of Romanisation. Structurally interlinked, they nevertheless had their roots in the political, social, and economic pressures which were the result of Roman conquest and influence. In the mountainous areas of Samnium and Lycia, we can begin to build up a picture of the way in which these developments interrelated. Exposure to Roman models of building, and the exemplary generosity of emperors and members of the Roman political elite led to an enthusiasm for competitive benefaction in cities; Roman taxation (in the case of Lycia), and the need for increased wealth for this kind of generosity on the part of the local elites led to an increase in estate sizes. This in turn led to a disruption of the rural population, and, I would argue, an increase in urban populations to match the scale of building. The possibility of further advancement within the Roman hierarchy, encouraged at first by individual acts of patronage, led to an increased level of competition within the towns, and intensified the developments which were already taking place. Advancement of the provincial elites to senatorial rank was in part the product of personal patronage by emperors - but the phenomenon also owed much to the more general social, economic and political effects of Roman rule, which set the whole complex of estate growth and urban competition in motion. The isolated mountains of Lycia and Samnium are areas we might least expect to be affected by Roman rule: the fact that the results of Roman control are so apparent even here shows the tremendous impact of the Empire on the Mediterranean basin as a whole.

Acknowledgements

I am very grateful to the editors, and to Dr J.J. Coulton and Professor M.H. Crawford, for their comments on drafts of this paper.

Bibliography

Balland, A. (1981), *Fouilles de Xanthos VII: inscriptions d'époque impériale du Letoon*. Paris.

Barker, G., Lloyd, J. and Webley, D. (1978), 'A Classical landscape in Molise', *Papers of the British School at Rome* 46, 35-51.

Bean, G.E. (1978), *Lycian Turkey*. London.

Bintliff, J.L. and Snodgrass, A.M. (1985), 'The Cambridge/Bradford Boeotian Expedition: the first four years', *Journal of Field Archaeology* 12, 123-61.

Birley, A. (1981), *The Fasti of Roman Britain*. Oxford.

Broughton, T.S.R. (1938), 'Roman Asia Minor', in T. Frank (ed.), *Economic Survey of Ancient Rome* 4, 499-950.

Brunt, P.A. (1971), *Italian Manpower 225 BC - AD 14*. Oxford.

Castrén, P. (1975), *Ordo Populusque Pompeianus*. Rome.

Champlin, E. (1981), 'Owners and neighbours at Ligures Baebiani', *Chiron* 11, 239-264.

Coulton, J.J. (1982), 'Termessians at Oinoanda', *Anatolian Studies* 32, 115-121.

Coulton, J.J. (1983), 'The buildings of Oinoanda', *Proceedings of the Cambridge Philological Society* n.s. 29, 1-20.

Coulton, J.J. (1986), 'Oinoanda: the Agora', *Anatolian Studies* 36, 61-90.

Coulton, J.J. (1987a), 'Roman aqueducts in Asia Minor', in S. Macready and F.H. Thompson (eds.), *Roman Architecture in the Greek World*, 72-84. London.

Coulton, J.J. (1987b), 'Balboura Survey 1986', *V. Araştırma Sonuçları Toplantısı* I (Ankara, 6-10 Nisan 1987), 205-11.

Coulton, J.J. (1987c), 'Opramoas and the anonymous benefactor', *Journal of Hellenic Studies* 107, 171-8.

Crawford, M.H. (1977), 'Rome and the Greek world: economic relationships', *Economic History Review* n.s. 30, 42-52.

De Benedittis, G. (1980), 'L'oppidum di Monte Vairano ovvero Aquilonia', in *Sannio: Pentri e Frentani dal VI al I sec. a.C.*, 321-57.

Duncan-Jones, R.P. (1982), *The Economy of the Roman Empire: Quantitative Studies*, 2nd edn. Cambridge.

Eschebach, H. (1973), 'Laconicum et destrictarium faciund ... locarunt': Untersuchungen in den Stabianer Thermen zu Pompeji', *Römische Mitteilungen* 80, 235-42.

Gabba, E. and Pasquinucci, M. (1979), *Strutture agrarie e allevamento transumante nell'Italia romana*. Pisa.

Gaggiotti, M. (1982), 'La gens Neratia', in *Saepinum: Museo documentario dell'Altilia*. Campobasso.

Gaggiotti, M. (1983), 'Il Sannio Pentro', in M. Cebeillac-Gervasoni (ed.), *Les 'bourgeoisies' municipales italiennes aux IIe et Ier siècles av J.-C.*, 137-50. Naples.

Gordon, A.E. (1953), 'Quintus Veranius, consul AD 49: a study based upon his recently identified sepulchral inscription', *Univ. of California Publications in Classical Archaeology* II, 5.

Halfmann, H. (1982), 'Die senatoren aus den Kleinasiatischen Provinzen', in *Epigrafia e Ordine Senatorio* II, 603-50. Rome.

Hammond, M. (1957), 'Composition of the Senate AD 68-238', *Journal of Roman Studies* 47, 73-81.

Hodges, E. and Mitchell, J. (1985), *San Vincenzo al Volturno: the Archaeology, Art and Territory of an Early Medieval Monastery*. Oxford.

Hopkins, K. (1978), 'Economic growth and towns in Classical antiquity', in P. Abrams and A. Wrigley (eds.), *Towns in Societies*, 35-77. Cambridge.

Hopkins, K. (1980), 'Taxes and trade in the Roman Empire (200 BC - AD 400) *Journal of Roman Studies* 70, 101-25.

Hopkins, K. (1983), *Death and Renewal*. Cambridge.

Jameson, S.E. (1966), 'Two Lycian families', *Anatolian Studies* 16, 125-37.

Jameson, S.E. (1973), 'Lykia', *RE* suppl. XII, coll. 265-308.

Keil, J. (1936), 'The Greek provinces: Lycia et Pamphylia', *Cambridge Ancient History* XI, 590ff. Cambridge.

Keppie, L.J.F. (1983), *Colonisation and Veteran Settlement in Italy, 47-14 BC*. London.

La Regina, A. (1968), 'Ricerche sugli insediamenti Vestini', *Memorie dell'Accademia Nazionale dei Lincei* VIII 13, 5, 361ff.

La Regina, A. (1970), 'Note sulla formazione dei centri urbani in area sabellica', in *Atti del convegno di studi sulla città etrusca e italica preromana*, 191-207. Bologna.

Levick, B.M. (1967), *Roman Colonies in Southern Asia Minor*. Oxford.

Lloyd, J. and Barker, G. (1981), 'Rural settlement in Roman Molise: problems of archaeological survey', in G. Barker and R. Hodges, *Archaeology and Italian Society*, 281-304. Oxford.

Magie, D. (1950), *Roman Rule in Asia Minor*. Princeton.

Mitchell, S. (1987), 'Imperial building in the eastern Roman provinces', in S. Macready and F.H. Thompson (eds.), *Roman Architecture in the Greek World*. London.

Patterson, J.R. (1985), 'The upper Volturno valley in Roman times', in R. Hodges and J. Mitchell (eds.), *San Vincenzo al Volturno: the Archaeology, Art and Territory of an Early Medieval Monastery*, 213-26. Oxford.

Patterson, J.R. (1987), 'Crisis: what crisis? Rural change and urban development in imperial Appennine Italy', *Papers of the British School at Rome* 55, 115-46.

Patterson, J.R. (1988), *Samnites, Ligurians and Romans*. Circello.

Piccirilli, G. (1931), *Atti e Memorie del Convegno Storico Abruzzese Molisano* 2, 460.

Robert, L. (1937), *Études Anatoliennes*. Paris.

Salmon, E.T. (1967), *Samnium and the Samnites*. Cambridge.

Shatzman, I. (1975), *Senatorial Wealth and Roman Politics*. Brussels.

Shaw, B. (1984), 'Bandits in the Roman Empire', *Past and Present* 105, 3-52.

Snodgrass, A.M. (1982), 'La Prospection archéologique en Grèce et dans le monde méditerranéen', *Annales - Economie-Société-Culture* 37, 800-12.

Stenton, E.C. and Coulton, J.J. (1986), 'Oinoanda: the water supply and aqueduct', *Anatolian Studies*, 36, 15-59.

Torelli, M. (1982), 'Ascesa al senato e rapporti con i territori d'origine', in *Epigrafia e Ordine Senatorio* II, 165-99. Rome.

Torelli, M. (1983), 'Edilizia pubblica in Italia centrale fra guerra sociale e età Augustea: ideologia e classi sociali', in M. Cebeillac-Gervasoni (ed.), *Les 'bourgeoisies' municipales italiennes aux IIe et Ier siècles av. J.-C.*, 241-50. Naples.

Walton, C.S. (1929), 'Oriental senators in the service of Rome', *Journal of Roman Studies* 19, 38-66.

Wiseman, T.P. (1971), *New Men in the Roman Senate 139 BC - AD 14*. Oxford.

Wörrle, M. (1988), *Stadt und Fest in Kaiserzeitlichen Kleinasien*, Munich.

Zevi, F. (1976), 'Alatri', in P. Zanker (ed.), *Hellenismus in Mittelitalien* I, 84-96. Göttingen.

7

Roman towns and their territories: an archaeological perspective

Martin Millett

Introduction

Contemporary archaeology is beginning to develop methods which enable the relationships between towns and their hinterlands to be explored. This paper attempts to review some of the methods used together with some results in order to illustrate their potential as a source of new evidence. To realise the scope and limitations of this archaeological work two important general points should be appreciated. First, since most archaeological evidence is the accidental by-product of past human activity, the information it communicates is latent, passive and static, so only articulated through interpretative models imposed by the observer, whether or not these are made explicit. In this lies both the strength and weakness of archaeology, for although its evidence is 'unbiased' in the sense that it does not suffer from the distortions that affect written sources, it is particularly prone to echo our contemporary views of the world. This observation has sometimes been overlooked by those using archaeological data, although its recognition has equal dangers for it has blinded us to other problems. Uncritical uses of archaeological information have been based on the assumption that the evidence about the past is 'unbiased'. In recent years an increasing awareness that this is fallacious has led archaeologists to develop methods of source criticism (analogous to those practised by historians) vital if we are to avoid naive interpretations. This has involved attempts at understanding the processes which have led to the formation of the archaeological record (Schiffer 1976). Such methodology has wide implications for those using archaeological data: they should be aware of the dangers of accepting archaeological evidence at face value.

Secondly, archaeologists have to use a chronology which is considerably less precise than that which is available to those reliant upon documentary sources. These chronologies make questions which examine causality or the interrelationships of individual events extremely difficult to address (Millett 1981a). Awareness of this has led many archaeologists to pose more general questions for which the evidence is more appropriate. These are often concerned with processes of long-term change and the varying composition of assemblages from different sites. In examining these questions the wide spatial and social range of archaeological evidence enables us to examine aspects of the past which are not otherwise easily approached.

These introductory comments are offered to show that archaeological 'rules of evidence' are necessarily different from those applied by ancient historians to their texts but that the strengths of our sources make them peculiarly appropriate to examining the changing relationships between ancient cities and their territories. As the range and scope of the sources differ, so will the reconstructions of the past produced from them. In examining town/country relationships, the realization of the complementary nature of archaeological and historical sources is important, for worthwhile new insights are likely when our different views of the past are contrasted.

The prime archaeological problem in examining urban centres and their surroundings lies in the fact that past social, economic and political systems were dynamic, whilst the archaeological materials - the rubbish by-products of society - are static. Archaeologists therefore need to use data which can give direct insights into the functioning of the systems under study. Here I have chosen to illustrate the investigation of these issues, first, through settlement patterns themselves, and, secondly, through the flows of goods between individual settlements. This discussion investigates both data from surveys and materials recovered from excavations. The latter comprise both objects produced by human populations (artefacts) and those from the natural environment exploited by them (ecofacts). These are merely illustrations of the scope of archaeological data and I have deliberately ignored potential information from a number of sources like the analysis of building types and epigraphy.

The settlement pattern

Given that there is an exploitative or symbiotic relationship between towns and their territories, the pattern of settlement around any town should provide evidence of the nature of the interactions between urban and rural sites. As settlement patterns are a result of a series of interrelated influences including ecology and past history as well as the nature of the socio-economic and political systems, their interpretation is likely to be complicated. Nevertheless, major spatial relationships can sometimes be discerned and interpreted archaeologically, although the results may not be unambiguous as it is common for different processes to produce indistinguishable patterns of distribution (Hodder and Orton 1976).

A critical awareness of the reliability of site distribution evidence is an essential prerequisite for any reliable analysis. When examining a distribution map of Roman rural settlement in a particular area (fig.1) our first question should be what the map represents: is it a result of casual knowledge, or information systematically collected? On fig.1 the concentrations of sites can be shown to result from at least two factors which distort the archaeologically recorded pattern. First, differential intensities of fieldwork have led to a more thorough knowledge of distributions in areas where work has been concentrated. Blanks in the known distribution are often simply the result of a failure to look for evidence. Secondly, not all archaeological sites are equally visible. Certain types of site - larger villas and sites with prolific finds - are more likely to have been noticed accidentally than, for instance, a peasant farm. Similarly, the more robust an archaeological object, the more likely it is to survive and be noticed on the surface of a ploughed field. Romano-British pottery, for instance, survives longer on the surface of ploughed fields than most prehistoric pottery which was less well made (Crowther 1983). The recognition of these basic factors lies behind recent attempts at more systematic data collection through regional field surveys, although it would be wrong to assume either that all survey evidence is reliable, or that non-systematic data are unusable.

The use of evidence which has not been collected systematically can be illustrated with the example of the spatial analysis of villa distributions. This study was based on first seeking patterning in the existing haphazard distribution data, then attempting to interpret it. The analysis examined the distribution of Roman villas in Britain in relation to towns and examined the variation in the relative density of sites with distance from towns (Hodder and Millett 1980; cf. Gregson 1982). Our work was based on the simple idea that the more important a town, the more attractive it would be to those constructing villas. A town with a high attraction would have more villas for a great distance away from it than would one with a low attractiveness (fig.2). This was pointed out by Rivet many years ago (1955), although it was not taken beyond the level of general observation.

We measured the decline of *density* of villas in bands with increasing distance from each town to enable their relative attractiveness to villas to be established. Since variations in density (i.e. villas per hectare) were being assessed, the importance of the absolute numbers of known sites was reduced. The validity of this approach clearly depends on the quality of the evidence, but as villas are generally amongst the most visible of archaeological sites, biases seem less important than they might be. This optimism is supported by the results of our study, the consistency of which inspires some confidence. They show that in general the towns most attractive to villas were not those of the largest size, but those which fulfilled a major administrative role. Since size is most likely to correlate with the economic success of the towns, and administrative status with their social and political pull, this result supports the idea that the villas (as opposed to the less Romanised farmsteads) were most appropriately located close to the administratively important towns. Thus although some high status towns (like London) lack substantial villa concentrations, these absences can be explained by reference to a complex of other factors (Millett, forthcoming, A) and do not contradict the general conclusion which underlines the formative importance of the administrative structure in the Roman system. It seems unlikely that new fieldwork will substantially alter this conclusion for Britain, although it would be extremely interesting to see comparable analyses for more central provinces.

In many areas evidence about the settlement patterns is less satisfactory, while elsewhere we may wish to undertake more systematic analyses than that just described, so it is frequently desirable to begin with the systematic collection of new data. This is

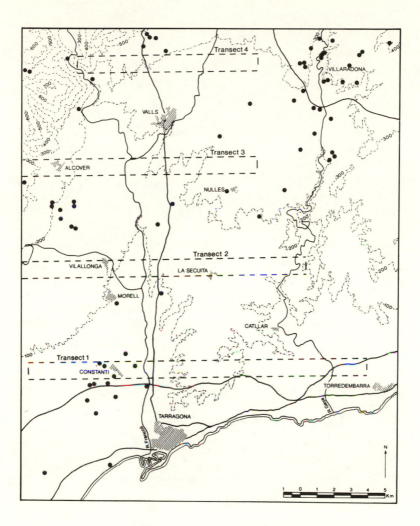

Figure 1: The *Ager Tarraconensis* Survey showing the distribution of sites known before work began together with the location of the survey transects. Note how the concentrations of sites reflect the intensity of work, especially in the north-east and south-west.

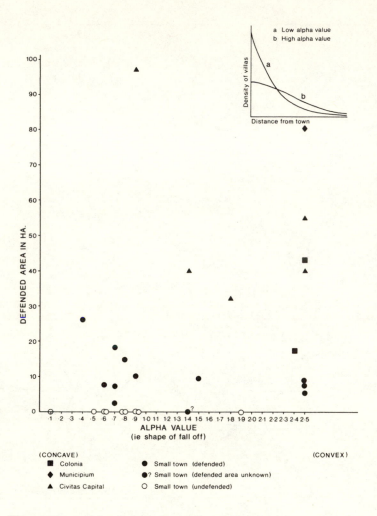

Figures 2a and b: Graphs illustrating the relationship between town size and villa distribution in Roman Britain (based on data from Hodder and Millet 1980).

2a: the defended areas of the towns compared with the shape of the fall-off in density of villas with distance away from them. A convex shape indicates a high attraction to villas, a concave one, a more limited spatial influence. Note how towns with a demonstrable administrative role tend to have more convex curves than those of the 'small towns'.

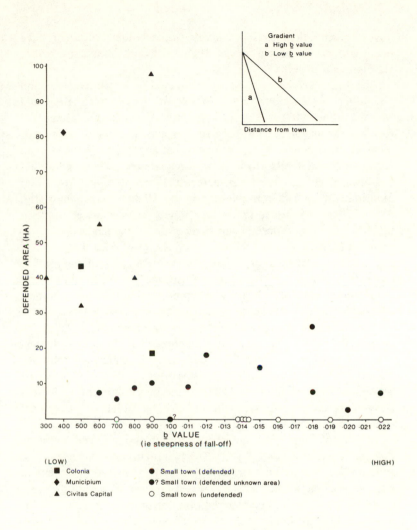

Figure 2b: The defended areas of the towns are compared with the steepness of the fall-off in villa-density away from them. The steeper the fall-off (i.e. the higher the b-value), the less attractive the town was to villas. This graph shows clearly that towns with an administrative role were more attractive to villas than the 'small towns'.

now frequently done by field survey, the techniques of which have been widely discussed (e.g. Macready and Thompson 1985; Haselgrove *et al.* 1985).

The *Ager Tarraconensis* survey (directed by Dr Simon Keay and the author), which provides an example of this approach (Keay and Millett 1986; 1987; 1988; forthcoming, A) aims to evaluate the Roman impact on the territory of Tarraco, provincial capital of *Hispania Tarraconensis*. In five seasons of approximately one month each, we are attempting to walk all the available arable land within four 1km-wide East-West transects which sample the landscape at 5km intervals inland from the city on the Mediterranean coast (fig. 3). These transects are designed to provide a representative sample of the different types of terrain across the grain of the landscape and at increasing distances from the coast and the city. Within this area a limited number of sites (principally major villas) was known prior to our survey. Given the importance of Tarraco we expected the rural landscape to have been heavily occupied, perhaps with the highest concentrations of villas in the immediate environs of the city.

The technique of fieldwalking used is for experienced walkers to traverse the fields about 5m apart, collecting all visible archaeological material from the surface. The bulk of this material comprises pottery, which is most densely distributed in the vicinity of settlement sites (Haselgrove 1985) so the distribution of settlement sites of different periods can be mapped by isolating the densest concentrations of pottery.

In principle, this is straightforward, but methodological problems do exist (Haselgrove *et al.* 1985). The two main problems result first from the fact that past human activity was not confined to settlement sites. Instead the whole landscape was used for a variety of different purposes. Finds of surface material often result from these uses - for instance through domestic refuse being mixed into manure - so a careful methodology is required to distinguish settlements from other traces. On a small scale such a methodology has been successfully used in the examination of a block of landscape on the Berkshire Downs, where different types of surface distributions of material have been correlated with settlement sites and areas of arable and pastoral agriculture (Gaffney *et al.* 1985a and b). On a regional scale we are attempting to tackle the problems of distinguishing settlement sites from the residues of agriculture in our examination of the *Ager Tarraconensis* by collecting all surface material and looking for

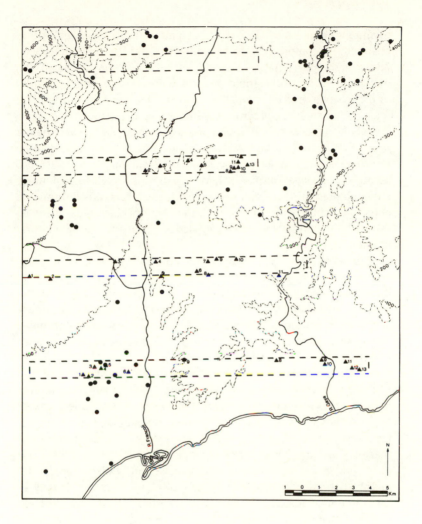

Figure 3: The *Ager Tarraconensis* Survey showing sites discovered to 1988 (triangles) in relation to those previously known (circles). It should be noted that although the survey is incomplete (especially in the north and west) the balance in site distribution has already been radically altered.

distinctive patterning. The types of patterning we are seeking to characterise comprise both the content of the assemblages (what fabrics and types of pottery etc. are present) and the nature of the material (densities of distributions and degrees of fragmentation). As in the Boeotia project (Snodgrass, above), our work is showing that most of the landscape is carpeted with varying densities of finds from the whole classical period. In the present stage of our research on the *Ager Tarraconensis* data, we can do no more than suggest that the information will enable us to postulate different land uses whilst also identifying changes in the settlement pattern through time. Indeed, although presenting us with interpretative problems, this information about the nature of human exploitation of the whole landscape is an invaluable potential source of knowledge about ancient agricultural practice.

The second problem, which archaeologists have only recently begun to broach, is that pottery is not always equally common in different archaeological periods and on different types of site (Millett 1985; forthcoming, B). This factor of varying intensity of pottery supply is obvious to anyone who has excavated a settlement occupied through a sequence of different periods, but has now also been shown to have an important effect on supply within periods. Thus studies of *terra sigillata* (samian ware) by Marsh (1981) and African Red Slip ware by Fentress and Perkins (forthcoming) show that there are very considerable variations in the volume of these wares supplied through time. Although such variations in the intensity of supply do not necessarily affect all pottery, it would be extremely unwise to assume that they do not. Thus, when presenting finds from surveys, one ought not to assume automatically that rises and falls in the density of findspots of pottery relate directly to changes in the density or distribution of human populations. Unfortunately this assumption has been made in the publication of some pioneer surveys (e.g. Potter 1979), the results of which now need calibration. If pottery is less common or is restricted in distribution to certain parts of the settlement hierarchy (as in early Roman Sussex - Millett 1981b), its distribution may represent only part of the settlement hierarchy. Methods to cope with this factor of varying pottery supply should thus be applied before maps of distributions of pottery are taken as an index of population.

The techniques used in the analysis of the *Ager Tarraconensis* pottery aim to cope with this variable, thereby enabling valid chronological comparisons to be made (Millett, forthcoming, B; Keay and Millett, forthcoming, B). In brief, all surface finds are collected by the fieldwalkers. Once classified and quantified according to the detailed standard typologies, the pottery is grouped into broad chronological ranges (e.g. Early Imperial) and the amounts of each are expressed as densities per hectare for each field walked. The *range* of the values present for each chronological group is then examined by dividing them into quartiles and octiles. Hence, if we have data from 79 fields, we first find the middle (or median) value (in this case the 40th from the lowest). This is more useful than the mean which is invalidated by the skewed graphical distribution which is a characteristic of this type of data. The scale is subsequently divided into quartiles (the 20th and 60th values in this illustration) and further into eights or octiles (the 10th, 30th, 50th and 70th values). By this method the same part of the range of values can be compared without concern for the absolute numbers of sherds found. Thus if we say that sites are defined as the highest density scatters of pottery, we may define them as the topmost octile, even though for the Republic this may represent 26+ sherds per hectare, compared with only 5+ sherds per hectare for the Early Empire. Thus, as we know that diagnostic Republican pottery is much more common than that of the Early Empire in the survey area, the results are scaled to allow for this in the definition of settlements. With the use of these methods it is possible to compare different periods and arrive at a more realistic assessment of population densities and changes than has hitherto been possible, whilst it is also possible to show whether or not pottery supply remained constant.

A preliminary analysis of the *Ager Tarraconensis* survey results (1984-8) suggests that we have a modest decline in the number of sites occupied through time (Iberian 28; Republican 22; Early Empire 19; Late Empire 16) but much less marked than would have been assumed had the raw pottery data been used. There does appear to be some dislocation of the settlement pattern as a result of the growth of Tarraco with a shift away from a dispersed inland pattern towards one more concentrated around the city, but these trends are as yet not fully tested. The pottery assemblages from these sites are being examined in detail to assess the changing trade-contacts of the sites through time (below).

All the results of recent field surveys have revealed remarkable patterns, with much larger densities of sites than has been hitherto expected and much larger populations than are allowed for in most conventional population estimates (e.g. Hopkins 1980, 116-20). Thus at some periods in the *Ager Tarraconensis* some areas have more than 1 site per km^2 suggesting a much more substantial rural population than has previously been recognised. A glance through the results of similar surveys in the Empire suggests that this density of rural population is not exceptional, undermining any residual belief that the Roman Mediterranean had a predominantly urban population. In time survey should provide more realistic estimates of the size of the rural and urban populations than those presently available.

In summary there are a variety of problems which mean that we should be extremely wary of simplistic interpretations of survey data. Principal amongst these are:

(i)   biases in existing distribution maps caused by haphazard data collection;

(ii)   the differential survival and visibility of varying types of archaeological evidence;

(iii) difficulties in distinguishing artefact scatters resulting from settlement and those which result from agricultural processes;

(iv)   problems caused by variations in the supply and distribution of datable artefacts at different periods.

Methods are being developed which enable us to cope with these problems, thereby producing a sharper source criticism. The combination of good data from surveys with systematic analysis of settlement distributions promises to have a major impact on the ways in which we can see the towns functioning in relation to the countryside.

Artefact distribution patterns

Like settlement patterns, artefacts from sites can also provide insights into the relationships between towns and the countryside since they represent tangible evidence about past movements of goods. Robust artefacts, like pottery, can be used from either surface survey or excavations, whilst other materials like bone are almost exclusively recovered from excavations. Whatever process leads to their recovery, they provide an index of interaction between urban sites and their rural hinterlands, provided that information about the place of production and the methods of distribution can be inferred from their study.

Most valuable in this regard are ubiquitous objects with a known place of manufacture, the distributions of which can be studied quantitatively. Pottery most often fulfils this role since its generally low value in the ancient world means that it was ubiquitous, and often had widespread distributions. These can be studied to provide reliable and chronologically differentiated distribution maps which may define the changing economic territories served by a town (fig.4). A reasonable number of such local or regional distribution studies are now available from Britain, and similar work is being

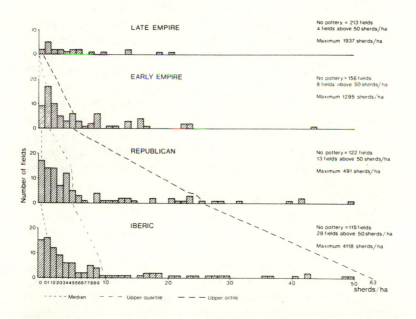

Figure 4: Graphs showing an example of the method used for scaling the pottery from the *Ager Tarraconensis* Survey. For an explanation of the method see text.

undertaken in other provinces. Valuable comparisons can be made between such local distributions and the administrative territories of towns whilst the distributions of more widely exchanged pottery (like the amphorae which contained staples such as oil and wine) can reveal interesting patterns of regional and local interdependency (fig.5). Work of this type on the pottery from the *Ager Tarraconensis* survey and Tarraco itself demonstrates divergent patterns of trade which make it clear that the town-country relationship changed considerably between the Republic and the late Empire. The preliminary results show that in the late Republic-early Empire Tarraco acted as a major economic focus for the sites in the hinterland, which were receiving large quantities of imports. Through the period from the first to the fifth-sixth centuries, the pattern changes: the town continues to receive imports, whilst many contemporary rural sites receive few, if any. Even the largest villas appear increasingly isolated from the urban market, suggesting the emergence of exchange networks centred on rural estates rather than Tarraco (Keay 1987; forthcoming).

With such data it is thus possible to map changes in a town's economic territory and to approach an understanding of the economic history of an area. This is particularly true where large quantities of pottery are recovered from field surveys. Work like this requires much time, but does provide evidence which is not available from other sources. Artefacts can also provide data about the relative status of sites, as there is strong reason to suppose that the nature (i.e. variability, quantity and quality) of the finds on a site are partly determined by its status. Provided we are not too naive in our expectations, valuable conclusions can be arrived at, as has been illustrated in a pilot study of the pottery from Roman sites in Sussex (Millett 1981b). Here it was shown that different types of site had varying access to specialised pottery supplies at different stages in the Romanisation of the province. As similar studies of material from surveys like the *Ager Tarraconensis* progress, it may be possible to estimate how far different elements in the population were involved in exchange with towns through time. This, of course, relates directly to the problem of varying archaeological visibility already discussed; if peasant farmers were not receiving pottery - they were working at a truly subsistence level - they would not generally be archaeologically visible. This problem of visibility may explain for instance, the

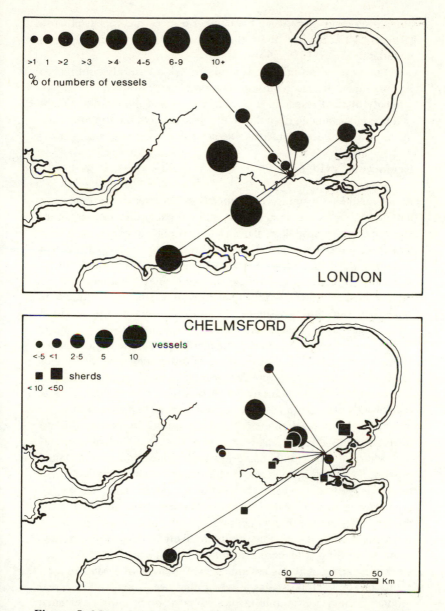

Figure 5: Maps showing the supply of pottery to later Roman London and Chelmsford, illustrating how pottery source studies can enable us to identify the regional territories they served.

noted discrepancies between the number of known colonists at Cosa (Brown 1980, 16) and the number of rural sites observed in its hinterland (Dyson 1978, 264).

At present the results of this kind of work are mostly confined to Britain where there is a strong tradition of pottery study and a high intensity of field research. It is to be hoped that more similar work will become available from the central provinces of the Empire, since the large quantities of data available provide an enormous potential.

Ecofactual evidence

Ecofact is the term some archaeologists use to refer to the remains of natural resources (such as cereals and animal products) which are recovered from archaeological excavations. Contemporary archaeology uses these sources of evidence from excavation to an increasing extent and they have considerable value in the study of town/country relationships. Used critically they can provide new information about their economic interrelationships as well as the more mundane aspects of diet and environment. The following examples will, I trust, point towards their potential value in this sphere. These sources of archaeological evidence are particularly appropriate to the debates about the extent to which the residents of urban sites were themselves engaged in agriculture or were dependent upon rural supplies.

Let us look first at the evidence of cereal grain which is now regularly recovered from samples of soil collected on excavations. By examining the assemblages of seeds found, it is possible to distinguish the different stages of crop processing which the samples represent. Thus the freshly harvested grain will contain roughly equal proportions of cereal, chaff and weeds. Samples which are dominated by weeds are likely to be the by-product of sieving and cleaning the crop prior to storage or use. In contrast, assemblages in which chaff predominates are the by-product of processing the grain by pounding it. Deposits containing mainly grain are likely to derive from storage prior to milling and consumption (Jones 1986, 94-100). Thus examining and classifying assemblages of grain from urban and rural sites can establish the stages at which they were involved in cereal production and consumption. Sites with all grain entirely cleaned were consumer sites, whilst those with waste products were producers. Furthermore, the weeds found with the grain sometimes have ecologically diagnostic growing conditions which enable the location of the fields to be suggested. At the Iron Age hillfort of Danebury, Dr Jones has been able to use this evidence to suggest that crops from damp ground some distance from the hillfort were brought to the site for processing (Jones 1986, 97). Careful analysis of cleaned grain from a Roman storehouse at York has identified a major infestation of beetles, the ecology of which suggested that the grain was imported from Southern Britain or the continent (Kenward and Williams 1979, 71). Similarly the grain varieties found in London (Straker 1984) and at South Shields (van der Veen 1988) suggest that grain was imported from abroad.

These examples should illustrate the potential of rather unprepossessing botanical data for contributing evidence about flows of food between sites. The clear implication is that sustained and systematic work on seeds from urban sites and their rural hinterlands could provide invaluable information about site interrelationships.

Animal bone evidence, if anything, has even greater potential, because bones have been much more widely recovered in quantity from archaeology excavations. Bone evidence is useful because the animals represented by the bones have a known anatomy and we understand the quality of the meat produced by a particular joint. Furthermore, it is possible to estimate the ages at death of the stock from the bones. These features mean that the study of animal bones can go a long way towards providing evidence of the dynamics of past economic systems. Thus, for instance, by examining the sheep bones from a settlement where flocks were kept, a pattern of ages at death can be established. This range of ages can be related to the different uses to which the flock was put. Young animals were culled for meat (lamb), whilst the middle-aged animals were kept for wool and milk and slaughtered only for meat (mutton) in old age.

Although care has to be taken in the interpretation of the bones because of complexities in their survival and deposition, it is clear that there is a high potential for examining patterns of animal exploitation. Thus the occurrence of all these age categories may indicate that a site was involved in rearing flocks as well as consuming the products. In contrast the presence of only prime meat (lamb) might indicate that the site was a consumer rather than a producer, whilst the presence of only the bones from the meat of old animals might suggest identification as a producer site which was exporting the prime meat.

When we look at the array of bones present in a particular

assemblage, we may be able to draw more detailed conclusions. Take, for instance, the assemblage of cattle bones which show marks of cutting from butchery and jointing. Since each beast had only a known number of each type of bone, absence or over-representation of certain joints can easily be measured. Thus the absence of feet and head bones may indicate that the bones arrived on the site as already dressed meat (having been butchered and prepared elsewhere). The presence of large quantities of bones from the best cuts of meat might indicate a higher status consumer than an assemblage dominated by the bones of the poorer joints. The study of the bones from any site can therefore give a good indication of not only how the site fits into the system of production, but also its likely status. The distinction has also been drawn between a highly organised economy with large numbers of bones of prime animals of the same age range occurring at a site, and a less uniform selection of material. Thus in Maltby's major study of the animal bones from Exeter (Maltby 1979) a change in the relationship of the hinterland seems to be indicated by a shift from the highly standardised supply system of the original military phase to the later, less organised supplies which arrived at the civilian town. Clearly similar work on material from other urban and rural settlements should provide important insights into economic aspects of their interrelationships.

Conclusions

In my introduction to this paper, I pointed towards some of the general characteristics of archaeological evidence, and indicated that if we are to use our data to its full potential, we must use it critically. In illustrating the use of settlement patterns and finds from surveys and excavations, I have tried to show some of the ways in which static evidence can help us understand past dynamic systems through relating the evidence to the processes which produced them. Whilst much of what I have presented is concerned with methods and potential rather than results, I hope to have succeeded in demonstrating that we have a series of potent sources of information.

Acknowledgements

I should like to thank my colleagues and students in Durham who have discussed the ideas with me. I am particularly grateful to Simon Keay, initiator of the *Ager Tarraconensis* survey and my co-director who is equally responsible for the evolution of our methodology there. Finally I am grateful for comments and advice offered by the editors and Dom Perring. The illustrations were drawn by Pauline Fenwick (figs.1,3,4) and Yvonne Beadnell (figs.2,5).

Bibliography

Brown, F.E. (1980), *Cosa: the Making of a Roman Town.* Ann Arbor.

Crowther, D.R. (1983), 'Old land surfaces and modern ploughsoil', in *Scottish Archaeological Review* 2, 31-44.

Dyson, S. (1978), 'Settlement patterns in the Ager Cosanus: the Wesleyan University Survey, 1974-76', in *Journal of Field Archaeology* 5, 251-68.

Fentress, L. and Parkins, P. (forthcoming), 'Counting ARS', in *L'Africa Romana V*.

Gaffney, V. Gaffney, C. and Tingle, M. (1985a), 'Settlement, economy and behaviour?', in Haselgrove *et al.* (eds.) (1985), 95-107.

Gaffney, V. and Tingle, M. (1985b), 'The Maddle Farm Project and micro-regional analysis', in Macready and Thompson (eds.) (1985), 67-73.

Gregson, M. (1982), 'The villa as private property', in K. Ray (ed.) *Young Archaeologist: Collected Unpublished Papers, Contributions to Archaeological Thinking and Practice*, 143-91 (Cambridge: Department of Archaeology).

Haselgrove, C.C. (1985), 'Inference from ploughsoil artefact samples', in Haselgrove *et al.* (1985), 7-30.

Haselgrove, C.C., Millett, M., and Smith, I.M. (1985), *Archaeology from the Ploughsoil.* Sheffield.

Hodder, I.R. and Millett, M. (1980), 'Romano-British villas and towns: a systematic analysis', *World Archaeology* 12/1, 69-76.

Hodder, I.R. and Orton, C.R. (1976), *Spatial Analysis in Archaeology.* Cambridge.

Hopkins, K. (1980), 'Taxes and trade in the Roman Empire', in *Journal of Roman Studies* 70, 101-25.

Jones, M.K. (1986), *England before Domesday*. London.

Keay, S.J. (1987), 'The impact of the foundation of Tarraco upon the indigenous settlement pattern of the Ager Tarraconensis', *De Les Estructures Indigenes a L'Organizacio Provincial Romana de la Hispania Citerior*, Jornales Internacionals d'Arqueologia 53-8. Granollers.

Keay, S.J. (forthcoming), 'The Ager Tarraconensis in the Late Empire: a model for the economic relationship of town and country in Eastern Spain?', in G. Barker (ed.) *Roman Agrarian Structure: Archaeological Survey in the Mediterranean*. London.

Keay, S.J. and Millett, M. (1986), 'The Ager Tarraconensis Survey: interim report 1985', in *Universities of Durham and Newcastle upon Tyne Archaeological Reports for 1985*, 44-5.

Keay, S.J. and Millett, M. (1987), 'Ager Tarraconensis Survey 1986', in *Universities of Durham and Newcastle upon Tyne Archaeological Reports for 1986*, 43-5.

Keay, S.J. and Millett, M. (1988), 'Ager Tarraconensis Survey: interim report for 1987', in *Universities of Durham and Newcastle upon Tyne Archaeological Reports for 1987*, 13-16.

Keay, S.J. and Millett, M. (forthcoming, A), 'Ager Tarraconensis Survey: interim report for 1988', in *Universities of Durham and Newcastle upon Tyne Archaeological Reports for 1988*.

Keay, S.J. and Millett, M. (forthcoming, B), 'Surface survey and site recognition in Spain: The Ager Tarraconensis and its background', in J. Schofield (ed.) *Artefact Scatters*. Oxford.

Kenward, H. and Williams, D. (1979), *Biological Evidence from the Roman Warehouses in Coney Street*. London.

Macready, S. and Thompson, F.H. (1985), *Archaeological Field Survey in Britain and Abroad*. London.

Maltby, M. (1979), *Exeter Archaeological Reports 2: The Animal Bones from Exeter 1971-1975*. Sheffield.

Marsh, G. (1981), 'London's Samian supply and its relationship to the development of the Gallic Samian industry', in A.C. and A.S. Anderson (eds.) *Roman Pottery Research in Britain and North-West Europe*, 173-238. Oxford.

Millett, M. (1981a), 'Whose crisis? The archaeology of the third century: a warning', in A.C. King and M. Henig (eds.) *The Roman West in the Third Century*, 525-9. Oxford.

Millett, M. (1981b), 'An approach to the Romano-British pottery of West Sussex', in *Sussex Archaeol. Collect.* 118, 57-68.

Millett, M. (1985), 'Field survey calibration: a contribution', in Haselgrove *et al.* (1985), 31-7.

Millett, M. (forthcoming, A), *The Romanization of Britain: An Essay in Archaeological Interpretation.* Cambridge.

Millett, M. (forthcoming, B), 'Pottery: population or supply patterns? The Ager Tarraconensis approach', in G. Barker (ed.) *Roman Agrarian Structure: Archaeological Survey in the Mediterranean.* London.

Potter, T.W. (1979), *The Changing Landscape of South Etruria.* London.

Rivet, A.L.F. (1955), 'The distribution of villas in Roman Britian', in *Archaeological Newsletter* 6, 29-34.

Schiffer, M.B. (1976), *Behavioral Archaeology* . New York.

Straker, V. (1984), 'First and second century carbonised grain from Roman London', in W. van Zeist and W.A. Casparie (eds.) *Plants and Ancient Man, Studies in Palaeoethnobotany*, 323-9. Rotterdam.

van der Veen, M. (1988), 'Carbonised grain from the Roman granary at South Shields, England', in *Der Prähistorische Mensche und seine Umwelt: Festschrift für Udelgard Körber-Grohne, Forschungen und Berichte zur Vor- und Frühgeschichte in Baden-Württemberg* 31, 353-65. Stuttgart.

8

Towns and territories in southern Etruria

T.W. Potter

In an archaeological sense, the landscape of southern Etruria is amongst the most closely investigated in the Mediterranean. Topographical studies have a very long history in the region, and have particularly benefited in this century from the work of first Thomas Ashby (1927; Castagnoli 1986) and, in the post-war era, of John Ward-Perkins (1962, 1968). Detailed field survey has provided the data for a remarkable series of period-maps, where the major centres, smaller settlements, individual farms and the successive road systems can be plotted (Potter 1979). No one would of course claim that every site has been identified, nor that surface finds always provide a tight chronology; but the information that is available does allow the construction of some interesting models for the history of settlement in the region, which have inspired many other comparable projects in Italy and elsewhere (Barker 1986). If one result has been to emphasise the extraordinary diversity of landscape histories, then it is an important antidote to any tendency to generalise from the South Etruria model. Topographical studies do show many similarities from one region to another in Italy (Potter 1987), and elsewhere in the western Mediterranean; but it is the differences in settlement trends that is the more striking feature.

Moreover, for southern Etruria, the proximity of Rome has exerted a profound influence upon its development since at least as early as the fifth century BC, if not before; for this reason alone, one is dealing with an unusual - if not unique - example of town-country relationships. Communications between Rome and southern Etruria have long been easy - a factor that indeed facilitated and encouraged the topographical work of the British School at Rome - and the relationship between city and its hinterland has thus been an intimate one. The countryside provided much of the building materials for Rome - *tufo*, travertine, basaltic *selce* and brick and tile - as well as agricultural staples: the latter were rarely sufficient, but there was always a ready market for the rural landowner. Equally, however, there were periods when Rome and the countryside came into opposition. Even today, parts of the Roman Campagna which remain isolated from the City maintain a distinct and particular identity, a feature which can be recognised far back in time. The cultural and linguistic independence of the Faliscans (a tribe whose leading city, Falerii, lay no more than 40 km from the gates of Rome) was worthy of note in Strabo's day (5. 2. 9), and was undoubtedly enhanced by the geographical isolation of the Treia basin, in which the tribe concentrated. Similarly, in the early Middle Ages, towns like Nepi fought to achieve independence from the Papacy of Rome, so that Popes such as Hadrian I (772-92) were obliged to take measures to maintain their control in the region (Christie 1987) - although not, as we shall see, with great success. Only in the classical period, and now in the modern era, was Rome able, it would seem, to integrate fully the countryside with the city, and even then it is a conclusion that may not be wholly sustainable, especially as far as the lower levels of rural society are concerned.

The territories of urban centres, especially in the vicinity of great cities such as Rome, may therefore be subject to considerable change over time, and it is important to resist the temptation of facile generalisation. In this paper, we shall attempt to assess these changes, insofar as they can be detected in the region immediately to the north of Rome, using in part some new evidence from an excavation that is currently in progress at the Mola di Monte Gelato, in the heart of the Ager Faliscus (Potter and King 1988).

The emergence of urban centres in southern Etruria (fig.1)

The territorial framework that governed this region during the heyday of the Etruscans and Faliscans seems to have emerged early. Towards the end of the second and early in the first millennium BC, naturally defended acropolis sites such as Veii, Narce, Nepi and probably Falerii Veteres were gradually established as major centres. Little is

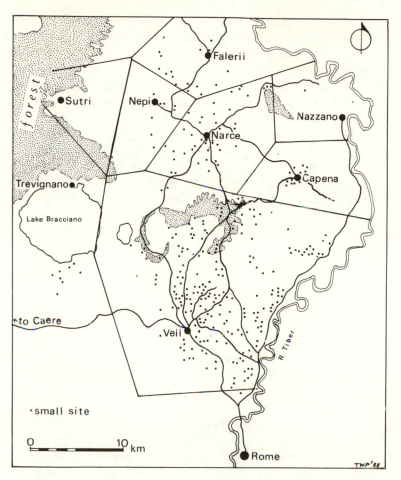

Figure 1: Southern Etruria showing hypothetical city territories as they might have been about 500 BC. Also shown are the major settlements, small rural sites, the roads and the areas of upland (stippled).

known about how they were organised (although Veii may initially have comprised a number of contiguous villages - perhaps five in all - within a plateau that covers some 190 hectares [Ward-Perkins 1961], although see now the rather different picture suggested by the new work of Guaitoli [1982]). Nevertheless they may be regarded as 'central places', with dependent rural sites in their vicinity (a feature which is to some extent apparent in the distribution maps). About the same time, other major settlements came into being elsewhere in south Etruria, especially at Cerveteri, Tarquinia, Vulci and Orvieto. Together with Veii, all were later to emerge as the urban foci of Etruscan city-states, with extensive territories and, in some cases, dependent towns. Indeed, by the sixth century BC, a complex network of roads linking these centres had come into being, and was to a partial extent designed to facilitate the passage of wheeled vehicles.

During the same period, there were also far-reaching social and economic changes. The present indications are that at later Bronze Age settlements such as Narce (Potter 1976) the economy was initially relatively uncomplex. Cereals were grown, and a variety of stock was raised, but there are few hints of anything more than a simple subsistence economy. Towards the end of the second millenium BC, however, cereal production seems to have expanded, traded items appear in the archaeological record, and the settlement itself grew larger. During the ninth and eighth centuries, the plant remains indicate a considerable pressure on land, implying a sharp increase in the size of population; a second acropolis, M. li Santi, was also occupied. Adequate funerary data from the Narce complex for this period is lacking, but contemporary cemeteries at Quattro Fontanili, Veii (Close-Brooks 1979, Toms 1986) and at Osteria dell'Osa, to the east of Rome (Bietti Sestieri 1979) provide clear evidence for the emergence of an elite element of society at these centres. The phenomenon is unlikely to be isolated; indeed, at all the major Etruscan and Latin sites, the signs are of a steady concentration of wealth in the hands of a few during the first part of the first millennium BC. Moreover, in the eighth century BC, significant changes were initiated in terms of the agricultural regime, most notably the widespread introduction of the vine and the olive tree. Whatever the origin of these changes (and the Greeks must surely here have played a significant role), they were to lead to the widespread adoption in the upper echelons of Etruscan society of the banquet as a manifestation of great wealth and status (Cristofani 1987). We may suppose that these social developments had a considerable impact upon the life of the farmer whose obligation it was to produce the agricultural surplus to support the nobility.

Modern scholarship lays stress on the way that Etruscan epigraphical evidence suggests that a two-part name came into general use in the second half of the seventh century BC. The appearance of the *gentilicium* whose function 'is to link people who are related by blood, religion or common political or economic interest' (Cristofani 1979) is thought to have had the effect of associating individuals and families with particular settlements. As this broadly coincides chronologically with the beginning of much more urbanised features in some of the major settlements in southern Etruria, it is possible to infer some relationship between the two: that, as properly urban centres began to emerge, so controls over the local population were tightened by the social elite. Similarly, it is often suggested that town walls, which were widely erected in southern Etruria and elsewhere in the fifth - fourth centuries BC, were put up not only for reasons of defence, but to regulate the urban population (e.g. Torelli 1974, 1981).

However, even in so well studied a region as southern Etruria, it is not easy to work out the boundaries between one town and another. If we can assume that in such a densely settled landscape, formal territorial limits did come into being at an early stage, defining the precise limits is still a matter of subjective conjecture. Nevertheless, there are some pointers. In the Ager Veientanus, Veii seems to comprise the only substantial settlement, and common sense demands that its *territorium* extended at least as far as the Monti Sabatini, 11 km to the north. Beyond these hills, the ground drops away to the north and east into the Treia basin, a topographical divide which may be plausibly (if unprovably) linked to political boundaries.

Within the Ager Faliscus, there are many more substantial settlements than in the Ager Veientanus, and it is not easy to evaluate their relationship. It is commonly assumed that all are Faliscan, but this is not necessarily the case: Faliscan epigraphic evidence is, for example, notably lacking from Narce (Giacomelli 1963), leaving open the possibility that it was under Etruscan control for some of its history. Moreover, many considerations suggest that there was a hierarchy of sites, presumably forming some sort of federation, with linguistic and cultural ties. A combination of literary and archaeological factors make it clear that Falerii Veteres was the leading city (Frederiksen and Ward-Perkins 1957), but the cemeteries of Narce, Nepi, Corchiano and Vignanello suggest prosperous communities. Similarly, in the adjacent Ager Capenas, Capena itself was an important place, and sites like Nazzano may have been not unwealthy centres (Jones 1962, 1963).

One way of placing these settlements in a ranking order is in terms of their size (Guidi 1985). This can only be taken as a very rough guide, since it is not clear how much of the interior was occupied (cf. e.g. the scattered buildings at Acquarossa: Ostenberg 1975, Nylander 1986), and it is therefore impossible to arrive at population estimates. Nevertheless, the figures (as calculated by Judson and Hemphill 1981) are interesting, and do serve to differentiate the major from the more minor settlements.

Site	Size in hectares
Veii	190
Falerii Veteres	26
Nepi	17.5
Narce	12.5
Sutri	7.5
Capena	4.6
Grotta Porciosa	3.0
Nazzano	2.8
Corchiano	2.5
Vignanello	2.5
Ponte del Ponte	0.4

The huge size of Veii, as measured within its Etruscan defences, is striking, and corresponds neatly with the impression of a very large *territorium*, controlled directly from the city. Unfortunately, we cannot yet arrive at any close figure for the area occupied by Rome at this time (although it is likely to have been bigger still), although figures are available for Caere (130 ha), Tarquinia (121 ha), Vulci (90 ha) and Orvieto (82 ha). Given that these are all 'big league' cities, there does seem to be some correspondence between their size and their notional position in a political ranking table of Etruscan cities.

In the territory of the Faliscans and Capenates, the size of Falerii also corresponds well with its evident position as the leading centre, although it is interesting that Capena, a not unnoteworthy place in the literary sources (Jones 1962), is forty times smaller than Veii - a warning, perhaps, of the difficulties of using size as a measure of rank. For the rest, Nepi, Narce and Sutri group together (as indeed we could conclude from the archaeological evidence), while the remaining sites would rank as minor places, playing perhaps some satellite role to the larger towns.

To sum up, the first half of the first millennium sees the

emergence of a considerable number of major settlements in southern Etruria, which by the fifth century had aligned themselves into a loose hierarchy. The Faliscans seemed to have created a series of centres which were perhaps semi-autonomous, but united by tribal ties. Falerii Veteres, and its successor, Falerii Novi, apart, only Fescennium is specifically named as another Faliscan centre, and its identification has long been in dispute (Shotter 1976); Narce must be the strongest candidate on its size and wealth alone, but diminutive Capena warns against too ready an acceptance of the hypothesis, despite the attractions. But nothing conflicts with the idea of a series of separate territories, within an organised and heavily exploited landscape which, by the fifth century BC, supported a large population (Potter 1979).

The expansion of Rome (fig.2)

The historical aspects of Rome's expansion into Etruria are well known and require little reiteration here. Veientines (as well as some Faliscans and Capenates) were incorporated into four new tribes, Stellatina, Tromentina, Sabatina, and Arniensis, after the conquest of Veii in 396 BC, Sutri and Nepi (both of which are described as Etruscan places) became Latin colonies soon afterwards, and Capena itself, and its territory, also came under Roman control (Livy 6.4.4; 5.8), perhaps as a *municipium foederatum* (Jones 1962, 124-5). The history of the Faliscans is more complex, but in 241 BC they too were conquered, and half their territory was confiscated (Zonaras 8.18).

In archaeological terms, the impact of these successive phases of Roman conquest are surprisingly clear, given the normal limitations of the material evidence. Within the territories of the Veientines and Capenates, very little disruption seems to have occurred; to judge from surface evidence (Ward-Perkins *et al.* 1968) many farms carried on much as before, with no appreciable signs of hiatus in the organisation of the landscape. Nepi was soon connected with Rome by means of a new highway, the Via Amerina (Frederiksen and Ward-Perkins 1957), but it is the continuity from Etruscan to early Roman that is the striking feature to emerge from both field survey and excavation. By contrast, in the Ager Faliscus disruption was widespread. Most of the larger settlements were abandoned, and in the

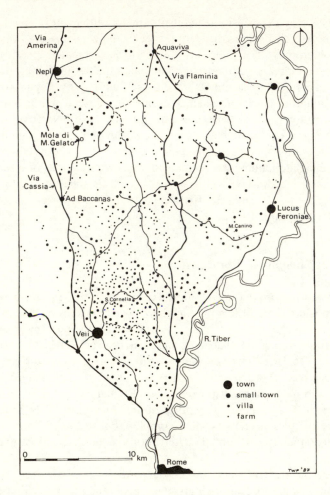

Figure 2: Southern Etruria showing roads and sites, including the Mola di Monte Gelato, about AD 100. Based on the British School at Rome field-survey.

countryside occupation terminated on 80% of the sites, and more than half were never occupied again (Potter 1979). Indeed, what lends credence to these figures - assembled, let it be said, from the manifestly imprecise data of field survey - is that the few sites that did apparently survive lay mostly close to Nepi, and were perhaps the farms of the Latin colonists.

Two symbols of the stamp of Roman authority in the Ager Faliscus are the Via Flaminia, laid out in 220 BC, and the town of Falerii Novi. Down to this day, the great walls of this newly created urban centre (Potter 1987, 32) are an imposing reminder of the power of Rome, and its foundation must be seen as an unambiguous statement of a new order of things. Even so, despite the severity with which the Romans treated the Faliscans, Falerii Novi was probably granted federate status, and thus remained formally independent (Frederiksen and Ward-Perkins 1957, 162). Moreover, Faliscan inscriptions are known from the site, including two which refer to a *praetor* (*CIE*, 8340, 8434), and we may reasonably assume that the indigenous component in the population remained substantial. Indeed, its *territorium* may well have been quite considerable, since epigraphic evidence (*CIL* XI, 3930) implies that it extended well to the south-east, as far as Rignano, more than a dozen kilometres away. This leaves open the question of the location and fate of the confiscated territory, but the creation of a new urban centre - however strong its Faliscan component remained - must have resulted in a substantial reorganisation of the landscape.

This is not the place to review in detail the absorbing problems of the later Republican archaeology of southern Etruria. The conventional picture is of a thickly settled landscape, with many smallholders, a few towns - Veii, Nepi, Sutri, Falerii Novi, Lucus Feroniae, Capena (a minor place) and probably Nazzano (? *civitas Sepernatium*) - and some road-stations. What seem to be lacking are the large villa estates which characterised, for example, the Ager Cosanus in this period (Carandini 1985). Moreover, the black glaze wares collected in the survey yield a consistent picture of an assemblage dominated by types of the third century BC, with little later material. Liverani (1984) has therefore argued that there was an economic and demographic 'crisis' in southern Etruria (and elsewhere around Rome) in the second century BC, stemming partly from the disruption brought about by the Second Punic War and also by a massive growth of Rome itself. As a result, he suggests, the villa system of agriculture did not become established until much later, while there may have been some truth in Propertius' (4.10.29) remark (made in the later first century BC) that Veii after the Roman conquest was a place of shepherds and cornfields.

The hypothesis is a stimulating one, although it seems inherently unlikely that the Roman Campagna should have become quite so depopulated at a time of pronounced expansion within Rome itself. But it is a matter which can, and must be, tested by excavation on carefully selected rural (and urban) sites - precisely the sort of 'question and answer' archaeology which, if elegantly approached, can be so rewarding.

What is unquestioned is the reality of a massive development of southern Etruria (and elsewhere) from the later first century BC, both by smallholders and by larger proprietors, many of whom, we might suppose, came from Rome itself, as we shall see. Veteran settlement is also likely. According to Cicero (*Leg.Agr.* 2.66) Rullus considered the Ager Faliscus as a suitable area for land allocation in 63 BC, and parts of the Ager Capenas and Ager Veientanus were similarly contemplated in 46 BC (Cicero, *Ad Fam.* 9.17.2). There was a comparable expansion in the towns, especially under the Julio-Claudians; this is clearly attested at Veii (Liverani 1987), Lucus Feroniae, Falerii Novi and Sutri, pointing to a considerable influx of people and wealth (Harris 1971, 316; Keppie 1983, 171). Some new light on this period has also been cast by the excavation at the Mola di Monte Gelato (Potter and King 1988). This site lies in the heart of the Ager Faliscus, in the valley of the River Treia. It is an attractive place, with lovely waterfalls which today bring many hundreds of weekend visitors from the city of Rome; this, it should be said, is largely a novelty of the last fifteen years, during which time the roads that connect the city with Monte Gelato have been considerably upgraded. This finds a close parallel with the situation in antiquity, when a country road, that originated in a large settlement (? a *vicus*) nearly one km. to the north of Monte Gelato, headed southwards to join with the Via Amerina, and thence to Rome. The road, which bridges the River Treia close by the Mola, was subsequently paved with *selce* blocks (perhaps as early as Augustan times, and certainly by the end of the first century AD), thus creating an easy all-weather route between Rome and this region of the Ager Faliscus (fig.2).

The Mola di Monte Gelato (fig.3) has long been known as a substantial Roman and medieval site - there is a castle overlooking the valley, and two standing towers, one a mill, - but systematic investigation began as recently as 1986. To date, the only structural remains of earlier Roman date to have been excavated comprise a small, apparently isolated, bath-house, constructed about AD 100 beside the road. However, later deposits have yielded an already remarkable collection of inscriptions and sculpture, dating mainly to

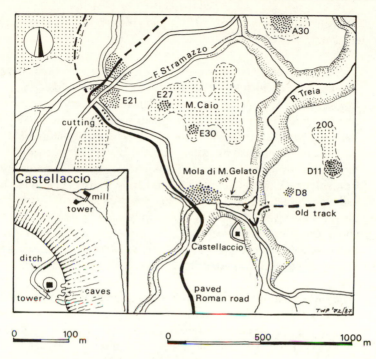

Figure 3: The Mola di Monte Gelato in its local setting, based on field survey. Sites (e.g. E21) are stippled.

the period between the late first century BC and the late first century AD. The outstanding pieces include (1) a marble nymph in the rare 'Virunum' series, dating to the first century AD; it is a fine product, presumably of a Rome workshop (Claridge 1988); (2) a building inscription on *nenfro*, set up by [IVS ET HILA] (RIO (?) who might have been officials of a local temple or village community; a late Republican or Augustan date best suits the formula and style; (3) parts of a tomb monument, of which some of the inscription, two of the *imagines clipeatae* and a complete portrait bust have been found. The inscription identifies, it would seem, two freedmen of the same patron, and both were called C. Valerius C.L.; but only one *cognomen*, Hilario, survives. The head represents one of the two freedmen, and a Julio-Claudian date is suggested for the monument; (4) fragments of a funerary inscription, bearing the name ACHILLI, presumably Achilleus; it may date to the mid first century AD.

Purcell's discussion (1988) of the inscriptions is well worthy of quotation:

> The building inscription gives the possibility of a valuable insight into the way in which this part of the Ager Faliscus worked in the late Republic, and opens up the possibility of a variety of interesting institutional parallels with other parts of Etruria and of Italy in general. But the low status of the officials, if that is what they are, is striking, and might be evidence for the dependence of this area on structures of patronage which went beyond the locality. Certainly the Valerius inscription is urban in its associations, style and type. It fits well in to the pattern of very close social interaction between Rome and its region which is suggested by the epigraphy of Veii and Capena and to some extent Falerii Novi; the excellent communications between Monte Gelato and Rome via a *deverticulum* of the Via Amerina are to be noted in this context.

The 'urbanisation' of parts of the Campagna by families with strong onomastic links with Rome may therefore well prove to be a common feature of early Imperial times: the great villa of the Volusii, on the outskirts of Lucus Feroniae, immediately comes to mind, as does the suggestion that the same family owned a large villa by the Fosso di Volusia, near the Via Veientana (Manacorda 1982). This is itself close to the Fosso della Crescenza site, excavated in 1962, which yielded a funerary inscription belonging to a servile family with the cognomen Hypora - a rare name, but attested four times in Rome and once in Naples (Fentress *et al*. 1983, 98).

Much more work on the epigraphic sources is required to develop this theme, but meanwhile we may suggest that the links between Rome and the countryside became significantly enhanced during the early Imperial period. At the same time, building inscriptions like the example from the Mola di Monte Gelato point to a more complex infrastructure of settlement than has hitherto been inferred from the material evidence on the ground. It has perhaps been too easy to interpret the remains of these larger rural sites as splendid villas: the Mola di Monte Gelato (and the Fosso Stramazzo site, a kilometre to the north), are probably not villas, but *vici* or even religious complexes. As ever, some of our seemingly secure assumptions may prove to be quite erroneous.

Rural settlement in the later Roman and early medieval periods

The pattern of landowning in the later Empire is extremely difficult to decipher from the archaeological evidence, and excavated sequences remain rare. At the Fosso della Crescenza site (Fentress *et al.* 1983), there seems to have been a marked degeneration in living standards by the third century, although the unpretentious villa at Crocicchie (Potter and Dunbabin 1979), which was extended at that time by the addition of a small bath-house, warns against generalised statements about rural decline. The excavations at the Mola de Monte Gelato are here proving of particular interest (fig.4).

The bath-house of early Imperial date continued in use down to about AD 400. It was then demolished (as were the monuments which provide the epigraphic and sculptural material, discussed above), and replaced by a large complex, apparently with a central courtyard. It is provisionally interpreted as a late Roman villa. This is in itself an interesting hint of renewed investment in the countryside, which finds parallels in other parts of the Italian peninsula, as at San Giovanni di Ruoti in Basilicata (Small 1980) and at San Vincenzo al Volturno, in the Abruzzi (Hodges 1985). At the Mola di Monte Gelato, a small church was added to one corner of the complex about AD 450, and the site seems thereafter to have continued in occupation through into the early Middle Ages. If the archaeological evidence has been correctly interpreted, this is a remarkable instance of a continuity of agrarian tradition that has long been inferred from the documentary sources but never properly demonstrated in southern Etruria.

About AD 800, the late Roman buildings were demolished to foundation level, and replaced by a complex of strikingly similar layout. The church was slightly realigned and enlarged, but otherwise the two periods of building are so remarkably close in plan as to point to continuity of function. It has been elsewhere argued that the early medieval complex was one of the centres of the Papal *domusculta* of Capracorum, erected by Pope Hadrian I in c. AD 774. The excavated site of Santa Cornelia, near Veii, provides a striking parallel (Potter 1979, 152). Moreover, it is suggested that Monte Gelato can be identified with the *castrum Capracorum*, mentioned in a bull of 1053:

*cum terris, vineis... et molaria sua cum ecclesia santi Johannis
que dicitur La Tregia... positam territorio Vegetano millario ab
urbe Rome plus minus vicesimo septimo.*

(Tomassetti 1913, 141; Partner 166, 75)

The finds from the excavation show that the early medieval church
was handsomely embellished with marble sculpture, and the quality
of the work suggests a wealthy and well-patronised community.

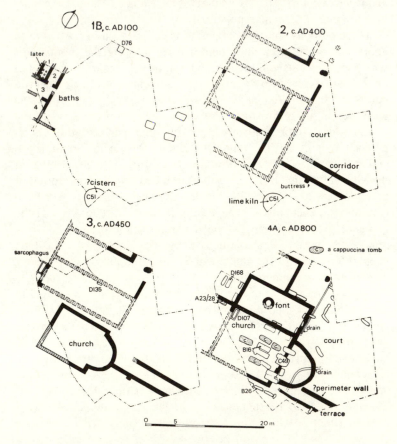

Mola di M. Gelato 1986-87: provisional sequence

Figure 4: The sequence of building phases at the Mola di Monte Gelato

Papal ownership is entirely consistent with this evidence, and it may be suspected that the sculpture is the product of craftsmen from Rome itself; once again, there are strong connections between the City and this rural dependency, as there were eight centuries or so before.

The Papal *domuscultae* (Partner 1966; Wickham 1978, 1979) which took the form of a series of estates that more-or-less encircled the City, have been usually thought of as a measure taken to prop up a flagging agrarian system. Indeed, the *Liber Pontificalis* describes in detail how the produce of *Capracorum* was to be distributed to the poor of Rome, and also the quantities involved (Duchesne 1886, 501, 506). However, as was hinted at the outset, recent commentaries have tended to stress another factor, namely the rise of the local lords at this time (Brown 1984; Christie 1987). Dukes such as Toto of Nepi (who endeavoured to establish his brother, Constantine, as anti-pope in Rome in 768) were constantly looking at ways to curb the power of the Papacy, and the loss of their lands to the Church was a continual grievance. Thus, in 816, the nobles organised the burning of some of the *domuscultae*, and by the early tenth century, although they provided some revenue, they were hardly a functioning concern (Partner 1966).

Seen in this light, it is scarcely surprising that the creation of *domuscultae* can be as readily interpreted as a political gesture as they can an economic measure (Marazzi 1988). The founding of the estate centres was intending to focus loyalty to the Papacy and, at the same time, establish a rural militia: indeed, the men of Capracorum worked on the building of the Leonine Wall in 846 (Tomassetti 1913, 109). The complex at the Mola di Monte Gelato, in the heart of a territory with a long tradition of independence, was thus well placed to fulfil this function, although it too was defunct and *diruta* by 1158 - a documentary date (Tomassetti 1913) that is wholly supported by the archaeological evidence. Indeed, it is during the 800s that many of the defended medieval fortified centres in the region come into being, once more effectively isolating the Ager Faliscus from the city and *territorium* of Rome. In some senses, therefore, matters had gone full circle, reverting to the situation in the pre-Roman period, not least since it was often the old Faliscan centres, such as that of Falerii Veteres (medieval and modern Civitá Castellana), that were reoccupied.

Today, the pendulum has once again swung back. In the course of the last thirty years, most of the villages have lost their isolation, and in some cases the medieval centres have been abandoned. In others, the houses have been bought up by inhabitants of Rome, seeking a country refuge. Even more recently, large parts of the countryside have been colonised by modern-day citizens of Rome, investing their wealth in the new 'villas' - not working farms, but places of weekend sojourn (and, increasingly, commuter travel). Once again, the City and its hinterland have become closely integrated, so that the wealth of Rome is spread deep into the surrounding countryside. Resistance to these changes exists, but even that is increasingly a thing of the past. Anachronistic analogy is always full of pitfalls but, in this case, the comparison between the Classical and the modern eras seems irresistible, especially to those who explore one and have witnessed the changes brought about by the other.

Conclusions

Southern Etruria is a remarkably interesting area of study, particularly once it emerged from the obscurity of prehistory in the later second millennium BC. At times, it has played a not insignificant role in the history of the Italian peninsula, while the diversity and variation within successive landscapes confers additional importance upon the region. However, it would be easy to assume that the interest of this region derives almost entirely from the proximity of Rome. In reality, the relationship between Rome and southern Etruria is much more complex, and there have been marked fluctuations over the last three thousand years. At times, the inhabitants of the countryside near to Rome have shared an intimate involvement with the history of the city; but in other periods the trend has been for a marked dichotomy between Rome and southern Etruria. Thus, the *territorium* controlled or influenced by Rome in effect has changed considerably over time, often as a result of moves initiated from small urban centres in the countryside. Whatever the legal definition of boundaries between one town and another, in practice these seem to have been relatively fluid.

It follows that there is still much to be learnt both from further study of the epigraphic and documentary evidence from southern Etruria and from well-placed excavations. The Mola di Monte Gelato - a site which escaped the large-scale despoliation of the last century, catering for a demand for classical sculpture and other works of art - has here proved a fortunate focus of enquiry. The rich remains of the

Roman and early medieval periods are of importance for the close links that they imply with the city of Rome, while the epigraphic evidence (which should be considerably extended by future seasons of work) holds particular promise as a major new body of information from a rural site. Above all, it is instructive that on-going investigation in this intensively studied landscape continues to result in so many new thoughts and fresh perspectives. Syntheses can, and must be, attempted; but the current and fruitful trend towards collaboration between historian (ancient and medieval) and archaeologist will surely ensure that they are outdated with remarkable rapidity.

Bibliography

Ashby, T. (1927), *The Roman Campagna in Classical Times*, 1970 reprint. Tonbridge.

Barker, G.W.W. (1986), 'L'archeologia del paesaggio italiano: nuovi orientamenti e recenti esperienze', *Archeologia Medievale* 13, 7-30.

Bietti Sestieri, A.M. (1979), *Ricerca su una communità del Lazio protostorico*. Rome.

Brown, T.S. (1984), *Gentlemen and Officers: Imperial Administration and Aristocratic Power in Byzantine Italy AD 554-800*. London.

Carandini, A. (ed.) (1985), *La romanizzazione dell' Etruria: il territorio di Vulci*. Milan.

Castagnoli, F. *et al.* (1986), *Thomas Ashby. Un archeologo fotografa la campagna romana*. Rome.

Christie, N.J. (1987), 'Forum ware, the Duchy of Rome and incastellamento: problems in interpretation', *Archeologia Medievale* 14, 451-66.

Claridge, A. (1988), 'La scultura romana', in Potter and King (1988), 291-4.

Close-Brooks, J. (1979), 'Proposal for a division into phases (at Veii in the Iron Age)', in D. and F. Ridgeway (eds.), *Italy before the Romans*, 95-106. London.

Cristofani, M. (1979), *The Etruscans: A New Investigation*. London.

Cristofani, M. (1987), 'Il banchetto in Etruria', in *L'alimentazione nel mondo antico: gli Etruschi* , 123-32. Rome.

Duchesne, L. (ed.) (1886), *Liber Pontificalis* I. Paris and Rome.

Fentress, E. *et al.* (1983), 'Excavations at Fosso della Crescenza 1962', *Papers of the British School at Rome* 51, 58-101.

Frederiksen, M. and Ward-Perkins, J.B. (1957), 'The ancient road systems of the central and northern Ager Faliscus', *Papers of the British School at Rome* 25, 67-208.

Giacomelli, G. (1963), *La lingua falisca*. Florence.

Guaitoli, M. (1982), 'Notizie preliminari su ricenti ricognizioni svolte in seminari dell' Institute', *Quaderni dell' Istituto di topografia antica dell' Università di Roma* 9, 79-87.

Guida, A. (1985), 'An application of the rank size rule to protohistoric settlements in the middle Tyrrhenian area', in C. Malone and S. Stoddart (eds.), *Papers in Italian Archaeology IV, vol. 3: Patterns in Protohistory*, 217-42. Oxford.

Harris, W.V. (1971), *Rome in Etruria and Umbria*. Oxford.

Hodges, R. (1985), 'Excavations at San Vincenzo al Volturno (Molise)', *Archeologia Medievale* 12, 485-500.

Jones, G.D.B., (1962), 'Capena and the Ager Capenas I', *Papers of the British School at Rome* 30, 116-207.

Jones, G.D.B. (1963), 'Capena and the Ager Capenas II', *Papers of the British School at Rome* 31, 100-58.

Judson, S. and Hemphill, P. (1981), 'Sizes of settlements in southern Etruria, 6th-5th centuries BC', *Studi Etruschi* 49, 193-202.

Keppie, L.J.F. (1983), *Colonisation and Veteran Settlement in Italy 47-13 BC*. London, British School at Rome.

Liverani, P. (1984), 'L'Ager Veientanus in età repubblicana', *Papers of the British School at Rome* 52, 36-48.

Liverani, P. (1987), *Municipium Augustum Veiens*. Studi archaeologica 45, Rome.

Manacorda, D. (1982), 'Una villa antica presso il fossa di Volusia', in *I Volusii Saturnini* (Archaeologia: materiali e problemi 6), 55-82. Bari.

Marazzi, F. (1988), 'Inquadramento storico del sito di Mola di Monte Gelato: suoi legami con le vicende dei possessi fondiari della Chiesa Romana nell'alto medioevo', in Potter and King (1988).

Nylander, C. (ed.) (1986), *Architettura etrusca nel Viterbese*. Rome.

Ostenberg, C.-E. (1975), *Case etrusche di Acquarossa*. Rome.

Partner, P. (1966), 'Notes on the lands of the Roman Church in the early Middle Ages', *Papers of the British School at Rome* 34, 68-78.

Potter, T.W. (1976), *A Faliscan Town in South Etruria*. London, British School at Rome.

Potter, T.W. (1979), *The Changing Landscape of South Etruria*. London.

Potter, T.W. (1987), *Roman Italy*. London.

Potter, T.W. and Dunbabin, K.M. (1979), 'A Roman villa at Crocicchie, Via Clodia', *Papers of the British School at Rome* 47, 19-26.

Potter, T.W. and King, A. (1988), 'Scavi a Mola di Monte Gelato, presso Mazzano Romano, Etruria meridionale', *Archeologia Medievale* 15, 253-311.

Purcell, N. (1988), 'Le iscrizioni', in Potter and King (1988), 284-91.

Shotter, D.C.A. (1976), 'Rome, the Faliscans and the Roman historians', in Potter (1976), 29-35.

Small, A.M. (1980), 'San Giovanni di Ruoti; some problems in the interpretation of the evidence', in K.S. Painter (ed.), *Roman Villas in Italy* (British Museum Occasional Paper, 24), 192-202.

Tomassetti, G. (1913), *La campagna romana, antica, medioevale e moderna* III. Rome.

Toms, J. (1986), 'The relative chronology of the Villanovan cemetery of Quattro Fontanili at Veii', *Archeologia e storia antica* 8, 41-97.

Torelli, M. (1974), Introduction, in F. Coarelli, *Etruscan Cities*, 11-28. London.

Torelli, M. (1981), *Storia degli Etruschi* . Bari.

Ward-Perkins, J.B. (1961), 'Veii. The historical topography of the ancient city', *Papers of the British School at Rome* 29, 1-123.

Ward-Perkins, J.B. (1962), 'Etruscan towns, Roman roads and medieval villages: the historical geography of southern Etruria', *Geographical Journal* 128, 389-405.

Ward-Perkins, J.B., Kahane, A. and Murray-Threipland, L. (1968), 'The Ager Veientanus north and east of Veii', *Papers of the British School at Rome* 36, 1-218.

Wickham, C.J. (1978), 'Historical and topographical notes on early medieval south Etruria, part I', *Papers of the British School at Rome* 46, 132-79.

Wickham, C.J. (1979), *idem*, part II, *Papers of the British School at Rome* 47, 66-95.

9

City, territory and taxation

Mireille Corbier

The Roman Empire of the first three centuries AD can be seen in three ways.

First, as a political and administrative space, where a privileged centre, Rome and Italy, is opposed to a periphery, the provinces.

Second, as a space of circulation and exchange marked by the development of axial routes and rivers, such as that following the Rhone valley in the direction of the Germanies, or the 'continental' route which links London to Byzantium via Boulogne, Cologne, Carnuntum, Aquincum and Sirmium. The network of roads, systematically extended and regularly maintained, is traversed by officials, travellers, traders and armies.

Third, at a local level, as a cellular space: with the model of the 'city' (*civitas,* polis), that is to say of town and its territory (*ager, territorium, pertica, chora*), which involves town/country relations. This model, repeated in hundreds of examples, was probably, for the Romans themselves, the prime unifying factor of their empire. In his 'Eulogy of Rome' (61), the rhetor Aelius Aristides represents the civilised world (*oikoumene*) as the *chora* of a single and unique polis, Rome, which has extended its territory to the limits of this same *oikoumene* and gives rise to the *astu koinon*.[1]

In the east, wherever the city model already existed, it received a boost in the Roman period. This extended as far as Egypt, by the very end of the period we are dealing with, on the standard view, but

---

[1]   The image is taken up by Dio Cassius 52.19.6 and the rhetor Menander, *De divisione generis demonstrativi* iii.360.

arguably much earlier.[1] In the west, certain cities, almost all in Britain, were creations *ex nihilo*, while others, like the majority of Gallic *civitates*, were the result of an evolution encouraged by the conqueror. This cellular structure was to leave a lasting mark on countries of the west such as Gaul and Spain, while in North Africa or in Britain, by contrast, the countryside was to take back its own.

This town/country relationship was in many respects new: the whole network of dependence and the levying of tax would tend to be structured at the level of the principal town. On one side, we have the town where the main landowners live, a defined space usually circumscribed by its ramparts and the ring of cemeteries. On the other is the territory, sometimes centuriated, and articulated, at least in the west, by *villae* (large farms, often containing a *pars urbana*, the temporary residence of the owner) and villages grouping together peasant labour. The distribution of cultivation reflects the power of the privileged unit of consumption represented by the town.

This chequerboard pattern was not imposed from above, but evolved gradually with the advance to city-status of village communities (*vici, pagi, oppida, castella, komai, katoikiai...*) enriched by the exploitation of their land. The pattern varied widely in different parts of the empire, especially on the periphery. Thus the density of cities was low on the Atlantic coast of Mauretania or in the interior of Asia Minor. The *koinon* of the province of Asia united Greek cities (*poleis, demoi*) and 'tribes' (*ethne*) living outside the framework of the city (Drew Bear 1972). Urbanisation, then, was not complete, and the fact that Rome helped to spread a 'town-and-territory' model of organisation of space and of social life must not lead us to forget the existence of zones of various size and population which are 'outside' the territory of the cities. Besides the 'tribes', 'peoples', or 'nations' (*gentes, nationes, ethne*) which we have already met, there were imperial domains granted their own administration, sanctuaries with their own lands (at which neighbouring cities tended to nibble away) and large estates of rich individuals enjoying the benefit, according to some *gromatici*, of special status linked to extraterritoriality. There were whole regions where the 'town and territory' model did not apply, including a part of Hauran (Sartre 1987), Galilee (Goodman 1984), the country of the Gorgoromeis and

---

[1]   This view was suggested to me by Alan Bowman.

of the Homonadeis in Galatia (Hall 1971), and many others besides, not to mention Egypt.

Despite these blanks, which one must not minimize, the cellular structure of the city weighed heavily upon the working of the empire itself; central power which relied on it had also to make allowances for it. Though a unifying factor, at the same time it generated economic and social inequalities, for example the imbalance between town and country, in which Rostovtzeff sought the explanation of the decline of the Roman empire. One of the keys to the interpretation of these inequalities is taxation; its assessment, the methods of its levying and payment, the relationship between local and imperial taxation.

There are two ways of approaching the idea of territory in the Roman empire: one 'fragmented' and the other 'global'. A fragmented approach, which was also that of Roman administrative practice, puts the main emphasis on those territorial units made up by cities. Above them are superimposed judiciary districts (*conventus*, dioceses), provinces and groups of provinces. Below came the small towns and their dependent villages. The cities themselves were differentiated by status (colonies, *municipia*, foreign cities), but these differences only indirectly concern our enquiry. This 'fragmented' administrative practice is reflected in the formula *coloniae et municipia non solum Italiae, verum etiam provinciarum, item civitates cuiusque provinciae* used by the emperor Claudius (*ILS* 214), or again in estimates (inaccurate in the eyes of modern historians) such as the 'five hundred cities of Asia' which we meet in Josephus (*Jewish War* 2.366) and later from Philostratus (*Lives of the Sophists* 2.1.4). The latter passage is in the context of a question of tribute: the procurators of Asia are recorded protesting against the expenditure of the tax of 'five hundred' cities for the benefit of one single city for which an aqueduct had been built. This same administrative practice is responsible for the emergence of the 'residual' categories which, wholly or partially, fail to fit this framework.

The alternative, global, approach was also employed by the Roman state, though less from the point of view of practice than of theory. To the multiplication of cities, it opposes the unity of the empire. A sign of this global approach is the concern to catalogue the resources of the empire which appears in the Augustan period and relies on one technique, the *census*. Carried out province by province, and within each province city by city, the *census*, a statistical return of men and goods, is a Roman innovation, whose aim is primarily fiscal. It serves as a basis for the apportionment of taxes between the provinces, and within them between the cities. The emperor Claudius gave a model justification for the *census:* 'to make our resources publicly known' (*ut publice notae sint facultates nostrae*, *ILS* 212, 38-40; cf. Nicolet 1988, 157). The beginnings of a statistical mentality are also revealed in the central establishment of balance-sheets of public revenues such as that *Breviarium totius imperii* left by Augustus on his death, but which unfortunately has not come down to us. Josephus (*Jewish War* 2.16) was certainly able to consult this type of document under the Flavians in order to set out a panorama of human resources and capacities for contribution in the Empire (Nicolet 1988, 192-9).

From this global approach derived the plan of a complete register of the area and its inhabitants, which left no more room for the least 'blank'. The state recognised immunities, which it had itself granted: some towns in the Empire (though not the richest) enjoyed the status of *civitates foederatae* or *civitates liberae et immunes*, and were thereby exempt from taxes, and a handful of colonies had *ius Italicum*, and so enjoyed the same fiscal privilege as the inhabitants of Italy. But no one could usurp immunity, as the Cietae discovered to their cost. This tribe withdrew to the Taurus mountains to avoid the census and taxes introduced when Cappadocia was annexed as a province, but were brutally subjugated by the governor of Syria (Tacitus, *Annals* 6.41). True, the emperor could exercise *indulgentia* in granting remissions of tax, particularly of arrears which were in fact lost (Corbier 1977 and 1988b); but the principle of liability for taxation could not be contested.

Taxation then exposes inequalities at several levels: between Italy, exempt from the *tributum*, and the provinces; between the cities themselves, a small number of which were exempt from taxation; between what was and was not 'city territory'; and within the city between the town and its own territory.

Roman administration for the purposes of its own accounting used wider divisions, the province or group of provinces. So the tax districts, like those for levying the inheritance tax which only affected Roman citizens, went beyond provincial boundaries. On the other hand, the scale of the *tributum* was fixed at the provincial level. But apart from exceptional cases, the city remained the basic unit in so far as it was at that level that tribute and many other dues were assessed. An example is the requisitioning of carts, mules, donkeys and even oxen, for the transport of officials, known as *angareia* or *vehiculatio* (Frend 1956; Zawadski 1960; Mitchell 1976). Each city, Italian or provincial, was liable to be requisitioned within the limits of its own territory, beyond which another community had to take on the relay. The island city of Thasos was thus called upon to contribute for the section of the *Via Egnatia* which crossed its territory on the mainland (Dunant and Pouilloux 1958, no.186). Villages on main roads could find themselves assigned the responsibility for their section. Much new light has been thrown on the subject by the edict of Sotidius Strabo, governor of Galatia, published at the beginning of the reign of Tiberius, which regulated the obligations of the city of Sagalassus in Pisidia and set up 'in each town and village a list of those services which he judges ought to be provided' (Mitchell 1976).

It is important to note that the role of cities in the Roman taxation system is distorted by the sources in various ways.

1 The most serious problem is that the sources are mainly concerned with *expenditure*, and take little interest in the collection of revenue.

A well-known social phenomenon, current in the east as a legacy of the Hellenistic age, which spread in Italy and started and developed in the western provinces, was euergetism, the generosity of notables towards their city. As a result of the cultural phenomenon of epigraphic commmemoration, euergetism bulks large in the surviving evidence. Inscriptions of various kinds testify in abundance to the expenditure of the benefactor (*euergetes*) towards his fellow citizens, ranging from the erection of public buildings to feasts, distributions of money or food, or even oil in the gymnasium. The same epigraphic practice records works financed by the municipal public purse, and, of course, the supreme *euergetes*, the emperor, finds himself glorified when he has granted some concession to the city.

The rare literary sources which provide concrete illustration of the city life of the early empire, such as the exchange of letters between Pliny the Younger and Trajan, or the discourses of Dio of Prusa which, by chance, concern the same region, Bithynia, only a few years earlier, tell us the same story of *expenditure* for aqueducts, public baths and so on. The question of the necessary financing, and the possible receipts, only emerges in outline, especially in Trajan's replies. As for the city curators introduced by the emperors in just this period, their primary function was apparently to prevent cities from ruining themselves by excessive spending.

2 At a local level, even when they touch upon financial returns, the sources only deal with contributions if there have been *changes*. We see this from the practice of posting up official documents such as imperial edicts, or by the custom of commemorating the services of a leading citizen, effectively ambassador for his city to Roman authority (emperor or provincial governor). In this way our attention is drawn to exemptions or alleviations of taxes which have been obtained, or conversely to authorisations to levy such and such new tax, or to increase, with the body of decurions, the number of people paying for the privilege of entry to the council or contributing to the *munera*.

These sources do not allow us to pinpoint the usual rates of taxation, which are taken for granted, but only the adjustments to the tax system. When established revenues are confirmed, the detail is not spelt out, a natural omission, since the context is always a reply from the emperor to a request from the interested parties (e.g. *ILS* 6092, one of a series of such documents linked to Flavian fiscal policies).

When, exceptionally, an inscription might indicate the scale of certain taxes, it must be interpreted with caution, for example the marble plaque of Ephesus (*Inschriften von Ephesus* 13), which gives a list of the cities and the peoples of the province grouped according to district - *conventus* - with an indication, following each tribe name, of the cause for deduction,[1] followed by a figure, with or without a unit of money, probably indicating the level of the levy in the territorial unit concerned. We would get to the heart of our subject if we could be sure of this point. At least, this document shows that the hierarchy city/ *conventus* / province is, under the Flavians, the territorial framework of the assessment of most Roman taxes.

3 A third problem, which would repay further investigation, concerns terminology. The use of the same terminology for the taxes paid to Rome and the local dues paid to the city creates, for us, a

---

[1] On the difficulties of interpreting these rubrics, see Habicht 1975 and Knibbe 1987.

certain amount of confusion. Latin usage of the period distinguishes broadly between the *tributum*, the direct tax (sometimes still called *stipendium*), which could take two forms, the *tributum soli* (land taxation) and the *tributum capitis* (personal taxation), and the other dues which are grouped under the name of *vectigalia*. But *vectigalia* can also cover revenues in general, like *prosodoi* in Greek. (The Greeks established the same kind of distinction between *phoros* and *telos*.) In literary works, the confusion may be made worse by the use of more or less appropriate synonyms. Thus the much discussed 'tithe' of the Bithynians which figures in Dio of Prusa *Discourse* 38 may simply be a word chosen to avoid repeating the word *phoros* which had already been used in the previous sentence (Jones 1978, 185 n.29).

Taxation casts a spotlight upon conflicts, which would otherwise mostly if not completely escape our notice, and which arise from the control of space as well as the appropriation and administration of its resources. Some go beyond the strict limits of the city. This is the case with populations and territories situated outside its legal or *de facto* control. It is also the case with population movements which affect the city's territory but are beyond its control, such as transhumance, which in the Abruzzi caused conflict between the cities of Saepinum and Bovianum and the *conductores* of herds to which the state guaranteed free circulation and access to pasture (Corbier 1983 and 1988b). It is also the case with the movement of armies, which created requirements for supplies far beyond the usual resources of cities. This explains the frequent intervention in this period of the benefactor to take responsibility for exceptional requirements of this nature. There is hardly a conflict, however, which, directly or indirectly, fails to involve one or more cities. Most occurred within the framework of the city and its territory: the argument will focus on these.

The city and its territory

The hierarchy of cities

The richness of a city is proportional to the extent and the population of its territory, or at least to the size of the revenue which the latter brings in: for the fertility of the soil, the exploitation of mines, quarries, salt-marshes, fishing zones, ferries etc., or the profits from customs duties can make up for smallness of size.

This richness is one factor determining the hierarchy of cities. A classic text on this theme is Dio of Prusa's eulogy of Celaenae-Apamea in Phrygia (*Oratio* 35.14-15; cf. now Jones 1974). The capacity of a city such as Celaenae to contribute, be it state taxes to Rome or its share of the expenses of the imperial cult to the provincial *koinon*, is at once the mark and the consequence of its wealth. A major element in the wealth of Celaenae is the number of 'cities without prestige' (*anonymoi poleis*) and 'affluent villages' which are 'in submission' to it (*hypekooi*). A similar phenomenon occurs at Nimes, whose importance was linked to its 24 dependent villages (Strabo, 4.1.12; Pliny, *Nat.Hist.* 3.37). Strabo speaks of these villages as 'subject' (*hypekooi*) to Nimes, the same word used by Dio of Celaenae's villages. He also describes them as *syntelousas* to Nimes, using a word with a telling ambiguity - it can mean both 'dependent' and 'contributory'. In another passage Dio (*Oratio* 40.10) makes the defining characteristic of a village *syntelein allois* - to be dependent on others which are not themselves dependent, except ultimately on Rome.

Uncertainty remains over the nature of the contributions made by villages dependent on cities like Celaenae and Nimes. Some instances are known of peoples and towns that actually paid tribute to another town (e.g. Caunos to Rhodes, Cicero, *ad Quintum fr.* 1.1.33: cf. Bertrand 1987; or the Carni and Catali to Trieste, *ILS* 6680: cf. Degrassi 1954, 81-3). Some suppose that this was the relationship of the 24 villages to Nimes (so Goudineau 1976; Christol and Goudineau 1988). An alternative, which seems to me more attractive, follows the model of the synoecism of Athens described by Thucydides (2.15.2), where the power of the city is linked to the centralisation of contributions (Van Effenterre 1985, 171f., 191f.). Nimes, as central city, benefited from the concentration of local contributions from the whole *civitas*; it could also act as middle-man, receiving the sums eventually due to the central government and passing them on to Rome.[1]

The Roman state applied the same reasoning to its subject cities as it did to itself; it was a *civitas* which grew larger with the

[1] On the problems, terminological and otherwise, posed by communities 'attributed' to cities see most recently Galsterer 1988. I shall return to this question elsewhere.

acquisition of new provinces and so acquired new sources of revenue. This is why, as late as the second century AD, Abdera on the Thracian coast gives thanks to Hadrian for extending its territory as far as the river Nestos and restoring a territory it regards as its own (Robert 1987, 137f.). In the last century of the Republic, we even see Italian towns receiving lands overseas. Thus Capua, deprived of a part of its own lands by Octavian for allotment to his veterans, was granted among other compensations land at Cnossos in Crete, whose revenues it was still drawing two centuries later (Ducrey 1969; Rigsby 1976).

The foundation of a city presupposes the assignment of revenues, as Hadrian confirms. Stratonicea on the Caicus, elevated to the rank of a city with the name of Hadrianopolis, received, in response to its request, a letter from the emperor agreeing its requests as being 'just and necessary for a recently created city', and adding, 'I grant to you the revenues from the territory (*ta tele ek tes choras*)' (*Syll.*[3] 837). To give a territory - a *chora* - is in fact to confer a revenue. For Rostovtzeff (1957, 698-9), '*tele* means of course the payments of the rural population of the territory of the newly created city.' 'Of course' is probably going too far; for uncertainty remains over the nature of these *tele*. They may correspond either to taxes levied on the inhabitants as a whole or on certain activities (of which some might even have been made over by Rome to the city's profit), or to the revenues from public lands let to people who cultivate or exploit them, or to a combination of the two, to which levies of corn could have been added. In either case, Stratonicea drew additional income from rents from villages and peasants under its authority. Louis Robert (1962, 65f.) offers a pointer in the same direction: a tribe, the *Indeipediatai*, formed a *sympoliteia* with Stratonicea until the time of Trajan. The two communities even minted money, sometimes together, sometimes separately. The foundation of Hadrianopolis-Stratonicea doubtless forced the *Indeipediatai* to pass under the administrative authority of their neighbour. Later, in the Byzantine era, the situation was to be reversed. Kalandos (modern-day Gelemba), the capital of the *Indeipediatai*, will have acquired importance as a staging-post on a caravan route, while Stratonicea vegetated and finally disappeared.

Importance as a staging-post is one of the arguments deployed by Orcistos in Phrygia (*MAMA* 7 [1956] no.305) in its successful request to the emperor Constantine. In order to be able to escape from the guardianship of Nacoleia of which it is a *vicus* (the context is eastern but the inscription is in Latin), it aspires to the status of *civitas* - with its own *ordo decurionum*, its own magistrates and the right to manage its own affairs by means of decrees, as detailed in the grant of *ius civitatis* to another city of Asia Minor, Tymandus in Pisidia (*ILS* 6090). In order to justify its request, Orcistos puts forward, following the rhetorical practice of the day, the economic advantages attaching to its situation: a crossing of main highways endowed with a *mansio* (a staging inn) and abundance of running water used to power water-mills (serving to mill the grain). There follows an *ad hominem* point (the addressee being Constantine): the inhabitants are all Christians. The irritations of being dependent on Nacoleia include a *pro cultis* tax - likely enough to annoy Constantine, if this 'tax for cult' was put to pagan purposes (Chastagnol 1981a and 1981b).

In default of revenue, a new town could find recognition by means of immunities. To encourage the creation of an *emporion* in Pizos in Thrace by the regrouping of nine villages, Septimus Severus granted a double dispensation: both from providing corn-supplies for the city, Augusta Traiana, of which it was a dependency (rather than for Rome, as scholars have imagined), and from various services like levying recruits[1] (specified as *burgarioi* and *phrouroi*), and payments under the head of *angareia* (*IG Bulg.* 3.2. no. 1690).

It could be important that one did not fall within the area of a city. A recently published African inscription (*AE* 1985, 972) affords an instance. The Thudedenses (or Thuddenses) inhabiting a *castellum* (a borough) within or on the edge of the territory of Tipasa in Mauretania received from Septimus Severus and his sons confirmation of an *indemnitas* once granted by king Juba, and of their borders guaranteed by a new boundary. Probably the *Thudedenses* were resisting the claims of the city of Tipasa to levy contributions from them.

---

[1] The term used is *synteleia*, according to the supplement of Rostovtzeff (1918, 29).

The city and exploitation of territory

Rivalries between neighbouring cities, like the *campanilismo* of medieval Italian cities, were a commonplace feature of the Roman world (Robert 1977, Syme 1981), and often the issues at stake were trivial, as in the conflict between Nicaea and Nicomedia which centred on Nicaea's claim to share with Nicomedia the title of first town in the province of Bithynia. 'We are not fighting for the sea or the land ... it is not a question either of revenue or of territory', as Dio commented in his speech on the conflict (*Oratio* 38.22). Territory and revenues, he implies, were serious prizes, and might be worth quarrelling over. They were in fact at the heart of many conflicts between cities, or betweeen cities and tribes, between cities and great domains, private or imperial, reaping the benefits of extraterritoriality, and between cities and individuals, as numerous inscriptions confirm.

Each city tended its territorial limits with great care, as its boundaries were of such great importance. The *lex Irnitana* (76.14-15: *JRS* 76 [1986], 173) associates the three terms, *fines, agri, vectigalia*, to designate both the space and the revenues which the municipal magistrates should inspect annually. We find the transcription in Greek of Roman terms relating to possessions and revenues in earlier documents emanating from the Roman authorities, such as the *senatus consulta* of 170 BC in favour of Thisbe (Sherk, no.2, 17-18), of 81 BC in favour of Stratonicea in Caria (Sherk, no. 18, 53-4 and 97-8), of 80 BC in favour of Thasos (Dunant and Pouilloux 1958, no. 174) and again that in favour of Aphrodisias (Reynolds 1984, no. 8, 58-9).

It is rare to find, among the epigraphic evidence of the first three centuries AD relating to territorial disputes, any which explicitly link demarcation with taxation, or rather with immunity from taxation, as in the case of the *Thudedenses* discussed above. The demarcation attested at Uchi Maius between the land of the *coloni* of the *pagus* and those of the *peregrini* of the *civitas* (*CIL* 8. 26274 = *IL Tun* 1370) was on Gascou's interpretation (see below) of precisely this type, though it is not spelt out explicitly.

Tax-immunity was particularly hard to defend: in 129 BC Pergamum, in dispute with the *publicani*, had to get the Roman senate to confirm the attachment to its territory of certain lands (royal or sacred?) and their exemption from taxation (Sherk no.12; Nicolet

1966, 348-9). However, the *gromaticus* Hyginus (114, 12 Lachmann) states explicitly: demarcations of territory take place *propter exigenda tributa* - on account of the taxes to be levied. But if we recall the Greek inscriptions which associate taxes with 'other dues', we should equally take into account conflicts, including boundary disputes, connected with the *angareia*, like the dispute between Thasos and Philippi (Dunant and Pouilloux, no. 186).

Disputes might also concern grazing-land, water-springs, waste-land or scrub, as, for instance, in the argument under the Republic between the city of Genoa and the Langenses (*ILS* 5946). For the city banked on the fact that only part of the land was cultivated, and could be privately owned. Thus in colonies the land which the surveyors left out of the centuriated zone was of considerable value in Mediterranean countries where the use of *saltus*, uncultivated ground, was necessary for the pasturing of herds, or for acorns for the pigs to graze, let alone the gathering of the wild fruits. Most cities had at their disposal a public domain which brought them revenue, but which the notables (who could guarantee its management) tended to monopolise or sell for private profit; the preservation or recovery of this land, to protect the financial interests of cities, was one of the major preoccupations of central government.

Among the images which evoke the way cities siphoned off resources from their territory, we may briefly recall two centripetal movements: the channelling of water and the stockpiling of grain. Running water was an element of Mediterranean sociability (the fountain functioning like the village pump), of urban comfort and of city culture. The aqueduct was often only a preliminary to the construction of baths, the function of which was not solely hygenic. Running water was above all an element of urban decoration, marked by the stamp of the sacred, notably at nymphaea. As Pausanias puts it in a famous passage (10.4.1): 'Can one give the name of city to a place which has neither public buildings, nor gymnasium, nor theatre, nor public square, nor water supply to any fountain?' Among monuments of material prosperity which made the status of the city visible, those connected with water occupied a special place. This was piped in, if need be, from far away, and at great expense. Benefactors often made a donation of springs which rose on their land, and of the *iter aquae*, the strip of land necessary for the canal and its banks. Failing donations, magistrates could resort to expropriation. Conversely, if the water derived from the territory of a neighbouring city, rent (*vectigal*) was payable. Thus an inscription found at Castrum Novum shows the payment by this little town in Picenum of a rental for water to its neighbour Interamna (*ILS* 5681; cf. Corbier 1984).

On the siphoning off of grain to make up reserves in town, the best text is that of Galen (6. 749ff.), who shows the peasants of the countryside of Asia Minor starving after the grain harvest - and also that of bean crops - had been transported to town. Certainly, the context is one of a famine, and Galen's aim is that of studying illnesses brought on by eating grass, leaves and other inedible plants (Garnsey and Saller 1987, 97). But Galen's aside, 'the city-dwellers, as it was their practice to collect and store enough grain for all the next year immediately after the harvest', is good evidence of the usual practice of stocking up grain in the town immediately after the harvest. In case of need, the town would not hesitate to add pure and simple requisitions to the usual delivery of land-rent to the owners.

Size of territory and the emergence of elites

In a society in which the census (fortune) required for access to the higher orders of the state (the senatorial and equestrian orders) tended to be identified with the inheritance of real estate, the extent of territory also played an important role in the development of social inequalities. It allowed for the upward mobility and consolidation of land-based fortunes of the local notables. Syme (1977) showed, and the work of Burnand (1982 and unpublished thesis) has since confirmed, how in Narbonensis cities like Vienne which had a vast territory at their disposal were the first to send senators to Rome, and did so moreover in relatively large numbers, while Roman colonies with smaller territory, having been allocated originally in equal plots, did not create the right conditions of social differentiation for the emergence of a very rich elite. Working from this, one might then be tempted to investigate, apart from 'de grandes possessions terriennes' (Syme 1977, 380), not so much commercial activities and public service as the profits of tax-gathering itself, and those of the management of the public lands of the city, of which a part ended up in the hands of a small number of families. The same contrast can be observed in Africa between Lambaesis and Cirta.

Territory and fiscal system

For Roman and local taxation alike, men held that in principle taxation should be fairly divided. This was affirmed in the Severan age by the jurists, and by Dio Cassius (52.28-29). But *actual practice*, as is well documented by sources both earlier and later than this period, reveals inequalities created or accentuated by the processes of the fiscal system.

For the fiscal system of the state, the terms of the *census* described by Ulpian (*Digest* 50.15.4) presuppose the theoretical equality of all lands which are not exempt, in respect to land tax at least. The Severan jurists throw into relief the actual character of land tax: Ulpian's terms (*Digest* 50.4.6) - *intributiones quae agris fiunt vel aedificiis* - or those of Papinian (*Digest* 49.14.36) - *tributum eorumdem praediorum onus* - specify that taxation is a burden on the land. Every *possessor* (proprietor) is subject, within the framework of the city, to taxes and services relating to his landed estates, even if he is not a member of the community because of his place of origin or of residence. They are aware that certain communities or individuals benefit from total exemption (*immunitas*). But they look upon them as a minority to be discounted (for example, they give lists, though incomplete, of provincial cities which enjoy the *ius Italicum*) and they establish a distinction which operates between immunity of property, which is perpetual and so transferable, and that obtained by an individual which lapses with the death of the beneficiary. Likewise they draw a nice distinction between such exemption, a privilege which could be conceded or confirmed by the emperor alone, and merely temporary dispensation (*vacatio, excusatio*)which, it is worth noting, was in the power of the governor of the province and not of the municipal magistrates.

At the municipal level too, financial charges were determined by principles of equality. The revenues of a city, however, contrast with those of the state: they are characterised by the rarity of direct taxation (but not its absence as used to be claimed) and the importance given by contrast to indirect taxation which was essentially directed at exchange and circulation (tolls, marketing rights, anchorage for ships) and at certain urban services (entrance to the baths, water rights). Another characteristic was the importance of inherited estates - at least for the biggest landowners - in the part played by *summa honoraria*, sums paid in the exercise of a magistracy or on the occasion of entry to the council, and the practice of liturgies (*munera*), which made the richest inhabitants of the city undertake its expenses in a way which was simultaneously voluntary and obligatory. Hence the interest in increasing the number of participants: Trieste probably had in view the double profit to be derived from *summa honoraria* and from *munera*, when they successfully requested from Antoninus access to its council and magistracies for the notables of the Carni and Catali (*ILS* 6680). But the promotion of elites who gained Roman citizenship on election to the aedileship did not exempt the group from the dues which brought in income to the city.

Apart from the payments of such 'tributary' peoples, the first impression of city finances could be of the low level of the flow of taxes from the country to the town; this fits in with the equality of legal rights recognised to the inhabitants of town and country, so long as they enjoyed the same status. Thus the *lex de Termessibus* of 70 BC in favour of Termessos specifies that the immunity recognised by Rome applies both to town and country (*FIRA*^{2} I. no. 11, col. II, 9: *in oppidum... agrumve*).

Three texts examined by Fergus Millar (1983) even suggest that theory tended to protect the inhabitants of the villages from liturgies to the exclusive benefit of the inhabitants of the town. One is the decision of Septimius Severus, requested by the villagers of the Arsinoite nome in the course of a trial before the prefect of Egypt in 250 AD (*SB* 7696, cf. Lewis 1985, 49-50), who apparently freed Egyptian villagers and countryfolk (*kometai* and *georgoi*) from liturgies to the advantage of the metropolis of the nome. There is also the exclusion of the inhabitants of the countryside by the jurist Modestinus (*Digest* 50.1.35) from the status of *incola*, and thus of the inherent *munera*, for the precise reason that they did not benefit from the privileges (*exaireta*, the Greek equivalent of *commoda*) of the town. We have too Ulpian's enumeration of these very *commoda* (*Digest* 50.1.27.1) - use of the forum, use of the public baths, attendance at shows, participation in religious festivals - in connection with the establishment of the *domicilium*, in other words, the definition of the status of *incola*. At any rate Ulpian makes no mention of the incompatibility of this status with residence in the countryside.

But, whatever the principles, practice generated manifold inequalities within the city, both in the case of state taxes and of local dues. I will call attention to some of these, drawing a distinction as far as possible between the different levels of basis of assessment, assessment of individuals, and actual collection.[1]

Basis of assessment

Roman taxes were not limited to the *tributum*, the main provincial tax, with its two sides of land tax and capitation. They also involved the *portoria*, taxes on the manumission and sale of slaves and one on inheritance, involving only Roman citizens. But the commercial and artisanal activities which dominated the town seem to have been less affected than agriculture (and so the peasants and/or the landowners) by the *tributum soli* which was calculated as a percentage of the capital value of land or its yield, not from income. Personal tax itself was in some cases imposed upon everybody (except Roman citizens, infants and the aged) on the same basis (e.g. the didrachma of the Jews, which was possibly a supplement to their capitation), in other cases adjusted according to the district and status of individuals (e.g. the *laographia* in Egypt), and possibly in further cases proportional to capital declared and so progressive.[2] In the first case, the poor pay the same amount as the rich. In the second two, capital is directly affected in all its forms (land, urban property and ships, duly counted at the time of the *census*).

Taxes collected by the cities are ill-documented. The capitation of one denarius authorised by Antoninus in a city of Macedonia (Oliver 1958 = *AE* 1956, 101 and 1958, 2) also affected the inhabitants of the city, as well as tolls[3] and sales taxes. Revenue-bearing property

---

[1]   *Translator's note.* French distinguishes two aspects of taxation, *assiette* and *répartition*: the first refers to basis on which the tax is levied, the second to the assessment of individual liability. Here 'basis of assessment' is used for *assiette*, and 'assessment of individuals' for *répartition*.

[2]   At least, this is the case if the phrase of Appian, *Syr.* 50, speaking of a 1% tax practised in Syria and Cilicia really does refer to the *phoros ton somaton* mentioned in the previous phrase. Some believe that this 1% tax refers to the *tributum soli*.

[3]   Dagron and Feissel 1987, 183-4 for a brief survey, à propos a fifth/sixth-century customs tariff from Anabarzus in Cilicia.

belonging to the city might be located in the town (e.g. the *merides* of Orange, identified by Piganiol 1962, 329-36 as the stalls beneath porticoes let by the city); more important were those in the countryside. These affected agriculture, stock-breeding and exploitation of quarries or mines which the state had not taken. Cadaster B from 'Orange' (actually Valentia according to Salviat 1986) reveals a link between the progress of development and that of local resources; the newly cultivated lands are subject to *vectigal*.

In large measure, then, the assessment of taxation depended in the provinces on land. Even the inheritance tax, the profits of which were, according to Dio Cassius (77.9.6), the motive for the extension of Roman citizenship in 212, was probably calculated on the basis of the fortune declared at the time of the census.

An initial source of inequality resulted from the taking of the census. The census took place within the framework of the city and the *forma censualis* was drawn up on the basis of the declarations (*professiones*) of the interested parties (Ulpian, *Digest* 50.15.4.pr.: *omnia ipse qui defert aestimet*). The declarer had to estimate everything himself: notably the type of development - cultivation of grain, of plants (with the number of vines or olive-trees), meadows, pastures or woodlands. The extent of properties made fraud easy. On this point, the owners showed solidarity amongst themselves, just as they did on the basis of their estimates. Tertullian (*Apology* 42.9) assures us of the Christians that *they* did not cheat.

The census created a basis for assessment, a cadastral valuation. The frequency of the survey is very important: fourteen years in Egypt, linked to the age at which boys became liable to capitation. The timing offered two possibilities for speculation, which could lead to inequality. The first was positive: if a piece of land was uncultivated at the time of the census, the tax would not be imposed until the following census, on the basis of lack of cultivation, even if the owners sowed or planted it immediately afterwards. In this sense, the census was an encouragement to agricultural investment. But the more frequent the census, the smaller was the potential profit. Conversely, someone who cultivated his land badly continued to pay on the basis declared at the census. The second was negative: the big landowner was far more at liberty to leave land fallow or turn it over to pasture in the year of the census than the little peasant-farmer who lived off it. The census created a situation in which the small property which was intensively and regularly cultivated ran the risk of being overtaxed, in comparison with the large estate exploited more extensively.

But the major inequality was that of the status of the lands, linked to that of their original owners, reflecting, in Gaul and Africa, a contrast between privileged Roman citizens and non-citizens. It affected the territory in Roman colonies which was partly allocated to colonists (veterans or civilians), and partly restored to the natives: lands belonging to the colonists usually enjoyed the immunities described above.

This inequality is visible in, and above all sanctioned by, the land register. In the three cadasters, which according to Salviat (1986) refer to the colonies of Arles, Orange and Valence, the lands allocated to the veterans are described by the expression *ex tr(ibutario solo)*, interpreted by the editor Piganiol (1962) as 'withdrawn from tributary land'. The posting of three cadastral plans on the walls of the same Tabularium tended to prevent constant legal actions over the lands and the revenues from them.

In the territory of the colony of Carthage, inequality in taxation was linked with the status of the populations and the lands which had been carefully marked out and assigned to it. According to Jacques Gascou (1984), the colony of Carthage, endowed with an immense territory, in 28 BC received *immunitas*, dispensation from Roman tax, in respect of its *pertica* - colonial territory. Within the boundaries of Carthage in the early empire, he suggests, there coexisted two fiscal categories of land: on the one hand, the lands of the *pagi* inhabited by citizens of Carthage (so Roman citizens), integral parts of the colony, and hence exempt from provincial taxation, and on the other the land of the foreign *civitates* or *castella* (obviously, the natives), who were subject to taxation. Moreover, on Gascou's interpretation, the revenues drawn by the State from these *castella* were assigned to the colony of Carthage, which entrusted their levying to a Carthaginian magistrate, whose title *praefectus iuri dicundo vectigalibus quinquennalibus locandis in castellis LXXXIII* proves that tax-collection properly speaking was conducted at a local level. If Gascou's interpretation is correct, native towns in the territory of Carthage became virtually tributaries of the colony. But another possibility is that Carthage was only charged with the collection of their taxes, in order to remit the total to Rome. Alternatively, the *vectigalia* concerned were municipal revenues naturally due to Carthage (cf. above).

The development of the fiscal status of these lands suggested by Gascou is also very interesting. For in some cases where two communities coexisted - the Roman *pagus* and the native *civitas* - the process of symbiosis seems to have resulted under Septimius Severus in the creation of *municipia* (so at Thugga, at Uchi Maius and at Thignica). Raising the status of the lands of the ancient *civitas* to the level of the lands of the ancient *pagus* (i.e. immunity) would have brought with it a consequent loss of revenue for Carthage. The concession, also by Septimius, of the *ius Italicum* could be, according to Gascou, a form of compensation. Possibly this was a purely honorific compensation, for it is hard to see from the tax point of view what more this status could offer than the *immunitas* in force for more than two hundred years.

Similarly, the basis of municipal *munera* lent itself to inequalities. The request presented to the prefect of Egypt in 250, discussed above, reveals a contradiction between principles and reality: the villagers have to appeal to him to resist the claims of the metropolis of the nome to impose liturgies upon them to its own benefit alone.

The city is also where religious cults were concentrated, to which the population of the territory was required to contribute. According to the important inscription recently published by Wörrle (1987 and 1988), the villages of the *chora* of Oenoanda in Lycia undertake to provide fourteen oxen to be sacrificed to Apollo at a new annual festival instituted in the city. Oenoanda controls a vast mountain territory: some thirty contributing villages are listed. But the degree of participation by these villagers in the civic ceremony, at Oenoanda itself, and of their share in the sacrificial meats, the counterweight to their tax-offering in kind, remains unknown.

Emperors would occasionally justify their refusal of a remission of tax by the fact that this would only be advantageous to the rich. This point has a wider bearing than on town/country relations, but it is also relevant in this context. The problem has been raised (Brunt 1981; Corbier 1985) à propos of the remissions of tax for the following *quinquennium* granted by Tiberius to the towns of Asia which were destroyed by earthquakes. If it meant the actual non-payment of tax by those who usually paid, the relief would have been valid for all, city-dwellers and peasants. But if these remissions meant the non-payment to Rome of taxes owed by the city, which could still levy these sums in the usual manner to use them at home, the burden of the reconstruction of towns would have fallen for the most part on the population of their *chora*.

Assessment of individuals

Even when based on the census, the assessment of taxes allowed these inequalities to become even more marked. A passage of Josephus is revealing (*Jewish War* 17. 404-5). King Agrippa has just dissuaded the Jews from revolting against Rome and finishes his speech by saying (404):

> You will free yourselves from the suspicion of revolt if you repair
> the porticoes and pay your contributions ... (405) The people
> [continues Josephus] returned to their right minds. All having
> gone up to the temple with the king and Berenice, they began to
> rebuild the porticoes, while the magistrates and the members of
> the Council having dispersed into the villages proceeded to collect
> the taxes. The forty talents which made up overdue contributions
> were rapidly collected.

The picture is of the magistrates being sent from the town to the surrounding villages to gather the taxes.

To what degree is this situation representative of the rest of the empire? Whatever the answer, the passage suggests a twofold inequality: the first is linked to the basis of assessment, which, we have seen, rests essentially on land as the primary sector of the economy. A second inequality appears to be possible at the level of assessment of individuals. Certain cities, according to the jurist Arcadius Charisius (*Digest* 50.4.18.21-5), had the privilege of raising each year a special levy of corn proportional to size of estate (*pro mensura agri*): who but the municipal magistrates could judge the extent of the lands under cultivation of each individual?

For the Roman *tributum*, though we have no definite evidence, the likely procedure for assessment is that a total sum was determined for the province, and then divided between cities or communities. Villages paid the state taxes to the city or its representatives. If the city reserved a degree of freedom in gathering the amounts due (though this was surely not the case where the tax was a percentage of fortune declared, like the one percent of Syria and Cilicia), the possibilities would arise of overcharging some while lightening the burden of others, with the effect of exaggerating inequalities built into the initial census. This is the picture of tyrannical *curiales* given us by fourth- and fifth-century Christian authors concerned for the humble (Lepelley 1983). They accuse the *curiales* who were in charge of the assessment and collection of taxes of abusing their power and of drawing a 'personal profit' from the 'collection of public taxes' (Salvian 5. 21-28). John Chrysostom gives specific evidence for Antioch, where tax collectors are depicted as exploiters of widows and orphans. But it is above all the Gallic monk Salvian who in his vengeful treatise *On the Government of God*, written between AD 440 and 450, is the author of the famous tag *quot curiales, tot tyranni*. I quote the following passage:

> What is worse, is that the majority sees its goods confiscated by individuals for whom the public collection of tax is a prey they make their own and who make private gain under pretext of fiscal debt ... Is there in fact a town, or a municipium, or a borough where there do not exist *as many tyrants as curiales*. Where is the place where, as I have said, the chief men of the cities do not devour the entrails of widows and orphans ...?
>
> (Salvian 5. 17-18)

Involved in establishing the basis of taxation, and in effective control of its assignment between taxpayers, the *curiales* could give advantages to the rich, wherever they were, and put the burden on the poor, even in towns, or the weak (widows and orphans). But the abuses inherent in assessment are intimately linked to those of collection.

Tax -collection

The city, wherever it existed, was the basic unit for tax-collection. This duty was entrusted to the local notables, and not to the representatives of central power. The two methods for which we have evidence are the liturgy (the *munus exigendi tributi*) and farming out.

The *munus*, which made the tax-gatherer responsible for the sum due, meant that he could always end up with a loss if the taxpayers refused to pay. To be exempted from the duty of tax-collection could be a privilege which was valued under the early empire: we know for example that the rhetor Aelius Aristides (*Oratio* 50) invested some cash in order to obtain from the proconsul of Asia confirmation of this exemption. This fact has sometimes encouraged modern writers, following Rostovtzeff, to underline the risks of tax-collection. These risks are illustrated in moving detail in the famous speech of the rhetor Libanius *On Patronages*, dated between 386 and 392 AD, describing the ruin of *curiales*, collecting tax in the name of the city of Antioch, who came up against an actual tax strike on the part of some villagers, protected by a military leader and his soldiers, and upon their return to Antioch, saw their land, their houses and their slaves sold by the provincial authorities. But the situation described by Libanius, who was himself a representative of the dominant social class, appears to more recent commentators rather atypical (cf. above, Lepelley 1983).

The farming out of Roman taxes as well as municipal revenues is attested, but without the sources always allowing us to distinguish the one from the other. At any rate, we encounter at the local level certain *vicensimarii, eikostonai, telonai* and *demosionai*, concerned with one or other. The cadastral registers at Orange publicise the names of adjudicators who rented lands or farmed the collection of the *vectigal*, together with the rates of rent (expressed in *asses* per *iugerum*), and sum total (in *denarii*). The *vectigalia* of the *LXXXIII castella*, whatever their destination (the colony of Carthage according to Gascou) and their precise nature, were certainly farmed out at the beginning of the principate under the care of a Carthaginian magistrate. The city of Munigua in Baetica proved a bad payer to Servilius Pollio, probably a native of the neighbouring Carmo, who undertook to farm its dues and agreed on making it an advance; the city was forced by the governor and the emperor Titus to pay up (*AE* 1961, 147 and 288; cf. d'Ors 1961).

In either case, liturgy or tax farming, the intermediary (the local notable) could make a profit: he could speculate both on the amounts collected and still outstanding; late payments could be used to bring in interest (the *usurae* so frequently mentioned in antiquity), as could advances agreed either to the state or to the taxpayer. He could lend, speculate on the cash (in Asia Minor, probably, on the exchange rate between bronze coinage and denarii), or speculate on payments made in kind (by selling more dearly in the town produce which he has accepted on the basis of country prices).

Important, though late, evidence for the question of loans and advances is a constitution of Theodosius II dated 415 (*CTh* 11.28.10). In 414 the emperor granted a tax remission to the provinces of the east for a period of forty years - from 367 to 407 (in fact of long-standing arrears which were unquestionably lost; emperors always hoped to recoup their more recent ones). He then published a new constitution to denounce those who had profited from *indulgentia* in matters of taxation in the previous year 'to make private debts which were public' (*ut fierent privata debita quae fuerunt publica*). If the *curiales* managed to convert amnestied public debts into 'private debts', it is probably by way of the advances and loans granted to the taxpayers by the tax-collectors. The emperor demands that the taxpayers should profit from the *indulgentia* (fiscal amnesty) *non nomine sed re ipsa*, not nominally but in reality.

Despite the lack of such an explicit text for the first three centuries we have no reason to suspect that social realities had fundamentally changed. As Brunt rightly observed (1981, 170), at least one case exists, the inscriptions dealing with the *angareia*, for which the conflicts which sprung from the requisitions of the second and third centuries seem no less acute than those which the legislative texts assembled in the Theodosian Code reveal for the later period. But there was good reason for inscribing settlements of conflicts of this nature, which involved the services to be provided on sections of the road: the communities liable had an interest in making the details of their obligations known, to stop those eligible demanding more services than they were entitled to. The problems of taxpayers falling into debt with the local notables hardly lent themselves to epigraphic commemoration, but we do find commemorations of 'advances' to cities (Migeotte 1984, 314-16) or of payment of cities' tax obligations by private benefactors, recorded on a few inscriptions both from the west (Ibiza, *ILS* 6960) and the east (Tenos, *IG* XII.5.946; Macedonia, *SEG* 17.315).

Conclusion

The hypothetical nature of much of this argument is justified by the silence of the sources, which vary according to the period, the province, the elements of the process of tax-collection and of expenditure, and also according to the type of taxation (state taxation, however little understood, is better documented in the sources than local taxation). One is often bound to base oneself upon indirect clues, and on particular instances from which generalisation may or may not be legitimate. For the papyrologist there is the evidence of tax-collection, at the humble level of fiscal receipts, rather than of taxation itself. For the epigraphists, there is euergetism, and luckily also the arbitration of certain conflicts.

The temptation remains strong to restate the case for an 'idyllic urban' vision of Roman society of the first centuries of the Empire. Yet cities could only live by siphoning off the resources of the country, and this did not only take the form of rents. They derived profit from the collection of taxes and its inequalities, and they also imposed more or less exceptional levies such as requisitions of grain. There is some point, then, in making a clear distinction between the three aspects. Roman taxation tended to reinforce the power of towns over their surrounding countryside, as indeed did the management of local finances, and in particular of the lands belonging to the city. Notables, unless forbidden by the *lex* of the city,[1] could farm the collection of dues, normally called *vectigalia*, then let them for long periods in five-year renewable (i.e. permanent) leases, sublet them, or appropriate them, by reimbursement for their advances to the city. Epigraphic documentation, which is simultaneously produced and controlled by the notables, continues to proclaim the generosity of their benefactions to their fellow-citizens, and their participation in *munera*.

The central state had scarcely the means to counteract this evolution. Its interventions had bearing on the terms and frequency of the census; on the regulation of allocation of taxes between cities as a result of the census (even if we imagine it firmly established by tradition); on restraint of their falling into debt; on the control of sale of the municipal patrimony and of the squandering of local resources by the banning of 'ambitious decrees' (which allowed the decurions to 'do each other favours'), by the despatch of city curators recruited from outside the local Curia, and finally by hearing, at the provincial level at least, complaints from village communities. In practice, the ordinary individual had scarcely any recourse other than at the level of the city: Aelius Aristides (*Oratio* 50) calculated the cost of his request

---

[1] e.g. the *lex Irnitana* ch. J, in the case of magistrates and apparitores, Ulpian, *Digest* 50.8 for decurions; even then they could operate behind front-men, cf. Piganiol 1962, 58.

at the assizes of the proconsul of Asia at Ephesus at 500 drachmas.

The imbalance of power between villagers and city-dwellers, or at least those whom the complaints refer to as 'the powerful men' of the cities, was not, however, the only inequality. Notable citizens in their turn could find themselves in a situation of inferiority to big landowners. The most typical instance has been discussed by Millar (1986): the city of Vicentia tried to get the Roman senate to refuse the authorisation requested by a senator to hold a weekly market on his land (Pliny, *Letters* 5. 4 and 13). The competition would have affected the Vicentians twice over: at the level of sales by individuals as well as that of market taxes levied by the city. Their advocate, the victim of heavy intimidation, ended up by defaulting on them and by finding himself in a position of being accused of having abandoned his clients after having received fees from them. The senator could not help winning such an unfair contest.

So the city could find itself in its turn in a weak situation, when faced with stronger forces, even in the case of a recalcitrant village. But as a general rule, it was the city that called the tune, for it is at the level of the city that the essential decisions were taken. In relation to taxpayers, it had the advantage of size. State taxation had the effective appearance of a milking of resources, left over from conquest, and destined for Rome and its armies - distant and partly strange entities, even if the authorities missed no opportunity of reminding them of the necessity of military defence. However, little of it was put back into circulation locally, except through the benefactions of those who grew rich, at least in part, on the profits of its collection: for example the individual known on the one hand for his liberalities to the city of Aquincum, and on the other for farming the *portorium* for the great customs district of the two Pannonias (*ILS* 7124a, 7124; *AE* 1968, 323; cf. Corbier 1985, 226f.). But in such a case, the revenue did not come solely from the city that benefited from the redistribution .

Local levies from cities, whatever their nature, in the form of tax or not, would to a large extent be spent *in situ*, by the authorities or benefactors, notably in the guise of public works. Areas so enriched leave visible remains of monuments, and give rise to a more or less wide scale of activities. Imperial intervention to limit this local expenditure was in this sense by no means disinterested, whatever principles they invoked. It aimed not so much to protect the taxpayer as to put a limit to 'unfair competition' which would restrict the collection of taxes destined for central power.

In each case, then, the stake was the control of territory and its resources. The Roman Empire relied, for its day-to-day functioning, on the structure of the city; by its foundations, and by the privileges or franchises it granted on the occasion, it favoured the implantation and multiplication of cities in the less urbanised regions. Equally, it sought, without ever reaching its goal, to unify or at least assimilate local situations, characterised by an infinite diversity which discourages and distracts the modern scholar. But despite all efforts to impose the will of the political and administrative centre, serving the cause of a Rome which claimed identity with the empire, the local level never ceased to make its impact. Whatever the ideals, it was day-to-day decisions and practices that made up the fabric of life of the inhabitants of the empire.

Bibliography

Bertrand, J.-M. (1987), 'Le statut du territoire attribué dans le monde grec des Romains', in Frézouls (1987), 95-106.

Brunt, P.A. (1981), 'The revenues of Rome', *JRS* 71, 161-72.

Burnand, Y. (1982), 'Senatores Romani ex provinciis Galliarum ortis', *Tituli* 5, *Epigrafia e ordine senatorio*, II, 387-437; and unpublished thesis.

Chastagnol, A. (1981a), 'Les *realia* d'une cité d'après l'inscription constantinienne d'Orkistos', *Ktema* 6, 373-79.

Chastagnol, A. (1981b), 'L'Inscription constantinienne d'Orcistus', *Mélanges de l'École Française de Rome Antiquité* 93, 381-416.

Christol, M. and Goudineau, C. (1987-88), 'Nîmes et les Volques arécomiques au 1er siècle avant J.-C.', *Gallia* 45, 87-103.

Corbier, M. (1977), 'Le Discours du Prince d'après une inscription de Banasa', *Ktèma* 2, 211-32.

Corbier, M. (1983), '*Fiscus* and *Patrimonium*: the Saepinum Inscription and transhumance in the Abruzzi', *JRS* 73, 126-31.

Corbier, M. (1984), 'De Volsinii à Sestinum: *cura aquae* et évergétisme municipal de l'eau en Italie', *Revue des études latines* 62, 236-74.

Corbier, M. (1985), 'Fiscalité et dépenses locales', *L'origine des richesses dépensées dans la ville antique*, ed. Ph. Leveau, 219-32. Aix-en-Provence.

Corbier, M. (1988a), '*Indulgentia Principis*', to appear in the proceedings of the Tarragona Colloquium, *Culto y sociedad en Occidente Romano* (6-8 October 1988).

Corbier, M. (1988b), 'La Transhumance entre les Abruzzes et l'Apulie: problèmes de continuité entre l'époque républicaine et impériale',to appear in the proceedings of the Naples conference, *La Romanisation du Samnium aux IIe et Ier siècles av. J.-C.* (3-4 November 1988).

Dagron, G. and Feissel, D. (1987), *Inscriptions de Cilicie*. Paris.

Degrassi, A. (1954), *Il confine nord-orientale dell' Italia romana. Ricerche storio-topografiche*. Berne.

D'Ors, A. (1961), 'Los bronces de Mulva', *Emerita* 29, 203-18.

Drew Bear, Th. (1972), 'Deux décrets hellénistiques d'Asie Mineure', *Bulletin de correspondance hellénique* 46, 435-71.

Ducrey, P. (1969), 'Trois nouvelles inscriptions crétoises', *Bulletin de correspondance hellénique* 93, 846-52.

Dunant, Chr. and Pouilloux, J. (1958), *Recherches sur l'histoire et les cultes de Thasos. 2. De 196 avant J.-C. jusqu'à la fin de l'antiquité*. Paris.

Frend, W.H.C. (1956), 'A third-century inscription relating to *angareia* in Phrygia', *JRS* 46, 46-56.

Frézouls, Ed. (1987), *Sociétés urbaines, sociétés rurales dans l'Asie mineure et la Syrie hellénistiques et romaines*. Strasbourg.

Galsterer, H. (1988), 'Romanizzazione politica in area alpina', in *La valle d'Aosta e l'arco alpino nella politica del mondo antico. Atti del Convegno Internazionale di Studi. St Vincent 25-26 April 1987*, ed. Mariagrazia Vacchina, 79-89. Aosta.

Garnsey, P. and Saller, E. (1987), *The Roman Empire. Economy, Society and Culture*. London.

Gascou, J. (1984), 'La Carrière de Marcus Caelius Phileros', *Antiquités africaines* 20.

Goodman, M. (1983), *State and Society in Roman Galilee A.D. 132-212*. Totowa.

Goudineau, C. (1976), 'Le Statut de Nîmes et des Volques Arécomiques', *Revue archéologique de Narbonnaise* 9, 105-14.

Habicht, C. (1975), 'New evidence on the Province of Asia', *JRS* 65, 64-91.

Hall, A. (1971), 'The Gorgoromeis', *Anatolian Studies* 21, 125-66.

Jones, C.P. (1978), *The Roman World of Dio Chrysostom*. Cambridge, Mass.

Knibbe, D. (1987), 'Zeigt das Fragment IvE 13 das steuertechnische Inventar des *fiscus Asiaticus?*', *Tyche* 2, 75-93.

Lepelley, Cl. (1983), 'Quot curiales, tot tyranni. L'image du décurion oppresseur au Bas-Empire', in *Crise et redressement dans les provinces européennes de l'Empire (milieu du IIIe - millieu du IVe siècle ap. J.-C.); Actes du colloque de Strasbourg (Decembre 1981)*, 143-56. Strasbourg.

Lewis, N. (1985), *Life in Egypt under Roman Rule*. Oxford.

Migeotte, L. (1984), *L'Emprunt public dans les cités grecques*. Paris.

Millar, F. (1983), 'Empire and city, Augustus to Julian: obligations, excuses and status', *JRS* 83, 76-96.

Millar, F. (1986), 'Italy and the Roman Empire: Augustus to Constantine', *Phoenix* 40, 295-318.

Mitchell, S. (1976), 'Requisitioned transport in the Roman Empire: a new inscription from Pisidia', *JRS* 66, 106-31.

Nicolet, Cl. (1966), *L'Ordre équestre à l'époque républicaine (312-43 av. J.-C.)*, I. *Définitions juridiques et structures sociales*. Paris.

Nicolet, Cl. (1988), *L'inventaire du monde*. Paris.

Oliver, J.-H. (1958), 'A new letter of Antoninus Pius', *American Journal of Philology* 79, 52-60.

Piganiol, A. (1962), *Les Documents cadastraux de la colonie romaine d'Orange*. Paris.

Reynolds, J. (1984), *Aphrodisias and Rome*. London.

Rigsby, K.J. (1976), 'Cnossus and Capua', *Transactions of the American Philological Association* 106, 313-30.

Robert, L. (1962), *Villes d'Asie Mineure. Etudes de géographie ancienne*, 2nd edn. Paris.

Robert, L. (1977), 'La Titulature de Nicée et de Nicomédie; la gloire et la haine', *Harvard Studies in Classical Philology* 81, 1-39.

Robert, L. (1987), *Documents d'Asie Mineure*. Paris.

Rostovtzeff, M. (1918), 'Sunteleia Tirônôn', *JRS* 8, 26-33.

Rostovtzeff, M. (1957), *The Social and Economic History of the Roman Empire*, ed. 2, Oxford, I-II.

Salviat, F. (1986), 'Quinte-Curce, les Insulae Furianae, la Fossa Augusta et la localisation du cadastre d'Orange', *Revue archéologique de Narbonnaise* 19, 101-16.

Sartre, M. (1987), 'Villes et villages du Hauran (Syrie) du Ier au IVe siècle', in Frézouls (1987), 239-57.

Sherk, R.K. (1969), *Roman Documents from the Greek East, Senatus Consulta and Epistulae to the Age of Augustus.* Baltimore.

Syme, R. (1977), 'La Richesse des aristocraties de Bétique et de Narbonnaise', *Ktèma* 2, 373-80 = *Roman Papers* vol.3 (1984), 977-85.

Syme, R. (1981), 'Rival cities, notably *Tarraco* and *Barcino*', *Ktèma* 6, 271-85.

Van Effenterre, H. (1985), *La Cité grecque.* Paris.

Wörrle, M. (1987), '*Polis* et *Chôra* à *Oinoanda* de Cibyratide. Perplexités d'interprétation devant un document nouveau', in Frézouls (1987), 115-16.

Wörrle, M. (1988), *Stadt und Fest im kaiserzeitlichen Kleinasien.* Munich.

Zawadski, T. (1960), 'Sur une inscription de Phrygie relative au *cursus publicus*', *Revue des Etudes Anciennes* 62, 80-94.

10

Elites and trade in the Roman town

Andrew Wallace-Hadrill

The Weberian model of the ancient city championed by Finley (1977) rightly lays emphasis on the tight nexus between urban centre and rural hinterland in Greek and Roman antiquity. One of the consequences of this nexus is to determine the character of the ruling elite. Because town and country were united politically, and because the locus of politics was the heart of the town, the *agora* or *forum*, the great landowners, who (on any account of the ancient city) formed at least the core of the political elite, lived in and played a dominant role in the organisation of the town. In its crudest form, the model makes the landowners the sole members of the elite; the corollary is that specifically urban economic interests carry virtually no weight in the political process, and that no specifically urban elite can emerge. In place of merchant princes, the town can only produce a frustrated elite of non-political and only partially enfranchised rich, in the form of metics and freedmen. The contrast with the medieval city, or at least that of northern Europe, is marked: the separation of town and country leads there to the development of two competing elites, the barons of the countryside and the big merchants of the town.

Those who reject the Weberian model prefer to reaffirm the scale and significance of commercial activity in the ancient city and to minimise the contrast with the medieval model. Frank and Rostovtzeff, impressed by the variety and liveliness of the non-agricultural activities implied by the archaeological record of cities like Pompeii, posited an emergent bourgeoisie, a picture taken to extremes in the fantasy of a Pompeii run by fuller bosses at the centre of a web of a complex cloth industry (Moeller 1976, demolished by Jongman 1988, 155ff.). Others, like D'Arms (1981) have more cautiously attempted to identify a quasi-elite in the freedmen Augustales of whom Trimalchio serves as the fictional paradigm.

Yet to gloss over the differences between the antique and the medieval (and 'the medieval' is as hard to generalise about as the antique, if not more so, cf. Miskimin, Herlihy and Udovitch 1977) is to abandon the best insights derived from Weber's bold comparative method. Paradoxically, one of the most valuable of these was his perception of the involvement of the rural elite in specifically urban activity. The towns of medieval and early modern England (which Weber knew from his reading of Maitland) make a particularly sharp contrast. The cleavage between urban and rural elite in England down to the beginning of the early modern period was pronounced. It was a major turning point for the English town when in the seventeenth century the country gentry started to take up residence there. Squalid and subject to plague, the medieval and early modern English town deterred the rural elite by the sheer unpleasantness of its habitat, over and above the undoubted political and economic divisions. 'A clean town was something to be remarked on', observed Patten of the early modern English town.

> Running water (was) largely non-existent and internal sanitary
> arrangements primitive in the extreme. Outside in the streets,
> which were often the ultimate destination of these primitive
> sanitary arrangements, mire, filth and butchers' offal mingled on
> unpaved and undrained surfaces rarely swept or attended to by the
> town scavenger.
>
> (Patten 1978, 32)

The arrival of the country gentry as residents in towns was marked by cultural transformation, the spread of new London fashions, assembly rooms, coffee houses, theatres and spas, by the emergence of distinctive elite housing zones like the ostentatiously 'classical' squares and terraces, and by economic transformation as new capital was injected into the urban economy (Clark and Slack 1976, 157f.; Clark 1984, 22f.).

Such transformation was unnecessary in antiquity. The city was characteristically the place of residence of the elite, the centre of their political, social and cultural life. The paradoxical implication is that the elites of antiquity had closer contact with and a better understanding of urban economic activity than did the medieval elites, at least of northern Europe (Italy is a different story, see Herlihy 1977). The ancient patrician lived in a proximity to the world of trade and craft quite alien to the feudal noble; the conditions of ancient politics frequently meant that the elite had also to cultivate the support of the urban poor, and not just remotely by liberal gestures, but directly and personally by canvassing, naming and handshaking. The comparison of the ancient and medieval city and their elites is a lopsided one: discussion of the ancient city naturally embraces the society as a whole, while discussion of the medieval city excludes the countryside, its elite and values. If the elite of the ancient city lacked the *homo oeconomicus*, for whom profit was a prime motive and military glory an irrelevance, it also lacked the feudal noble or the country gentleman, who shunned and looked down on city life. Just as the attitudes of the Greco-Roman elites to trade were very different from those of the medieval merchant, they differed from those of the country-based medieval nobility.

It is these attitudes which I wish to pursue in the following pages for the case of the elite of the Roman town of the late Republic and early Empire. I want to suggest that we have been too ready to identify the ideology of the Roman elite with that of a country gentry to which urban commerce was alien and repulsive. I also wish to shift the focus of discussion away from the 'seaborne commerce' which, thanks to its apparent status as 'big' business has attracted most attention (e.g. D'Arms and Kopf 1980), and towards the sort of petty and largely quite local trade that went on in the little *tabernae* so often met in the archaeological record. I shall approach the question of attitudes from two disparate yet convergent angles. First I shall look at the attitudes of the elite to the town through the evidence of the literary sources; and though it is indeed possible to detect the contempt of the landowner for sordid urban trade, it is equally important to understand the ambiguity of elite attitudes to the town (I). The second and longer section attempts to get at attitudes through the organisation of physical space. Excavation of houses and shops offers valuable evidence of the degree to which the elite did or did not seek to distance itself from trade; and in taking the Vesuvian towns as a test case, the attitudes imported to their material by the excavators are illuminating for the gap in understanding between ourselves and the Romans (II). Finally I make some suggestions about the way in which the treatment of urban property in the legal sources might be brought into closer connection with both the archaeological and the literary evidence (III).

I Roman attitudes to town and country

> Those great men our ancestors rightly preferred rustics to urbanites. They reckoned those in the country who spend their lives within the villa to be lazier than those who are actively busy in the fields, and similarly those who sit about in the town to be more idle than those who cultivate the country. And so they divided the year to attend to urban business only one day in eight, and to devote the remaining seven days to agriculture.
>
> (Varro, *Rerum Rusticarum* 2.1.1)

> All craftsmen are engaged in mean trades, for no workshop can have any quality appropriate to a free man. Least worthy of all are those trades which cater to the sensual pleasures: 'fishmongers, butchers, cooks, poulterers and fishermen', as Terence says; to whom you may add, if you please, perfumers, dancers and pantomime performers.
>
> (Cicero, *De Officiis* 1.151)

The rejection of trade as sordid in the gentleman's code formulated by Cicero is a familiar focus of discussion. Agriculture not trade was the proper occupation for a gentleman. For Finley (1985, ch.2) such attitudes are normative: for D'Arms they are 'something more than a fiction, and something less than a norm' (1981, 47). Similar attitudes were in force, as D'Arms shows, in the early modern period: 'hee loseth the quality of a nobleman that doth trafficke' (1606). They were also applicable, as Weber was at pains to bring out, in precisely the medieval societies to which he contrasted the ancient city: 'in ancient and medieval cities families considered to be noble were forbidden the role of entrepreneur' (1958, 155). Weber saw the definition of the 'patrician' (i.e. the elite of the ancient and medieval city) as a matter of life style, a status etiquette of knightly manners; that by no means excluded the pursuit of profit ('the Roman nobility and medieval families were as eager for gain as any other historic class'), but it did involve being seen not to transgress the line separating them from the conduct of the entrepreneur. Weber's critics may show us Roman senators pursuing profit (he would not have denied it): but they do not show them transgressing the line of etiquette, or not without incurring the reproach of their peers, as did Vespasian in his descent to profiteering worthy of a slavemonger (*mangonicos quaestus*, Suetonius, *Vesp.* 4).

It is no surprise that Cicero and his contemporaries regarded the trades of fishmonger or slavedealer as sordid. But this did not prevent them from making use of their services, or even necessarily from deriving profit from them. Revealingly, it was precisely the trades which 'served the pleasures' of the elite which Cicero regarded as most inappropriate to the freeborn: to serve another man's pleasure is by definition servile. To look down on an activity as servile is by no means to shun it. Hence an ambiguity of attitude, which comes out particularly in Roman views of the town as centre of sordid trades and services. The most forceful and explicit spokesman of a long tradition of moralising rejection of the town is Varro. In the preface to the second book of the *Rerum Rusticarum* (quoted above), he endorses the ancestral contrast of the country as the seat of virtue with the town as the seat of idleness, *ignavia* and *desidia*. The theme is resumed in the preface to the third book: of the two ways of life, *rustica* and *urbana*, the rustic is the original, and the product of divine nature not human artifice. Agriculture is therefore not only older but better. 'It was not without reason that our ancestors used to drive back their citizens from the town to the fields, since it was the countrymen who provided food in peace and recruits in war' (3.1.4). This moral differentiation of town and country is a pervasive topic in Roman literature (cf. MacMullen 1974, 28ff.). In defence of Roscius of Ameria, Cicero pours scorn on the attempt to blacken his client by the charge that he was a rustic who never visited the town:

> Rustic manners, frugal living, a rough and uncivilised life are not generally the birthplace of such crimes (i.e. parricide).... The city creates luxury, from luxury avarice inevitably springs, from avarice bursts audacity, the source of all crimes and misdeeds. On the other hand, this country life, which you call boorish, teaches thrift, carefulness, and justice.
>
> (Cicero, *Pro Roscio Amerino* 75)

The town is characteristically the home of idlers and scoundrels. So Plautus' *Curculio* 467ff. offers a vivid topographical survey of the Roman Forum as the ideal place to find perjurers, liars, wastrels, whores, gossips, usurers, tricksters and male prostitutes. Conversely, when Horace tries to dissuade his bailiff from longing for the life of the town, he exposes him as yearning for the red lights:

> nunc urbem et ludos et balnea uilicus optas.
>   ... fornix tibi et uncta popina
> incutiunt urbis desiderium

> (Now you are a bailiff, you want the town and games and baths. ... The brothel and the greasy cook-shop fill you with yearning for the town.)
>
>   (Horace, *Epistles* 1.14.15, 21f.)

The theme of city vice versus rural virtue is abundantly developed throughout the satirical tradition, stretching from Horace's town and country mice to Juvenal's Rome. The antitheses adumbrated by Varro remain constant: town versus country means vice against virtue, modernity against ancestral values, luxury against industry, the idle and lying entrepreneur against the labouring peasant, the foreign import against the homegrown Roman, man-made disorder against divine and natural order (Braund 1989).

Traditional Roman morality is firmly rooted in agrarian values. But that is very different from saying that the Roman elite shunned the town and felt themselves demeaned by its contact. The one antithesis that is wholly absent from the town/country moralisation is that of class: no suggestion that the gentry belong in the country and the bourgeoisie in the town. On the contrary, the moralising contrasts affect all statuses alike. It is the peasantry which Varro obviously thinks will benefit from being sent back to the fields: that is in effect what contemporary agrarian legislation was supposed to achieve. It is a slave bailiff who displays his inconsistency to Horace by longing for the town, though he had longed for the country when a town slave. Indeed, slaves provided the ultimate test-case for the town versus country stereotype: the rural slave is the hard worker, the town slave the idle and pampered supplier of his master's pleasures. Freedmen, it is true, might be confined symbolically to the voting tribes of the *plebs urbana*, and were doubtless more numerous in town than countryside; but that did not render the town a no-go area for the freeborn, and even Juvenal's Umbricius (*Satire* 3) retreats from Rome against his will, in exaggerated despair at the difficulty of earning a respectable living in the city of vice. The moral contrasts of town and country cut across status contrasts, of slave and free, of high and low. By contrast, the medieval town/country divide coincides with a status contrast, setting the nobility or gentry on one side as a separate class.

At the same time, the Roman moral devaluation of the town is counterbalanced by an inverse set of values. The town is the home of *urbanitas*: the polish and culture of a civilised man that expressed itself in cultivated manners and wit of expression, and contrasts with *rusticitas*, the uncouth conduct of the uneducated rustic (Ramage 1973). Cicero and Quintilian have no hesitation in endorsing urbanity in the orator: to cultivate a rustic accent in order to sound old-fashioned was not unknown, but Cicero does not approve (*De Oratore* 3.42f.). Quintilian draws on the essay *On Urbanity* written by Domitius Marsus under Augustus:

> the urbane man is one who frequently produces neat sayings and responses; who in conversation, social gatherings, dinners, and similarly in public meetings and in fact in all circumstances speaks wittily and appropriately.
>
> (Quintilian, *Institutio* 6.3.105)

The city of Rome was the supreme centre of urbane values, and it was longed for as such, whether by Cicero's friend Trebatius on service in Gaul (*ad Familiares* 7.6.1), by Ovid at Tomi (*Ex Ponto* 2.4), or by Martial mouldering in Bilbilis (12 pref.).

Urbanity was an ambivalent virtue, because it posed a threat to traditional Roman morality. That ambivalence was clearly felt (some orators *did* cultivate rusticity) and could be exploited. Thus when Ovid mocks the rusticity of the Rome of Romulus, and praises the cultivation of the present, he succeeds in undercutting the virtue of the Augustan golden age:

> simplicitas rudis ante fuit, nunc aurea Roma est.
> ... cultus adest, nec nostros mansit in annos
>   Rusticitas, priscis illa superstes avis.

(Rude Simplicity belonged to days of old: Rome is golden now.
... Culture is with us, and Rusticity, that relic of erstwhile
ancestors, never survived into our times.)

(*Ars Amatoria* 3.113, 128ff.)

To devalue traditional rustic virtues in this way, particularly in the
context of a work celebrating sexual promiscuity, was provocative:
but Ovid can exploit the essential contradictions in the Roman
attitude to town and country, that make the rustic as easy to mock as
to idealise, the urban as easy to recommend as to denigrate.

This ambivalence of attitude does not allow itself to be resolved
into an ideological conflict between classes. The same urban elite
which idealised the ancestral values of the land defined its own elite
status by its urbanity. The circumstances in which Domitius Marsus
sees the need for urbanity, from the social gathering to the public
meeting, are those in and through which the elite dominated. By
attributing rustic ideals to their ancestors, they partly succeeded in
distancing themselves from them. There is no case for suggesting
that the nobility clung to traditional values while the new rich
embraced urbanity: on the contrary, it was the nobility who led the
field in innovation, and were criticised for betraying their ancestors by
their luxury, while the new men like Cato or Thrasea Paetus tried to
corner the reputation of rustic frugality.

If we return to Varro, we can see how even the rustic world he
praises is fraught with this ambivalence. The villa in its late
republican development encapsulates the tension. The moralising
remarks that preface both the second and third books lead directly into
complaints about the urbanisation of the villa: failure to exercise
properly by tilling the soil leads to need for the *urbana gymnasia* of
the Greeks, and villas now tinkle with the sound of Greek room
names (2.pr.2). The second passage elaborates the contrast between
the urban attributes of the villa, its paintings and fine plaster, its
bronze and marble statuary, its mosaics and intarsios, its citrus wood,
gold, vermilion and azure, and its rustic attributes, haylofts, grain-
bins, mills and mattocks (3.2.1-10). A villa with no rustic attributes,
teasingly suggests one speaker, would prove to be a town house in
disguise (3.2.7). It is revealing that the Romans chose the word
'urban' to label the luxurious features of their country houses (the
usage persists in the *Digest*). The use of the word in itself implies a
scale of values. In leaving the town for their country seats they left

the place of vice for the place of old Roman virtue; but they also left behind the comfort and the culture of the town. It was therefore necessary to import the culture of the town into the countryside. On the one hand to be a Roman gentleman it was necessary to be a good farmer; on the other hand, to avoid being a rustic, it was necessary to be seen as urbane even in the country (cf. Purcell 1987).

When it came to imposing order on the barbarians, the Romans left no doubt of their commitment to the town as an instrument of civilisation. Urbanisation is the unmistakable result of Roman control, and indeed without the self-governing mechanisms of the city-state Roman imperial government could scarcely have operated (Garnsey and Saller 1987). Municipal charters disseminated from Rome imposed administrative structures based on the town, and explicitly required the residence of members of the ruling *ordo* within the town or the first milestone. However questionable the morality of the amenities of city life, there could be no doubt of the advantages of introducing them to the local barbarian elites of Britain. So much is clear in Tacitus' classic account of Agricola's work in urbanising Britain (*Agricola* 21):

> To induce men who were scattered and uncivilised and so swift to war, to take to the pleasant ways of peace and leisure, he gave private encouragement and public assistance to the construction of temples, fora and houses.... Gradually they were led astray to the temptations of vice, porticoes, baths and elegant dinners. The inexperienced called it humanity, though it was an aspect of enslavement.

Tacitus deliberately makes play of the Roman ambivalence about the town: place of vice and corruption, or place of civilisation and order? The answer given by an elite with its ideology rooted simultaneously in town and country was 'both'.

II The fabric of the town

The elite of a Roman city were perforce resident in the town for at least part of the year. A multiplicity of social ties involved them in contact with the commercially active population. As private patrons, partly of freeborn clients but most conspicuously of freedmen, they were drawn into advising and supporting traders. As candidates for office, unless the electoral programmata of Pompeii are grossly misleading, they benefited from the support of groups of traders, whether or not these formally had the status of *collegia*: if the *quactiliarii* could declare their support for Vettius Firmus in his candidature for the aedileship and underline their identity with a vivid depiction of felters at work (Rostovtzeff 1957, 100, plate XVI), then, whatever Vettius' own involvement in the felting trade, it is clear that trades could represent themselves as having a sufficiently powerful group identity to be worth cultivating for political ends (Schulz-Falkenthal 1971; Jongman 1988, 283ff; Angelone 1986). Once elected, as magistrates, they were involved in the adjudication of commercial disputes, such as are now illustrated by the dossier of the freedmen Sulpicii from Murecine.

Socially and politically, contact with the commercial world of the towns was inevitable for the elite. It stands to reason that the economic dimension was also vital. Both as patrons of freedmen engaged in trade, and as property owners drawing rents from the lease of *horrea* and *tabernae*, a substantial portion of the urban elite must have derived at least part of their income from trade, even if they did not actually run businesses. Garnsey (1976) has made a powerful case for seeing urban real estate as a vital element in the income of the elite (this includes of course rental of apartments). Compared to land, such investment was high-risk, thanks particularly to the dangers of fire; but the returns were also high, and perhaps there were other compensations, such as a spread of cash-income through times of year when no agricultural returns were forthcoming. One may also hypothesise that such economic ties intermeshed with the social and political ties. In the countryside landlords could enjoy social and political support from their tenants. Not the least of the advantages of property ownership in the towns must have been to extend a nexus of social and political influence along the lines of economic power. Traders were thus a simultaneous source of revenue and social position.

Archaeological evidence ought to betray something of such links, and I want to look at the evidence of Pompeii and Herculaneum to illustrate the potential of archaeology in this respect. First however it is necessary to expose a number of questionable assumptions which underpin debate about these sites, formulated in their most uncompromising fashion by this century's dominant excavator,

Amedeo Maiuri.

One great strength of Maiuri's excavations is that they were conducted in full awareness of their potential importance for revealing the social and economic fabric of a Roman town. On the one hand, as was perhaps inevitable under the *età fascistica*, he was concerned to find glorious monuments: the Villa dei Misteri and the Casa del Menandro were the jewels in his crown. On the other hand, he looked for social and economic change, influenced by historical debate and particularly by Rostovtzeff, who drew on close knowledge of the site in his account of the supposed rise of a commercially and industrially based bourgeoisie in early imperial Italy. Maiuri evolved a thesis of a major social and economic transformation of the area under the early empire which came to a head after the earthquake of AD 62. The case was argued in *L'ultima fase edilizia di Pompei* (1942): the old patriciate was in decline, unable to stem the rising tide of commerce; its tasteful residences were invaded by industry, or broken up into squalid shops and flats; the new men who pushed out their old masters displayed their vulgar taste in the new styles of decoration. The earthquake delivered the coup de grâce to the patriciate, who retreated to their country estates, leaving the field clear for the *nouveaux riches*.

> But it is also in this period (i.e. post-earthquake) that we witness the transformation of many upper-class houses (case signorili) into *officinae*, the intrusion of shops, *cauponae* and *thermopolia* into the interior of and along the facades of patrician residences, the splitting up of a single grand upper-class house into several modest dwellings, the change and perversion of taste in type and style of the decoration of the rooms, sacrificing beautiful and noble old paintings for banal and poor redecoration, in short the invasion by the mercantile class of the structure of the old Romano-Campanian patrician class of the city.
>
> (Maiuri, 1942, 216f.)

The same thesis emerges repeatedly in Maiuri's numerous guide books and popular works on Pompeii. One may be struck by the warmth of his language, his sympathy for the taste attributed to the old patriciate and his resentment at the 'brutal invasion' of the commercial world:

Shops ... defaced the simple and severe architectural forms of
patrician houses by plastering garish trade signs on the wall; they
pressed against the sides of noble portals as if to launch a final and
triumphant attack against the whole edifice after having completed
the conquest of some of its less important rooms.

(Maiuri, 1960, 188)

His picture of Pompeian society read from the physical remains is
certainly lively ('this motley crowd of enriched merchants, secondhand
dealers, bakers, fullers, decayed patricians, and thrusting industrialists
dabbling in politics', *ibid*. p.138) but it rests on unwarranted
assumptions. He has been criticised from a variety of angles.
Castrén's careful study of the prosopography of the Pompeian elite
(1975) showed some at least of the picture of an invasion of the elite
by 'industrialists' to be sheer fantasy. Andreau (1973) questioned his
picture of the economic effects of a major earthquake: comparison
with the well-documented effects of comparable disasters in Catania
(1693), Lisbon (1755) and Messina (1783 and 1908) suggests that the
picture of a commercial boom in the aftermath of a quake is most
implausible. On the other hand, there are parallels for an exodus of
the rich to their country estates, a crisis of accommodation leading to
splitting up of grand houses into apartments, as well as for long
delays in reconstructing the city's public and private buildings,
stretching over twenty years and more. On this showing, there is at
least some plausibility in Maiuri's suggestions. What is hard to
estimate is the extent to which an exodus of the rich would have been
likely in an ancient as opposed to modern town, with its very
different conditions of political participation.

The fundamental obstacle, as has been stressed by a number of
scholars including most recently Verena Gassner (1986) is the
inadequacy of the archaeological evidence on which Maiuri's thesis
rests. Excavation that fails to penetrate below the AD 79 levels
cannot allow genuine comparisons with the situation before the
earthquake. Maiuri's case is anecdotal, not statistical: he points to the
installation of new shops, yet of some 600 Pompeian shops
catalogued by Gassner, only 20 on her reckoning demonstrably
postdate the earthquake (p.25). Again, Maiuri points to 14 cases of
'industrial' establishments (half of them bakeries or fulleries) installed
in the last phase in private houses. But this is no basis for inferences
about the social fortunes of their owners. In view of the fact that

nowhere in Pompeii do we find specialist 'industrial' establishments constructed for the purpose, bakeries and fulleries and workshops are bound to be discovered in the fabric of private houses. Given ownership of multiple properties, and patterns of death and inheritance, the decline of individual properties cannot be used as an index of the fortunes of the elite as a whole. To sustain Maiuri's thesis, it would be necessary to demonstrate an absolute decline over time in the number of elite properties in the city. The frequency of grand houses in the city decorated in later styles of painting tells strongly against this hypothesis; and to suggest that only 'new men' lived in houses decorated in new styles, while old styles point to old families, is manifestly absurd.

There may well be considerable elements of truth in Maiuri's account of the development of the city. More careful and systematic investigation may indeed confirm a tendency to split up properties, instal flats in upper storeys, open out shops in front rooms (Ling 1983). But what is particularly interesting in the context of this discussion is the nature of Maiuri's model of Roman society, and of his assumptions about the relations between the elite (or 'patricians') and trade. As Ettore Lepore observed in a subtle and penetrating critique (1950), the model is simply too rigid. What justifies the assumption that the old aristocracy was based purely on landed property, rather than being 'simultaneously landed and commercial'? Why should only freedmen *nouveaux riches* have been involved in trade, and how, in view of the transitional social status of the freedman, can they constitute a class with interests in conflict with those of the old elite?

It is worth looking at some examples to see these assumptions at work in detail. Maiuri's publication of his excavations in Herculaneum (1958) is a valuable test-case because here he was able to incorporate in detail in an excavation report the thesis of economic change previously evolved and selectively illustrated in his Pompeian studies. The handsome two-volume publication of the best part of six blocks of houses is also an essay in social and economic interpretation. The very structure of the volumes is significant. Rather than presenting his material topographically, block by block, as was traditional, Maiuri sorted the houses by social class. His classification creates eight divisions, which are presented in a hierarchical order:

1. Patrician houses of traditional type.
2. Middle class (del ceto medio) houses of traditional type.
3. Grand houses (case signorili).
4. Residential houses of non-traditional type.
5. Middle-class houses with attached shops/workshops.
6. Multiple-residence houses.
7. Mercantile houses and shops with dwellings.
8. Shops/workshops in a multi-storey block.

Implicit in this classification are two assumptions. One is that houses with shops or workshops incorporated are socially humbler than those without; the second is that houses of traditional (i.e. *atrium*) construction are socially superior to those of non-traditional type. Thus all the houses in the bottom four categories include shops/workshops. Among the residential houses, traditional houses are preferred to non-traditional, with the bizarre result that the three largest and most opulent houses are put in the third class. Among the houses with shops, those of most traditional structure (5) are preferred to those of the least traditional structure, the Ostia-type multi-storey *insulae* (8).

Once these assumptions have been incorporated into the classification system, it throws up a whole series of misfits, and these are all taken as evidence for the thesis of social change and degeneration. The Casa Sannitica (V.1) with its stately *atrium* is the first specimen: it must have belonged in the early empire to a family 'del più nobile patriziato ercolanese' (p.198). But this is a surprisingly small house, with no peristyle. Its reduction to the traditional nucleus therefore demonstrates that it was shaken by the 'grave crisis provoked by the increase of overseas trade in the patriciate of the city' (*ibid.*). Nevertheless, the rooms clustered round the *atrium* of this household in reduced circumstances manage to 'keep themselves pure of mercantile invasion' (p.204): there are, in a word, no shops in the facade.

The anonymous house V.11 (see fig.1) is another relatively small house of classic symmetrical *fauces/atrium/tablinum* construction. The 'nobility' of its *tablinum*, which is indeed decorated with rich paintings and a handsome marble inlay floor, confirms that it was originally an upper-class (signorile) residence.

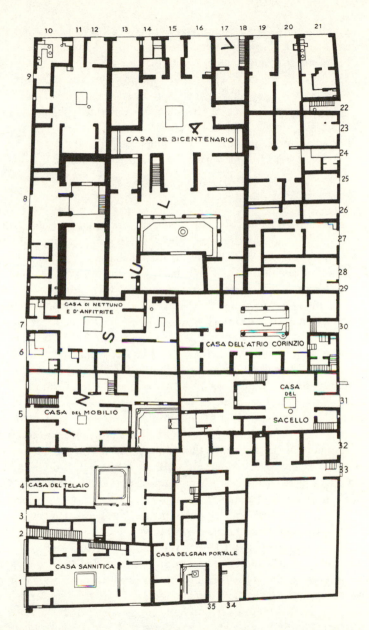

Figure 1: Herculaneum Insula V

But after upper-class occupation lasting possibly as late as the Claudian era, the profound transformation which the commercial life of the city had to undergo with the new arrangement of the Via del Foro, the grave crisis which the new currents of overseas commerce and earthquake damage produced in the class of the oldest patrician families of Herculaneum, and finally the need to withdraw from the noisy and plebeian commercial life of the Forum, were the multiple reasons which determined the decay of this house from an upper-class residence to the practical use of a lodging with shops.

(*ibid*. p.248)

The evidence for the decline consists in the 'conversion' of both front rooms of the house to shops, and the 'vulgar patching' of the *tablinum* decoration, damaged in the earthquake, which indicates the level of taste and priorities of the final owner (p.250).

But the prime specimen of degeneration is the neighbouring Casa del Bicentenario (V.15, fig.1), a show-house of the modern tourist trade, and findspot of the much-discussed Petronia Iusta dossier. Apart from the luxurious houses that engross the views from the sea-wall of the town, this is the largest excavated house. On the other hand, it has no less than four shops built into its facade. The thesis of 'decline' is rolled out to account for this supposed contradiction. Built in the early Julio-Claudian period with its magnificent *atrium* and richly decorated *tablinum* by a rich and noble family, it suffered towards the late fifties AD from the major social changes of the rise of commercial fortunes and the collapse of the old landowning aristocracy. The rooms fronting the forum were opened up as shops under freedmen or tenants. Ownership passed from the hands of a patrician to a rich freedman, and the house was split up into shabby flats. Its focus shifted from the noble quarters at the garden end to the commercial frontage, and there new flats were built and decorated. The lack of taste of the new owner emerges from the crude repairs to the beautiful Daedalus and Pasiphae painting in the *tablinum*, and from the absence of the sort of handsome furniture to be expected in a patrician house at the time of excavation (pp.222ff.).

Throughout, Maiuri's assumptions are consistent, and involve a simplistic correspondence between architectural and aesthetic features and the social standing of the inhabitants. Good quality decoration reveals the social quality of the owners; crude repairs indicate vulgar owners. The traditional *atrium* points to patricians, irrespective of the size of the house. The presence of shops is taken to be completely incompatible with the presence of 'patricians': thus where we find shops, as in the anonymous V.11, they are assumed to have withdrawn, where we do not find them, the old patricians are envisaged as still huddled in their reduced circumstances, taking refuge from the surrounding tide of change.

All these assumptions are arbitrary. There is no reason why a fine *atrium* should point to a patrician, let alone a landowning family. The Casa Sannitica is plausibly the reduced core of a once larger house; the anonymous V.11 is not. What sort of 'patrician' can have inhabited a house of these dimensions? What is the basis for the claim that the shops along the frontage of the Via del Foro are converted front rooms? The anonymous V.11 stands on a street corner close to the forum: it is the classic location for a corner shop. No archaeological evidence is offered for the 'conversion'. It is pure surmise, based on the logical chain of inference that a fine *tablinum* indicates noble inhabitants, and noble inhabitants exclude commercial usage. Similarly, no archaeological evidence is adduced for an earlier phase of non-commercial usage of the frontage of the Casa del Bicentenario. Its long *fauces* seem ideally designed to allow the incorporation of shops in the frontage, and to set back the *atrium*. Without a detailed structural and archaeological examination, it is impossible to refute Maiuri's account of the house's development; but as it stands, it rests on a substructure of unexamined assumption.

An alternative set of assumptions deserves consideration: that wealth of architectural and decorative detail is indeed a pointer to wealthy owners, but can indicate nothing whatsoever about the sources of that wealth, whether rural or urban; that good taste is no indicator of status, and could be found among freedmen as well as aristocrats; and that the urban elite, best defined by their tenure of public office, drew revenue from trade and agriculture without discrimination, and distanced themselves from commercial activity by the pattern of their lives (i.e. by not engaging in 'sordid occupations' in person) without feeling any need to distance themselves physically. Can these alternative propositions be tested?

If all these propositions were true, it would follow that it would be impossible to distinguish on architectural and aesthetic grounds between the houses of members of the local *ordo* and those of rich freedmen traders excluded by their birth but not their wealth from membership of the *ordo*; or indeed between members of the *ordo* whose families had held public office for generations and had a firm capital basis in agricultural holdings, and first generation decurions who owed their wealth to commerce. This is a position which should be susceptible of refutation: if it could be demonstrated that two contrasting groups of houses could be distinguished, one of which shunned commerce and the other of which embraced it, and if differential ownership were the most likely explanation of the contrast, the propositions would collapse. Is this the case?

Now of course there are some grand houses 'untainted' by commerce, and others with shops in their facades. To take Herculaneum, there is a clear pattern whereby the largest houses with the largest peristyles along the seawall (i.e. Case dell' Albergo, del Atrio a Mosaico, dei Cervi, della Gemma, and del Relievo di Telefo) are free from shops, while another group of smaller, but nevertheless grand houses, with *atria*, peristyles, and fairly elaborate decoration, open onto main thoroughfares, and incorporate shops in their facades (Case del Tramezzo di Legno, del Bicentenario, del Salone Nero, and della Colonnata Toscanica). But can we plausibly attribute the contrast between the two groups to the social standing of their owners? The distribution of shops makes complete sense topographically: they cluster on the main thoroughfares and thin out and disappear towards the periphery. There would be little point in trying to open up shops in any of the seawall group of houses. On the other hand, the potential for shops along the Via del Foro is obvious, and none of the three large houses that front it miss an opportunity. This was precisely Maiuri's dilemma. He was unwilling to admit that such fine houses could have been built by anyone other than members of the elite, and was so driven to posit the introduction of shops as a secondary stage. But where were the shops in the early Julio-Claudian period if not along the main streets? Was Herculaneum once a town without shops?

Or if we admit that it had to have shops, even at the beginning of the first century AD, and that they were bound to be along the main streets, why were grand houses ever built there? The answer lies to hand: the forum was the centre of political as well as of commercial life, and in any Roman town some (but not all) of the political elite could be expected to live in its close proximity. This might be supported by consideration of the distribution of electoral programmata, which cluster along the main shopping streets, most conspicuously along the via dell' Abbondanza in Pompeii. Programmata are scarce in Herculaneum, but there too they are found close to the shops of the via del Foro (Pagano 1987 for a recent programma opposite the C. del Bicentenario). Of course the presence of programmata does not prove that the candidates named lived nearby (though della Corte frequently identified house owners on that assumption alone). But they do illustrate the way in which the worlds of public life and of commerce intertwined. If there was any contrast between the owners of the mainstreet houses and the seawall houses of Herculaneum, it is as likely to be between the politically active and those pursuing the life of *otium* (e.g. visitors from Rome) as between the commercial class and the ruling elite. If we accept the attractive conjecture that the exceptionally rich Casa dei Cervi belonged to the family of M. Nonius Balbus, proconsul and patron of the town, whose funerary altar the house overlooked (Tinh 1988, 121ff.), we may take it as an example of a household that stood above, if by no means outside, the operations of local politics.

The same set of questions can be asked of Pompeii, and here a statistically controlled answer would be desirable. One investigation already to hand is that of Raper (1977 and 1979). Basing himself on the methods of study of urban geography, he conducted an analysis of distribution of landuse in Pompeii, dividing the whole area into equal squares on a 100-metre grid. The proportions of commercial, residential and public usage vary considerably from square to square in the grid. Nevertheless, as Raper observes, the spread of the commercial is pervasive: 'The commercial structures tended to be constant in their association with private houses and mansions suggesting a continuum of indiscrete usage of space' (p.208). While there are several squares with public usage to the exclusion of all else, there are none with any significant degree of residential usage which have not also at least some commercial usage. Raper's analysis is now borne out by that of La Torre (1988) based on the new computer database of Pompeii. He succeeds in distinguishing the city centre as more heavily commercial than the peripheries; nevertheless, residential and non-residential usage intermingle in all regions of the city.

Raper accounted for this pattern by reference to the theory of commercial invasion (pp.192-3, apparently derived from Maiuri's popular work *Pompeii*) though he puts it in a less critical light by calling the process 'democratisation'. He follows blindly the assumption that the upper class cannot have engaged in trade.

> Simultaneously came the decline of the aristocracy as they did
> not enter into trade or business.... By AD 79 the composite
> character of the city with its elegant neighbourhoods and
> business streets was not particularly distinct but intermingled.
> The archaeology serves to illustrate this social phenomenon.
> There were great contrasts between the aristocratic elegance of
> certain dwellings and the vulgarity of the trades or businesses
> established in them.
>
> (Raper, 1977, 192-3)

An alternative explanation is that it is modern taste, not ancient, which finds the juxtaposition of the elegant residential and the crudely commercial surprising and shocking. It is the post-industrial city that has evolved the fullest differentiation of residential and industrial areas, and with that differentiation our expectations have taken firm shape. On what basis can we assume that a Roman 'patrician' (let alone the local municipal elite) found the proximity of trade disturbing?

Closer examination of potentially elite housing in Pompeii shows no more trace of a social pattern of the avoidance of the commercial than do the Herculaneum houses. In an analysis described in detail elsewhere (Wallace-Hadrill 1990 and forthcoming), I have examined a sample of some 182 Pompeian houses, partly from the supposedly residential Regio VI, partly from the supposedly commercial Regio I, comparing their area, decoration, usage of space etc. Commercial usage (i.e. shops and workshops) is widespread among houses of all sizes, though naturally it is most common in the smallest units, which are almost exclusively shops. Taking this sample, we may try to isolate those houses which are potentially those of the elite. Selecting only those in the top quartile in terms of area (i.e. larger than 350m^2), and which have both an *atrium* and a peristyle and at least some decoration surviving, a group of thirty houses emerges. Of these, thirteen lack any form of commercial usage. Yet they are very difficult to distinguish as a group from those which have commercial usage. The average size is virtually the same (798m^2 for the non-commercial, 823m^2 for the commercial), both groups have an average of 17 ground floor rooms, of which a similar proportion are decorated (average 11 rooms for the non-commercial, 10 for the commercial) and the same proportion have mosaic floors (average 3 rooms in both groups). Even the average area of their open space enclosed by peristyles is almost identical (121m^2 in the non-commercial, 122m^2 in the others). Is there any reason here for supposing elite avoidance of the commercial among the thirteen? Again the critical factor is location. The large houses that front on busy thoroughfares, the via dell' Abbondanza, via Stabiana and via di Nocera, tend to incorporate shops, those remote from main roads lack them. There is a distinct group in the heart of Regio VI of splendidly decorated houses away from the thoroughfares (e.g. in Ins. 9 the Case del Meleagro, dei Dioscuri etc.), and this is indeed the area which on Raper's analysis scores exceptionally high for residential usage and low for commercial. But even if some of the elite did cluster here, it is manifest that others were scattered throughout the city in less secluded surroundings.

The archaeological evidence adduced here is insufficient by itself to allow us to build a model of the relations between the elite of a Roman city and its trade. Naturally Pompeii and Herculaneum may have been untypical in this as in other respects, and the earthquake of AD 62 will be one factor to be borne in mind. What is still needed is a wide-ranging investigation of the links between *tabernae* and grand houses in the numerous published sites of the Roman world, from Delos and Ephesus to Glanum and Silchester (cf. Bates 1983) and above all the towns of Roman Africa (Thébert 1987). As Garnsey (1976, 129f.) pointed out, the well-published excavations of Volubilis suggest strongly the same sort of admixture of the commercial and residential as at Pompeii (cf. Etienne 1960, pl.III). But pending more systematic investigation, the evidence is at least sufficient to cast considerable doubt on traditional assumptions about the way a Roman elite was likely to distance itself from commerce.

But perhaps the strongest evidence against these assumptions derives from the city of Rome itself. One might well argue that the elites of Pompeii or Herculaneum were a poor model of the likely behaviour and attitudes of the high aristocracy of the metropolis. The gulf between a local decurion of Herculaneum and the senatorial elite of Rome, let alone members of those gentes who could properly call themselves 'patrician', is vast. And indeed, Rome is often regarded as a prime example of 'zoning', the Palatine representing the most exclusive residential quarter for the nobility, in contrast to predominantly 'plebeian' areas like the Aventine. As Ovid puts it explicitly in his image of the abode of the gods as the Palatine of the heavens, the plebs lived elsewhere (*plebs habitat diversa locis, Metamorphoses* 1.173). Whatever may have happened at a second-rate colony like Pompeii, let alone little Herculaneum, can we image a Scipio or a Cicero enduring the proximity of petty commercial activity?

The answer is that we must, since it is clearly indicated by both literary and archaeological evidence. A vivid picture of the gradual transformation of the Roman Forum, particularly in the second century BC, is evoked by the annalistic tradition preserved by Livy (cf. Morel 1987, esp. 133ff.). As late as 210 BC, when a major fire swept the Forum, there were no basilicas, and behind the rows of shops, the Veteres on the south and the Novae on the north, were private houses (Livy 26.27.2). They were constructed with the characteristic 'Maeniana' or balconies from the houses behind projecting over the shops, from which people could watch the gladiatorial games below (see Platner-Ashby 1927, 504-5). In the course of the next century, the private houses were gradually replaced by ambitious public buildings. In 184 BC Cato as censor bought up private property in the area known as 'the Quarries' (Lautumiae) immediately adjacent to the Curia in the north-western corner of the Forum for his Basilica Porcia: the property purchased consisted in two *atria* or private houses, the Maenium and the Titium, together with four *tabernae* (Livy 39.44.7). This sounds very much like the standard Pompeian pattern of a house flanked by two shops (Boethius 1934, 164). A little later, in 170 BC, Ti. Sempronius Gracchus as censor constructed the Basilica Sempronia in the south-east of the Forum, on the corner of the Vicus Tuscus behind the temple of Castor and Pollux: this involved the purchase and demolition of the house of no less a man than his old *inimicus* Scipio Africanus, together with its adjoining shops, *lanienasque et tabernas coniunctas* (Livy 44.16.10). Butchers' shops had been a feature of the early republican Forum - it was outside one of them that they believed Verginius had saved his daughter from the advances of the decemvir Appius (Livy 3.48.5) - and Varro (ap. Nonius 532) saw the replacement of the butchers by bankers (*argentariae*) in 310 BC as the first increase of *dignitas* in the Forum. But though butchers were excluded from the state-owned Veteres and Novae, they evidently continued to trade in privately owned shops nearby. The image of the great Scipio living with a butchers' at his front door should in itself be enough to refute Maiuri's assumptions about 'patrician' houses.

The private houses that surrounded the third-century and earlier Forum cannot be wished away on a commercial bourgeoisie, though evidently the shopkeepers lived there too, and there was one *argentarius* who caused public outrage during the Punic Wars by appearing at his *pergula*, the room above his shop, at midday, garlanded with roses for a drinking party (Pliny, *Natural History* 21.8). Perhaps one day the levels below the Basilica Julia may be excavated to reveal how a Scipio lived. Meanwhile, we may turn for confirmation to the dramatic excavations currently being conducted at the foot of the Palatine by Andrea Carandini (1989 for a preliminary report). Along the stretch of the Sacra Via between the Atrium Vestae and the Clivus Palatinus, Carandini has revealed a series of private houses of considerable dimensions (c. $900m^2$), built astride the ancient Palatine *pomoerium* and dating back to a remarkably early period, possibly the sixth century BC. These he identifies plausibly as residences of the republican nobility, inhabited with a striking degree of structural continuity down to the end of the first century BC. If the hypothetical identification with the setting of Cicero's *De Domo Sua* is accepted, we may provisionally pinpoint not only the houses of Cicero and Clodius, but those of powerful families like the Aemilii Scauri and Octavii. Two points relevant to the present argument emerge from the preliminary results. One is that the basic pattern of *atrium* construction with narrow *fauces* seems to go back to the archaic period. The other is that at all periods from the archaic to the late republican these large houses had *tabernae* incorporated in their frontages on the Sacra Via.

It would indeed be surprising if a thoroughfare as prestigious as the Sacra Via were not flanked with shops. This was a prime location, and by the late Republic, the businesses must have been highly profitable. The large houses behind them similarly represented a prime location for the political elite, whether or not we count Cicero and Clodius among their number. Moving closer to the Forum was an established technique of maximising the popular following (cf. Plutarch, *Gaius Gracchus* 12.1, *Marius* 32.1). It does not follow, of course, that other Palatine houses, more secluded from the main roads, also included shops. But, like the literary accounts of houses of Scipio and others on the Forum, the excavations indicate that there was no perceived incompatibility between elite housing and the presence of petty commercial activity. It helps to explain the location of a grand house like the Casa del Bicentenario on the road leading to the forum of Herculaneum: it directly imitated a style current among the political elite at Rome.

III   Urban property in the lawyers

A model which predicts a basic spatial disjunction between the residential spaces of the elite and the commercial spaces of the petty trader must surely be rejected. In evolving an alternative model, it would be necessary to pay close attention to patterns of property ownership in their legal setting, and to explore the way in which these are reflected in the archaeological evidence. Frier (1980) has shown how fruitfully the archaeological evidence of the *insulae* of Ostia and Rome can be related to discussion of landlord/tenant relationships in the *Digest*. It may be imagined that the *Digest* has more bearing on the multi-storey blocks of the high empire than on what is often taken to be a rather dated housing pattern in Pompeii and Herculaneum, with still a heavy predominance of republican *atrium*-structure housing. But looking at the empire as a whole, it is the multi-storey blocks of Ostia that are the exception, made possible by the exceptionally high land-values of the metropolis. Large and complex concrete blocks required a high level of capital investment; in most cities of the empire the returns would have been inadequate. It is notable that the one multi-storey block in Herculaneum is part of the Palaestra complex and therefore presumably financed by the *municipium*. The lawyers of the *Digest* were concerned with applying the principles of civil law to the practicalities of life throughout the Roman world: what they say is as relevant to Pompeii as to Ostia.

A couple of observations are in place. The first is about the meaning of the term *insula*. The *Digest* consistently distinguishes two types of urban property, the *domus* and the *insula*. These are treated by archaeologists as architectural technical terms: *domus* referring to the classic grand single-occupancy residence, and *insula* inconsistently to the multi-storey multi-occupancy concrete structure block as at Ostia, or to the area isolated by (typically) four surrounding streets as at Pompeii, containing many separate properties. But it is clear from the references both in the *Digest* and elsewhere that the *insula* is a legal term for a unit of ownership. Just as the *domus* has a *dominus*, so does an *insula*. The *dominus insulae* entrusts supervision of his unit of ownership to a caretaker, an *insularius*, just as the owner of a rural estate entrusts supervision of his *villa* to a *vilicus* (e.g. Pomponius at *Dig*. 7.8.16.1 and 50.16.166). That is obviously applicable to the situation at Ostia, but equally it should be applicable at Pompeii and Herculaneum.

The block defined by surrounding streets is not properly an *insula* unless it is a unit of ownership. This evidently was the case with the 'insula Arriana Polliana Cn. Allei Nigidi Mai' (i.e. the Casa di Pansa and the surrounding properties at VI.4 in Pompeii) where *tabernae* with their upper rooms (*pergulae*), 'equestrian apartments' (*cenacula equestria*), and a house or houses (*domus*) were available for rent (*CIL* iv.138). But a street block might also logically include several *insulae*. For instance, it is conceivable that the Casa del Bicentenario formed part of an *insula* which extended over (say) the group of shops and flats to its east (V.17-29) and possibly also over the houses and shops to its west (V.8-12, see fig.1), with which there are traces of previous interconnecting doors. The problem with housing of the Pompeian type is that it is virtually impossible to demonstrate such *legal* boundaries. Perhaps the block I have suggested round the Casa del Bicentenario was three separate *insulae* or blocks of ownership. Or perhaps it had once been a single *insula* but had by AD 79 been split up into several. Archaeology cannot give an answer to questions about legal ownership. But we can bear in mind the legal background, and remember not to assume (as Maiuri appears to) that every physically separate unit was a legally independent owner-occupied unit.

Following from this, we may observe that the relationship between ownership and occupation was a complex one. Urban property is subject to constant change over time. It was not simply owned by 'families' which continued as single units from generation to generation, allowing us to infer the rise and fall of family fortunes from the fortunes of the house. Houses were subject to all the complications of the patterns of Roman inheritance, transmission and sale. For instance, you might leave the usufruct or right of habitation (*habitatio*) in a house to a spouse, or to another legatee, creating a problem over whether the heir as owner or the legatee as usufructuary was responsible for repairs to the roof (*Dig*. 7.8.18). You might sell a house, but preserve the rights of habitation of your freedmen in it (18.6.19). Since it was common to divide a house in two by building a partition (8.4.6), you might leave two houses with one common roof to two separate legatees (8.2.36); or you might leave one house to your heir and one to a legatee, and impose a servitude on one house with respect to the other (8.2.35), e.g. restricting its rights to lights, or allowing the insertion of beams in its walls etc. Such complex possibilities for the legal fortunes of a house make it quite illegitimate to infer from the splitting up and renting off and changing usage of a house that its owner has fallen on hard times. If Cnaeus Alleius Nigidius Maius, one of the outstanding elite of Pompeii, *princeps coloniae* and giver of games, rented out shops, flats and houses in a block he owned, it does not mean that he was desperate for money, or that he had left the city in disgust, but that he was realising the value of a unit of property which had come into his hands by whatever means, inheritance, sale, or even as dowry with his wife.

Finally, the occurrence of *tabernae* in the legal sources could be studied with profit. Shops (which frequently overlap with 'businesses', *negotia*) are seen as a valuable source of rental income. The usufructuary of a house might be anxious to establish his claim to rent out the shops which the testator had run himself (7.1.27.1). To open a shop in a house added to its value, and in assessing liability for repayment on expenses, e.g. on a dotal property, it was necessary to distinguish 'useful' expenses (*utiles impensae*), such as adding a bakery or a shop to a house, from expenses for pure pleasure (*voluptariae impensae*) such as adding pleasure gardens, fountains, marble cladding or mural decorations (25.1.6 and 50.16.79). The lawyers adopt a fairly high moral tone with regard to 'luxuries', disallowing for instance extravagant claims for repairs to decoration on a collapsed common wall (Ulpian, 39.2.40 pr, 'non immoderata cuiusque luxuria subsequenda'), but show no disapproval of *tabernae*, except such houses of ill-repute as a *popina* or gambling den (47.10.26, cf. Hermansen 1982).

The context in which *tabernae* are most frequently considered is that of the *actio institoria* in the fourteenth book. *Tabernae* are normally envisaged as run by slaves or freedmen who act as *institores* for the owner, so committing him to legal liability for their financial contracts (cf. Harris 1980). You might use the same slave to run two businesses, say a cloak business and a linen cloth one, or to run two branches of the same business, one at Buccinum and the other across the Tiber (14.4.14-16). A shop left to you in a will may come as a package, with its slave *institores* and the rest of its equipment, *instrumentum*, including the stock (33.7.13). Of course, you might also leave a shop to a freedman or slave: such as the blacksmith's left with its *instrumentum* to Lucius Eutychus and Pamphilus (who is thereby manumitted) for them to run (31.88.3).

These are only intended as examples of a highly complex picture. I would suggest that there is room for more thorough investigation, that would look at shops and urban property in general in legal, literary and epigraphic sources, and attempt to relate the results to the archaeological remains. But the possibility to which this legal evidence points for Pompeii and Herculaneum is that the many separate physical units of various size may have made up a much smaller number of units of ownership. Clusters of shops, flats and houses may have formed, as *insulae*, units of ownership which were valuable sources of rental income. Such clusters could have formed the basis not only for a variety of economic relationships, ranging from rental, through indirect running of businesses through freedmen, to direct running through *institores*, but also for a variety of social ties of obligation and political support. Although freedmen were clearly prominent in the trade of the area, and may indeed have emerged as important property owners, both through their own efforts, and as beneficiaries of their masters' wills, it is likely that the ruling elites represented by the members of the local councils were also major owners and exploiters of urban property. If so, there is no need to see in this evidence of a decline of a hypothetical elite that originally owed all its income to the land.

Conclusions

My argument has sought to break down some of our assumptions about the ideological and physical distance between the elite of the Roman town and commercial activity. My concern has been with attitudes, not with the economy. None of the evidence here discussed undermines the proposition that agriculture was dominant in the economy or that agricultural interests were dominant among a landowning political elite. Nor does it suggest the emergence of an urban bourgeoisie that regarded itself as economically, socially and culturally distinct from the landowners. But it may come some way towards explaining how towns and trade could flourish in a world dominated by agricultural interests, and why a situation of antagonism and conflict between bourgeoisie and landowners did not arise. The Ciceronian gentleman could afford to despise trade, while at the same time stimulating it by his luxurious lifestyle, staffing it by the importation of slaves and their subsequent liberation, providing it with premises within his own properties, even his own home, milking it of profits, and even turning to the tradesman for political support.

Weber pointed to, and Finley reaffirmed, a structural contrast between the ancient and the medieval city. There seems to me little advantage in watering down that contrast and attempting to demonstrate that the ancient city was more 'modern' than they allowed. Both perhaps underplayed the importance of trade in antiquity and overplayed its importance in the middle ages for the sake of the contrast; they may also have oversimplified both the ancient and the medieval in order to establish 'ideal types' or 'models'. But the underlying argument is that the town/country relationship of the Greco-Roman state was fundamental to its politics, society and culture, as well as its economy, and that this relationship was historically distinctive. The desire to pin down that elusive distinctiveness was surely right (cf. Hopkins 1978).

To Maiuri, who was no Weberian, the physical evidence of Pompeii and Herculaneum, with their often surprising juxtaposition of rich and poor, of the beautiful and the commercial, the luxurious and the squalid, suggested patrician cities in decline. But the same evidence could point to quite different conclusions. We must start by thinking away the assumptions of the industrial city of the modern western world, with its patterns of social contact and interaction. We must reconstruct a world in which the rich lived in close contiguity with their dependants, slaves and freedmen, clients and tenants, the sources of their economic and social power. In this respect, it may not be the Roman world that proves to be strange, but our own. Investigation of the cities of preindustrial Italy could teach us much - from the *vicinie* of the medieval Genoese clans vividly described by Jacques Heers (1977), to the *palazzi* of Renaissance Rome with their ground floor arcades occupied by shops. Or we may think of the France recalled by Proust's description of the Hôtel de Guermantes:

> It was one of those old town houses, a few of which are still to be found, in which the court of honour - whether they were alluvial deposits washed there by the rising tide of democracy, or a legacy

from a more primitive time when the different trades were
clustered round the overlord - is flanked by little shops and
workrooms, a shoemaker's, for instance, or a tailor's ... ; a porter
who also does cobbling, keeps hens, grows flowers, and at the far
end, in the ancient building, a 'Comtesse'.

(Proust, *The Guermantes Way* , *ch.1*)

Even today such patterns are not unknown. Strangely enough, a
corrective to Maiuri's assumptions lay to hand in contemporary
Naples. So much, at least, is suggested by the contrasts drawn by the
Naples-born Luciano De Crescenzo, through the mouthpiece of his
twentieth-century Neapolitan Socrates, Bellavista, defending Naples
with its basement slums (*bassi*) and tangle of interconnecting
washing lines, in contrast to the sanitised Milan:

Have you ever reflected that Naples is the only great city in the
world that is without exclusively popular quarters? The ghettos of
the subproletariat, typical of the heavily industrialised cities, like
Turin or Chicago, have never existed in our city. In Naples, the
working class lived in the basements, the nobles on the so-called
'primo piano nobile' and the bourgeoisie on the upper floors. This
social stratification of a vertical type has obviously favoured
cultural exchanges between the classes, avoiding one of the worst
evils of class, that is the ever greater cultural divergence between
the poor and the rich.

(De Crescenzo, *Così parlò Bellavista,* 1980, 100)

Acknowledgements

This chapter has benefited greatly from the criticisms of John Rich and Peter
Garnsey. I would also like to acknowledge in more general terms the
stimulation and instruction derived from many discussions with two Leicester
colleagues, Professors Peter Clark, Director of the Centre for Urban History,
and Charles Phythian-Adams, Head of the Department of English Local
History.

Bibliography

Andreau, J. (1973), 'Histoire des séismes et histoire économique: le tremblement de terre de Pompéi (62 ap. J.-C.)', *Annales E.S.C.* 28, 369-95.

Angelone, R. (1986), *L'officina coactiliaria di M. Vecilio Verecondo a Pompei.* Naples.

Bates, Wendy (1983), 'A spatial analysis of Roman Silchester', *Scottish Archaeological Review* 2 (2), 134-43.

Boethius, A. (1934), 'Remarks on the development of domestic architecture in Rome', *American Journal of Archaeology* 24, 158-70.

Braund, S.H. (1989), 'City and country in Roman satire', in S.H. Braund (ed.), *Satire and Society in Ancient Rome,* 23-47. Exeter.

Carandini, A. (1989), 'Le origini di Roma', *Archeo. Attualità del Passato* 48 (Febbraio) 48-59.

Castrén, P. (1975), *Ordo populusque Pompeianus. Polity and Society in Roman Pompeii.* Rome.

Clark, P. and Slack, P. (1976), *English Towns in Transition 1500-1700.* Oxford.

Clark, P. (ed.) (1984), *The Transformation of English Provincial Towns.* London.

D'Arms, J.H. (1981), *Commerce and Social Standing in Ancient Rome.* Harvard.

D'Arms, J.H. and Kopf, E.C. eds. (1980), *Roman Seaborne Commerce: Studies in Archaeology and History*, *MAAR* 36, Rome.

Della Corte, M. (1965), *Case ed abitanti di Pompei.* 3rd ed. Naples.

Etienne, R. (1960), *Le Quartier nord-est de Volubilis.* Paris.

Finley, M.I. (1977), 'The ancient city: from Fustel de Coulanges to Max Weber and beyond', *Comparative Studies in Society and History* 19, 305-27. Reprinted in *Economy and Society in Ancient Greece* (1981), 3-23. London.

Finley, M.I. (1985), *The Ancient Economy.* 2nd ed. London.

Frier, B.W. (1980), *Landlords and Tenants in Imperial Rome.* Princeton.

Garnsey, P.D.A. (1976), 'Urban property investment', in M.I. Finley (ed.), *Studies in Roman Property,* 123-36. Cambridge.

Garnsey, P. and Saller, R. (1987), *The Roman Empire. Economy, Society and Culture.* London.

Gassner, V. (1986), *Die Kaufläden in Pompeii* (Diss. Univ. Wien 178).

Harris, W.V. (1980), 'Roman terracotta lamps: the organisation of an industry', *JRS* 70, 126-45.

Heers, J. (1977), *Family Clans in the Middle Ages*. Amsterdam, New York, Oxford.

Herlihy, D. (1977), 'Family and property in Renaissance Florence' in Miskimin, Herlihy and Udovitch (1977) 3-24.

Hermansen, G. (1982), *Ostia. Aspects of Roman City Life*. Alberta.

Hopkins, K. (1978), 'Economic growth and towns in classical antiquity', in P. Abrams and E.A. Wrigley (eds.), *Towns in Societies: Essays in Economic History and Historical Sociology*, 35-77. Cambridge.

Jongman, W. (1988), *The Economy and Society of Pompeii*. Amsterdam.

La Torre, G.F. (1988), 'Gli impianti commerciali ed artigianali nel tessato urbano di Pompei', in *Pompei. L'informatica al servizio di una città antica*, 75-102. Rome.

Lepore, E. (1950), 'Orientamenti per la storia sociale di Pompei', in A. Maiuri (ed.), *Pompeiana. Raccolta di studi per il secondo centenario degli scavi di Pompei*, 144-66. Naples.

Ling, R. (1983), 'The insula of the Menander at Pompeii: interim report', *Antiquaries Journal* 63, 34-57.

MacMullen, R. (1974), *Roman Social Relations 50 B.C. to A.D. 284*. New Haven.

Maiuri, A. (1942), *L'ultima fase edilizia di Pompei*. (Italia Romana: Campania Romana II). Rome.

Maiuri, A. (1958), *Ercolano. I nuovi scavi (1927-1958)*, 2 vols. Rome.

Maiuri, A. (1960), *Pompeii*. Novara.

Miskimin, H.A., Herlihy, D. and Udovitch, A.L. (eds.) (1977), *The Medieval City*. New Haven.

Moeller, W.O. (1976), *The Wool Trade of Ancient Pompeii*. Leiden.

Morel, J.-P. (1987), 'La Topographie de l'artisanat et du commerce dans la Rome antique', in *L'Urbs. Espace urbain et histoire* (Coll. Ec. Fr. Rome 98), 127-55.

Pagano, M. (1987), 'Una iscrizione elettorale da Ercolano', *Cronache Ercolanesi* 17, 151-2.

Patten, J. (1978), *English Towns 1500-1700*. Folkestone.

Platner, S.B. and Ashby, T. (1927), *A Topographical Dictionary of Ancient Rome*. London.

Purcell, N. (1987), 'Town in country and country in town', in *Ancient Roman Villa Gardens*, ed. E.B. MacDougall, 187-203. Dunbarton Oaks.

Ramage, E.S. (1973), *Urbanitas: Ancient Sophistication and Refinement*. Norman, Oklahoma.

Raper, R.A. (1977), 'The analysis of the urban structure of Pompeii: a sociological examination of land use (semi-micro)', in D.L. Clarke (ed.), *Spatial Archaeology*, 189-221. London/New York.

Raper, R.A. (1979), 'Pompeii: planning and social implications', in B.C. Burnham and J. Kingsbury (eds.), *Space, Hierarchy and Society: Interdisciplinary Studies in Social Area Analysis*, 137-48. BAR International Series vol. 59.

Rostovtzeff, M. (1957), *Social and Economic History of the Roman Empire*. 2nd edn. Oxford.

Schulz-Falkenthal, H. (1971), 'Die Magistratenwahlen in Pompeji und die Kollegien', *Das Altertum* 17, 24-32.

Thébert, Y. (1987), 'Private life and domestic architecture in Roman Africa', in P. Veyne (ed.), *A History of Private Life. I. From Pagan Rome to Byzantium*, (trans. A. Goldhammer), 319-409. Cambridge, Mass. and London.

Tinh, Tran Tam (1988), *La Casa dei Cervi a Herculanum*. Rome.

Wallace-Hadrill, A. (1990), 'The social spread of Roman luxury: sampling Pompeii and Herculaneum', *Papers of the British School at Rome* (forthcoming).

Wallace-Hadrill, A. (forthcoming), 'Houses and households: sampling Pompeii and Herculaneum', in B. Rawson (ed.), *Marriage, Divorce, and Children in Ancient Rome*. Oxford.

Weber, Max (1958), *The City*, translated and edited by D. Martindale and G. Neuwirth. New York.

11

Spatial organisation and social change in Roman towns

Dominic Perring

The complexity of urban society is reflected in the physical complexity of the town. Social and economic relationships demand a structured environment; the client must know to wait on his patron at a certain time and place, the shopper must find the market during trading hours, and so on. The need for this structure is at its greatest in large settlements, where the number and range of possible social relationships is greatest. Much of the most important information for the city user is visual. In order to make use of urban facilities they first need to be recognized; distinctive forms of public building and common approaches to the location of certain types of structure will add to the user-friendliness of the urban area. Different patterns of social behaviour are made more or less appropriate by the perceived suitability of the surroundings, and buildings are consequently designed and decorated to elicit specific responses. Since space is structured to meet the needs of society, and gives shape to social life, the spatial organisation of a city ought to shed light on its social organisation.

The study of urban society through the evidence of spatial organisation has generated a considerable literature and contributed to a variety of social theories (see Saunders 1986, for a critical review). This paper will not give detailed attention to such theoretical issues (although it should be acknowledged that it owes much to the influence of structuralist thinking), but will instead concentrate on a particular attempt to reconstruct changing social arrangements from changing spatial ones.

Space within most classical towns was very evidently regulated.

The rigorously ordered street plans, the continued adherence to street and property boundaries, and the clear demarcation between urban and rural all testify to the existence of firm controls over the use of urban space. These controls were instituted primarily to facilitate the division of land, the resolution of property disputes, and the assessment of taxation liability. The way in which space was organized also contributed to the creation of a controlled urban environment and helped shape the social institutions and attitudes vital to the maintenance of order in the otherwise unpoliced ancient city (Nippel 1984).

For the purposes of this paper two basic forms of spatial organisation can be defined. In the first of these space is structured to encourage public use; social cohesion is promoted by developing activities attached to specific and identifiable locations. In such an approach, a strategy of inclusion, social order is encouraged by the identification of community interest in urban space which is supervised through public use. In contrast it is possible to develop strategies of exclusion where space can be structured to exclude or deter unwanted peoples and activities, and thereby reserve it for uses deemed more acceptable. This division is not necessarily the same as that between private and public: public space can exclude as much as private can include, although attitudes to privacy will reflect the different strategies. These forms of spatial organisation can be the intentional result of public building programmes and legislation, or be the unconscious (but no less socially revealing) consequence of economic and social pressures; however inspired, they find physical expression and can therefore be studied through the evidence available to archaeology. All towns will incorporate some design elements which invite involvement and others which exclude it. Piazzas, porticoes and broad avenues may welcome resident and visitor into some spheres of civic life, but elsewhere town walls, property restrictions, and the absence or expense of essential facilities may discourage if not directly prevent certain types of use. There are however important differences in the respective emphases placed on these strategies at different times and places, and these differences have relevance in the study of urban society.

Drawing principally, but not exclusively, on the evidence of Roman Britain and Gaul it is the intention of this paper to argue that in those Roman towns which had an administrative role the elite groups were generally able to maintain control over space and that, according to the town's status, location and date, there was a broad change in emphasis from strategies of inclusion to ones of exclusion. These changes, it is suggested, formed part of a process which eventually saw most towns decline in significance as centres for social cohesion, a decline which was matched by an increase in the importance of the private house or villa as the centre for elite social interaction. The changes can also be seen to be linked to a reduction in the role of town-based trade as a means of generating wealth and promoting social change; there is evidence to suggest that some later Roman towns were positively inhospitable to marketing activities. Although some elements of change were evident from the first century BC the process was most rapid during the course of the second and third centuries AD and it might seem, at least in part, to result from a reaction of the municipal aristocracy to their altered fortunes in this period.

Town planning and town plans

Until recently most studies of ancient town planning were, with a few important exceptions (as Rykwert 1976), concerned with the genesis of urban morphology. For Roman Italy this has involved a hunt for Greek and Etruscan influences (Boethius 1960; Ward-Perkins 1974), whilst in the frontier provinces attention has concentrated on the influence of the army and fort planning (Frere 1977; Crummy 1982). The way in which street systems were conceived and perceived as settings for urban life has received less attention. MacDonald has recently attempted to redress the balance in his analysis of the architecture of public open space in Roman towns: in particular he explores the significance of a 'path-like core of thoroughfares and plazas' which he calls an 'armature' (MacDonald 1986, 3). Through a series of examples, most of which are drawn from the Mediterranean provinces, he is able to demonstrate the importance attached to the creation of visual and spatial foci along main routes into Roman towns. Most of his examples owed their architectural complexity to a process of organic growth. The towns had been laid out with a single focus around a central forum, agora, or group of public buildings, but secondary foci had developed, most commonly outside gates, as the town grew. The result of this process was to ensure that visitors to these towns were immediately drawn to public open space and a path to the centre of town was clear, despite any irregularity in the street plan caused by the urban growth. The architectural emphasis of these towns leaves little doubt that visitors were to be expected and welcomed into the urban area. Where possible, public life was concentrated in a single core or otherwise along a clearly linked series of spaces leading to and from such a core. Supervision of these spaces was guaranteed by the flow of people through them and by the involvement of the community in the various rituals and festivals which were conducted in them (it is worth recalling that most religious and civic ceremonies took place in front of rather than inside public buildings). These open spaces were not left empty and uninviting but were filled by small monuments, mostly statues, which reduced the space to a human scale whilst reinforcing the ideologies which promoted social cohesion.

This impression of integrated urban space designed both to welcome visitors and provide areas for the socializing of the urban population does not seem to be supported by the evidence of some town plans of the north-west provinces. Richard Reece has noted that the grid-iron street plan can be applied in two ways: the principal roads (the *cardo maximus* and *decumanus maximus*) can lead up to a central block or piazza or they can cross unimpeded from one side of the town to the other (Reece 1985). He found few instances where the main streets did not carry right across the urban area. These towns, unlike those considered by MacDonald, had no evident spatial foci other than at their gates and offered no help, no recognisable visual pattern, to the visitor.

The studies of MacDonald and Reece would therefore seem to have identified two contrasting approaches to urban design. It is tempting to account for these differences on the basis of general cultural and climatic differences between the study areas. Such factors have undoubtedly influenced regional trends in town planning, but it is also possible to identify an evolution from one urban form to the other. This evolution is suggested by the study of the road junction arrangement at the core of the town (where *cardo* and *decumanus* meet). In some early Italian towns the streets led directly into the forum, as at Ostia and Pompeii (fig.1), and even through traffic would have been taken across the forum piazza. This was not a design favoured in the urban foundations of the north-west provinces, in most of which the forum was retained as the focus of the street system, but traffic was discouraged from crossing the centre of the

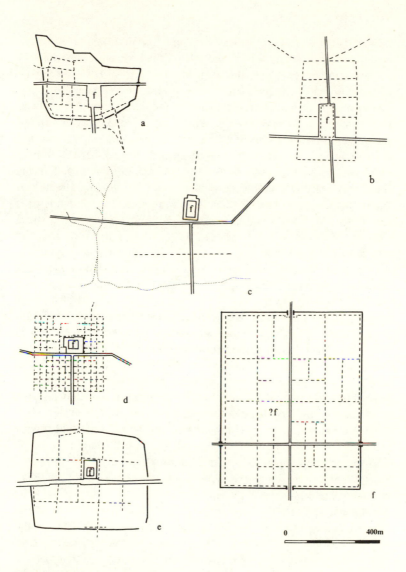

Figure 1: Plans of selected Roman towns:
a: Pompeii (early town only)
b: Milan (prior to the construction of the late Republican walls)
c: London (earliest street plan with the early Flavian forum)
d: Timgad (planned settlement only) e: Caerwent f: Aosta.
Minor streets are indicated by broken lines. f = forum

piazza. This was usually achieved by directing the *decumanus* across one of the ends of the forum and by building a basilica, portico, or temple complex to block the path of the *cardo*. This frequently resulted in the *cardo* and *decumanus* meeting in a T-junction at one end of the forum whilst the extension of the *cardo* from the opposite end of the forum was often treated as a minor road or even omitted altogether. Plans broadly of this type can be found at Verona and Milan (fig.1), and seem to have provided the model for the Roman fort. This T-junction plan brings to mind the comment of Servius that every real town should have three gates, three main streets and three temples (*Ad Aen.* 1.422). Although the roads did not pass through it, the forum was nonetheless a clear focus for the street system. MacDonald's description (1986, 18) of the forum as the centre of the town 'not only because of its functions and symbolic prominence, but also because of its direct, unimpeded connections with the main gates and the larger world beyond' remains applicable. Towns of this type were still being built up until the end of the first century AD (as Timgad) but from the Augustan period a new and significantly different approach was also employed. In these towns the fora were no longer at the centre of the street system but had been set in one of the *insulae* with angles formed by the central crossing of *cardo* and *decumanus*. This was the type of town plan, lacking a central block or piazza, described by Reece which was widely adopted in the north-west provinces (Aosta is an early example, see fig.1).

In Roman Britain two of the earliest and most important towns, London and Verulamium (both dated c. AD 50), had street plans focused on public open space (fig.1). Philip Crummy (1982) has also drawn attention to some instances where the fora of coloniae were placed over the *principia* of earlier forts and consequently provided a focal point for the town. At Exeter, however, the *principia* had been demolished in order to link the *via principalis* (equivalent to the *cardo*) with the *via decumanus* and hence turn the core of the town into a crossroads. Perhaps the most telling alteration was that made at Silchester (fig.2), where the early Roman *cardo* led directly to the entrance of the forum but in the late first century was redirected to pass along its side (Boon 1974, 55). Most of the other Romano-British fora were adjacent to the crossing of the principal streets but did not provide a pivotal point for the street system; an arrangement illustrated in the plan of Caerwent (fig.1).

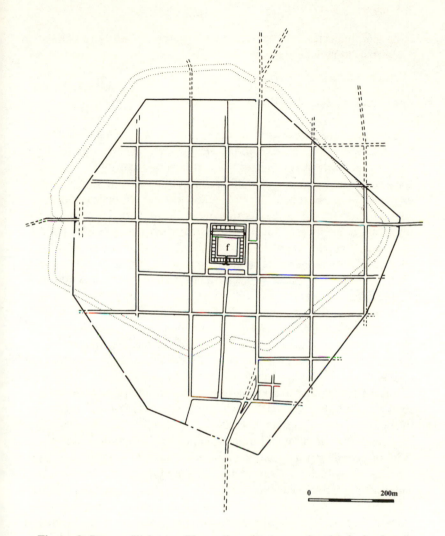

Figure 2: Roman Silchester. The earliest element on the plan is the dotted outline of the 'inner earthwork', the latest is the town wall.
f = forum

The type of plan adopted seems to reflect both the status and the date of the settlement. Public space in the more important towns seems to have been better designed to deal with visiting traffic than in the lesser sites (compare Milan with Aosta or London with Caerwent). The evidence from Britain, and especially the case of

Silchester, indicates that the difference in approach to town planning
was also a chronological development.

Fora and public buildings

The design of the forum itself seems to provide further illustration of
the change in approach seen in the arrangement of the surrounding
streets. The earliest fora were often little more than open spaces,
surrounded by a variety of public and commercial buildings, but
progressive alterations were to create a more comprehensively
enclosed and formal space (as illustrated in the remodelling of the
forum at Pompeii, sometime after 150 BC, when a portico was added
to enclose the piazza and conceal the muddle of buildings behind).
The more formal approach is shown by the imperial fora at Rome
where ceremonial space was separated from market areas (as in
Trajan's forum), and curtain walls were used to cut off surrounding
slums (as in Augustus' forum). The forum in north Italian and Gallic
towns of the late republic and early principate usually consisted of a
piazza enclosed by rows of shops behind a portico, and was entered
through fixed gateways. It was normally dominated by a basilica at
one end with a temple to the Capitoline triad opposite or in an
adjoining piazza. In most Romano-British fora the piazza had been
reduced to a fully enclosed courtyard in front of the basilica, reached
in some cases through a single gateway.

The early style of open forum would clearly have allowed a free
flow of people and it would have been difficult to impose controls
over its use, whether as a place of assembly or market. By contrast
the gateways into the later enclosed fora were easily closed or policed
(a potential shown by the episode of the trial of Milo at Rome when
Pompey was able to ensure that order was maintained by placing
guards at the entrances to the forum). It is of course impossible to
establish to what degree the architectural innovations in forum design
were a conscious response to the problems of policing open assembly
areas: they could equally reflect a more general change in social
attitudes to the role of public space.

Other forms of building defined space in ways to encourage and
control public activities, notably the temple precinct (not otherwise
discussed here but see, for instance, Price 1984). This is shown by
the use of the amphitheatre, an increasingly important site of popular

congregation and social interaction in the cities of the early empire. Gladiatorial contests originated as an element in funeral games and took place in the open forum. The transfer of such festivities to the amphitheatre, an enclosed building with organized seating, would have allowed them to be subject to a greater degree of control. The seating arrangements within the amphitheatre, where different areas were assigned to different classes and social groups, are in themselves a clear illustration of the way in which spatial arrangements can reflect social ones (Rawson 1987). It has been observed of theatres in Augustan Rome that

> rien n'évoque mieux le déplacement effectif des centres de la convergence populaire, et les nouvelles modalités de l'exercice du pouvoir, que ces édifices où le *princeps* se donne à lui-même et au peuple rassemblé le spectacle d'une puissance sacrilisée.
>
> (Gros 1987, 343)

Many amphitheatres were built on the very edge of, if not directly outside, the urban area. At Trier, for instance, the amphitheatre was set on the town boundary and could be entered from both inside and outside the town. Whilst such locations can in most cases be explained by the availability of suitable land it might also indicate a desire to remove the crowd from the core of the town.

In Britain amphitheatres and theatres were few and modest by comparison with such buildings in other provinces, and most were abandoned within the Roman period (as at Chichester, Dorchester and Cirencester, Esmonde-Cleary 1987, 177). This last fact would suggest that these buildings were considered unimportant to the town rather than that they had been too expensive to build. The comparative scarcity of public buildings in most of the towns of Roman Britain may therefore reflect the reduced value placed on collective activities by the time that the British elites were investing in competitive social display. Britain is an extreme case but civic building programmes were also comparatively unusual, after a second-century peak, throughout the empire (see Johnston 1985, 125; Ward-Perkins 1984). Given the changed economic and political circumstances of the later Roman world this is in itself hardly surprising, although it is also important to recognize that the decline of investment in most types of public monument was not matched by equivalent reductions in all areas of urban expenditure (see below).

It should also be noted that there was an increase in public building activity in some rural areas at a time when spending in towns was apparently in decline (see, for example, Horne 1981 on temple building in third-century Britain, and Blagg 1981 on the more widespread diversion of building activity from town to country). It is therefore possible to conclude that the changed attitudes to spending on public building were not simply in reaction to economic circumstance.

The evidence of public buildings can be used to illustrate an evolution from strategies of inclusion to ones of exclusion. The design of the areas set aside for public assembly in the earlier cities, the open forum and religious precinct, assumed a free mixing of the community. One consequence of the architectural patronage of the late republic was to direct some public activities into buildings and spaces which reinforced awareness of social divisions, and over which control could be more easily exercised. Through the location and design of such buildings, and restrictions placed on their use, it was possible for the municipal elites increasingly to control any public activities seen as threatening or otherwise undesirable. The exploitation of such possibilities may partly account for the treatment of public buildings in some later Roman towns.

Town walls

Town walls have an obvious effect on urban space, and the motives for their construction and effect of their presence require careful consideration. Whatever military function may or may not be ascribed to the walls of a city (an issue considered further below), they presented a clearly defined boundary to an urban area. Boundaries were used to separate and order society from the earliest days of Rome and their importance was recognized by a variety of rules and rituals. Rykwert, in particular, has drawn attention to the force of the town boundary: 'a forbidden tract of earth charged with menacing power', and the way in which entering through the gates of a city could be seen as a religious act (Rykwert 1976, 137-9). The concept of the boundary and the sanctity of the urban area were consequently powerful instruments in shaping social behaviour within the town. Although such boundaries needed to be marked, and hence the considerable importance attached to gates, doorways, and arches in the

Roman world, it was not always seen as necessary to define them with walls. In the early empire the republican and Augustan tradition of providing cities with walls was largely abandoned, only to be revived in the late second and third centuries. This chronology lends support to the view that the main purpose of wall building was defensive (a rather blunt form of social control). However when the evidence is studied in detail it is clear that in most cases prior to the last quarter of the third century town walls were not planned and arranged with defensive considerations paramount.

The walls of Romano-British towns have been subject to sufficiently detailed attention to demonstrate that from a tactical point of view they were poorly designed. At London, for instance, the wall built c. AD 200 enclosed a much larger area than was then in occupation. The mid-second-century contraction of the city had been ignored and the walls were built to enclose the earlier built-up area, creating an unnecessarily long barrier, and a consequent waste of defensive manpower. Furthermore the potentially vulnerable riverside was left unprotected until late in the third century. Elsewhere, as at Colchester, it has been noted that construction work started on the gateways before the walls. There is, in general, no evidence for the clearance of houses from around the walls of Romano-British towns and no evidence for the movement of people from suburban areas to within the protected area (Esmonde-Cleary 1987, 170-1). It is consequently difficult to assert that these walls were built from fear of attack, although a more general attempt to restore confidence in the security and status of the city is likely.

The importance placed on gateways and recognized boundaries, and the lack of a serious concern for defensive needs, in some second- and third-century Romano-British wall building programmes can perhaps be better understood through reference to a study of the Aurelian wall of Rome (Palmer 1980). In his paper Palmer suggests that the wall was conceived as much to secure and extend a customs barrier as to defend the city, and that it was essentially built in response to fiscal problems. The customs frontier of Rome may have been first established under Augustus. Inscribed stones indicate that it had been restored in AD 175 or shortly thereafter, and its line was followed by the Aurelian wall. Tolls were levied on market goods at the gates, and replaced the earlier taxation of sales in the marketplace itself. Clearly the town walls would have helped municipal administrators to control commercial traffic, whatever the motives for their construction (see also Jones 1964, 825). Other forms of traffic could also be controlled and exploited at gateway checkpoints; from the writings of Libanius we know that the animals of peasants visiting fourth-century Antioch could be commandeered at the gates in order to carry building rubble from the city (Libanius, *Oratio* 1). It is possible to argue that the growth of small extra-mural settlements outside some late cities was a direct consequence of the avoidance of tolls and impositions at town gates.

Urban housing and society

In most studies of urban space a lot of attention has been given to the identification and significance of urban zones. In the ancient city, however, there is little evidence for such zoning. Studies of the economic and social indicators presented by the evidence of the houses of Pompeii (Raper 1977, Wallace-Hadrill this volume) suggest that, beyond a general attraction of commercial activities to principal streets and corner locations, most areas showed mixed uses and accommodated rich and poor alike. This might suggest a society in which the clan-like ties of *familia* and *clientela* were more essential than any identification with class or economic interests; the clustering of houses of dependants around the large house of a *paterfamilias* has been observed to be a characteristic of clan-based society in Mediterranean cities of the Middle Ages (Heers 1977, 146). The shift of architectural emphasis from atrium to peristyle in the Pompeian house and the tendency towards a more formalized organisation of space, as in the layout of gardens (Jashemski 1979, 43-8), might reflect changing social attitudes in the Augustan period. The more hierarchical and formalized use of space implies an increased concern for social distinctions (see further below).

The evidence from Pompeii permits little consideration of change through time. At Ostia, however, a clear change in the nature of the housing is evident; from a mix of rich and poor, commercial and residential in the early imperial *insulae*, to a city dominated by the *domus* houses of the rich in the later empire. There is also plenty of epigraphic evidence to illuminate the social context of these changes; from social fluidity and commercial vigour in the early empire to a widening gulf between rich and poor later on (Meiggs 1973, 235-62). Ostia, however, was subject to far too many particular and unique forces to be reliable as a model for the period.

The study of changing approaches to architectural detail, in particular the comparison of evidence for the display of elite status with evidence for commercial vigour, reveals more widespread change in the character of urban housing. The large body of information retrieved from urban rescue excavations in Britain is particularly useful because shops and yards have been accorded as much attention as palaces and temples, and full sequences are usually studied. One of the most archaeologically evident changes noted on such sites is in the preference for building materials used in wall construction. In the major towns of south-east Britain a development from wooden walls to mud walls to masonry walls generally took place during the second century (Perring 1985). At the same time, and probably as part of the same process, there was a marked increase in the popularity of mosaic pavements and new and more complex forms of building were first adopted. Walthew (1975) has observed that in Britain the most sophisticated town house plans did not emerge until the mid-second century and were derived from the plans of earlier villas. It therefore seems reasonable to concur with Walthew's conclusion that the second century finally saw the British curial classes, previously resident in the countryside, accepting town life and building urban property for their own use. What is perhaps not so immediately evident is that the changes outlined above coincided with the start of a decline in the commercial vigour of the towns concerned. In many cases the new, supposedly curial, houses took up sites previously occupied by properties engaged in some form of commercial activity. This could be seen as no more than an illustration of the social upgrading of the particular area of settlement under study were it not for the fact that the commercial properties do not seem to have been replaced elsewhere. At Colchester, Verulamium and London considerably more buildings were in occupation and more industrial hearths and ovens in use in the late first century than in any equivalent period (data drawn from Crummy 1984 for Colchester, Frere 1983 for Verulamium, Perring and Roskams forthcoming for London). Alterations in late Roman Caerwent saw shops and workshops along the main roads into town give way to larger courtyard buildings (as in insula XVIs, Ashby *et al.* 1911, 427-48), and the proportion of commercial to elite property clearly declined. At Verulamium the rebuilding after a mid-second-century fire frequently saw houses built to cover over eight times the area of the earlier small houses and contain perhaps three times as many rooms (Frere 1983, 14). In the later fourth century the once densely occupied town may have contained no more than twenty or thirty houses, most of them the houses of the rich. The mid-second-century contraction of London resulted in the burial of many buildings, mostly shops and workshops, beneath a dark earth which is most likely to have been laid to extend gardens and fields around a comparatively small number of large houses (Perring and Roskams, forthcoming). All towns continued to house commercial activities. Strip buildings and workshops never entirely disappeared, but fewer such buildings would have been needed to service the urban population. Some towns and surburban areas were able to show a more continued commercial vitality, particularly those which had acquired increased status in late imperial administrative reforms, but the general picture would suggest that Ostia was not quite as unusual as might be assumed.

In many towns, and indeed in the countryside, later houses placed great emphasis on status display. Many activities which had previously been concentrated in public buildings may have been redirected towards the private house, as suggested by the more widespread provision of private bath blocks and places for religious worship in the house. It is notable that bath-houses in Byzantine and medieval towns were mostly small and private rather than large and public (Heers 1977, 160). MacMullen (1976, 72-3) has noted that in the third century there was an increase in attention to forms of interior decoration which distanced those in power from their clients, and he sees this as part of an attempt to reinforce perceptions of imperial and magisterial authority. Many other late Roman developments (as in rhetoric), give the impression of an elite seeking to establish cultural boundaries between itself and the rest of society (Brown 1971, 64-6), and these suggest a context for the changes in urban housing. Leone, in a discussion of Georgian domestic architecture which seems equally appropriate to the Roman house, points out that in conjunction with other aspects of material culture 'the individualisation and privatisation achieved through doors, distance, chairs, hyphens, wings, place-settings, and gardens - all created the inhibitions, withdrawal and isolation needed to prevent any attack on the established order' (Leone 1984, 27; see also Isaac 1982). These elements had long been evident in the houses of the rich, but in the later Roman town which contained fewer shops and houses of the poor, and cared less for its public buildings and spaces, the social uses of the houses of the rich must have dominated urban life in a way that would not previously have been possible.

The economic context of change

It is widely accepted that commercial interests in the ancient city were subordinate to those of the municipal aristocracies. However it is still broadly assumed, with no little encouragement from ancient sources, that to be worthy of its name an ancient town would have been a major market place (cf. Noviomagus Regnensium, the new market of the people of the kingdom, modern-day Chichester). It is, however, an important part of the argument presented here that some later towns were effectively excluded from the exchange networks. Studies of the distribution pattern of traded goods suggest that towns were not engaged in economic competition. In a study of early Roman pottery from sites around the neighbouring towns of Silchester and Savernake the differences in the size and status of the two sites showed little effect on their respective success in marketing locally produced wares (Fulford 1982). The implication is that the more important town was not a more important marketplace. In a more general review of the evidence from Gallia Belgica, Wightman saw the tribal capitals of Roman Belgica, paramount as centres for Romanisation and social status, as having only a limited economic function (Wightman 1985, 99). She also saw a diminution in economic activity in the later period when most aspects of production and distribution were controlled by the great landowners or imperial estates (Wightman 1985, 240). It is possible to argue (as Millett 1982, 427-8) that in later Roman Britain some trade patterns were structured to avoid the social constraints of the town. This finds support in the suggestion that from the late third century the economic functions served by the *vici* of Gaul were taken back into the direct control of large estate owners (Wightman 1981, 241). The references of Ausonius to Philo, a freedman merchant working out of the countryside and largely dependent on the patronage of villa-owning producers, support this picture of a rural economy which had largely bypassed the town (Ausonius, *Epistles* 26). Most larger scale production was based in the countryside and, through using freedmen and other dependants in the marketing process, producers were able to develop exchange networks independently of the town (see Whittaker 1983 on the control of trade by late Roman domanial estates and institutional proprietors, and on the growth of internal supply and reciprocal exchange between estates).

Merchants had always been subject to a variety of constraints in the Roman city but in the early and expanding empire trade generated sufficient wealth to guarantee an accommodation between the interests of commerce and those of the landed aristocracy (D'Arms 1981). The direction of marketing into controlled public space, increasingly evident from the end of the Republic (Morel 1987), can be seen as a reaction to mercantile success. The provision of public market buildings (note also the *macella*) ensured that the elite retained control of the aspect and economy of the city, but served to encourage rather than exclude marketing activities. This accommodation of interests seems, however, to have been placed under increasing strain as time progressed. The early-second-century riots in Tarsus by a mob of native craftsmen, apparently responding to the monopolistic tendencies of an aristocratic class (Dio Chrysostom, *Oratio* 34, and see Ruggini 1980), merit mention. Diminished profits required the elites to increase controls over trade to ensure that essential supply-routes were maintained and that their own revenues were not too adversely affected. It is possibly significant that the chronology of imperial interference in the grain supply of Rome (for which see Rickman 1980), is similar in outline to the chronology of change in urban form summarised here. These controls both diminished the importance of markets and increasingly removed them from the urban sphere. Even a town such as Antioch, despite the convergence of important oriental trade routes and imperial supply lines and despite its status as an imperial residence, does not seem to have been a significant marketplace in the fourth century (Liebeschuetz 1972, 58). The surrounding communities had their own fairs and made good each others' deficiencies with little need for the city (Libanius, *Oratio* 11. 230). The economic pressures brought to bear on urban trade are illustrated by a variety of legal and taxation measures (notably the imposition of the *collatio lustralis*, see Jones 1964, 871-2). Such measures were in part designed to relieve the financial burden on the municipal aristocracies, who were under increasing financial strain from the early second century onwards (see Garnsey 1974, who also notes the use of legislation to restrict the exemption of traders and *incolae* from financial obligations). These changes in the relationship between the landowning elites and urban trade provide a context for the changes in approach to urban space seen in the late second century.

Conclusions

In its original state the Roman city was the device which structured and gave coherence to society. The nature of the institutions of Rome required the day to day presence of citizens for innumerable activities and formalities; ceremonies which provided a complex range of ways in which the public could express themselves (Nicolet 1980), and which emphasized the benefits conferred on all members of society by the maintenance of the traditional social order.

> These institutions and ceremonies made of the city 'a structured complex of symbols'; in which the citizen, through a number of bodily exercises, such as processions, seasonal festivals, sacrifices, identifies himself with his town, with its past and founders.
>
> (Rykwert 1976, 189)

Space in the city was designed around and encouraged these activities and identifications.

The increase in wealth and social complexity that came with empire contributed to the development of an increasingly segmentary society in which the aristocracy was less able to integrate all parts of the urban population socially and politically (Nippel 1984, 29; Nicolet 1980, 390). Architectural innovation in the late Republic, and particularly under Augustus, can be seen as a response to these social changes. Urban design continued to presume a considerable degree of integration between the different classes of city users, but recognized a need to limit and control those activities in which the community was brought together. Interaction was not casual, but was directed into a supervised and ordered environment.

The development to empire permitted the emergence of political and social systems less dependent on attitudes derived from the city state, although initially the prosperity of the early empire drowned potential conflict in municipal munificence. It encouraged the evolution of a society in which individuals no longer identified so exclusively with a specific urban community. The city continued to be an essential element in the administrative system but this system no longer required the presence of more than an elite group. These changes had only a limited effect on the nature of urban society so long as the city remained a focus for other collective activities, as in the market or outside the temple. The emergent economic problems of the second and third centuries, and the consequent tightening of controls over trade, had a much more decisive impact on attitudes to the city. A few cities within the later empire were sufficiently important to vital supply routes and as administrative centres to sustain a successful trading community and a large urban population, but these were exceptional (although they tend to dominate the historical record). Across the empire the municipal elites found it increasingly difficult, unprofitable or undesirable to accommodate traders and peasants, more readily controlled in the countryside and perhaps unsightly in the city, in urban space. This process was more extreme in those provinces where traditions of urban life, along the earlier pattern, were less deeply rooted (as Britain), and seems to have been more rapid in those towns which had benefited most from the earlier profitability of trade (as Ostia, Lyons and London). The towns which emerged from this process were places where the elites could meet and compete, and were therefore filled by the houses and gardens of the rich and their dependants (in addition to the presence of a small service population). There was, however, little need for public space, public buildings, and public interaction in these towns. Such cities were preserves of *romanitas* from which most aspects of the barbarian world could be excluded. Superficially, therefore, they seem the very picture of prosperity; the display of prosperity was, after all, an important part of their *raison d'être*. In truth, however, the fortunes of most of these towns were dependent on a small cultured elite; and when the cultural values of that elite could be challenged and undermined (whether in the third century or at the end of the Roman period), so too could the role of the city.

Acknowledgements

I would like to extend my thanks to all those who contributed to the seminars at Leicester University where this argument was first presented, and to Andrew Wallace-Hadrill, Tim Potter, John Rich and Rob Young for their highly constructive comments on an earlier draft of this paper.

Bibliography

Ashby, R. *et al.* (1911), 'Excavations at Caerwent, Monmouthshire, on the site of the Romano-British city of Venta Silurium, in the years 1909 and 1910', *Archaeologia* 62.2, 405-47.

Blagg, T.F.C. (1981), 'Architectural patronage in the western provinces of the Roman empire in the third century', in M. Henig and A.C. King (eds.), *The Roman West in the Third Century*, British Archaeological Reports, S.109, 167-88. Oxford.

Boethius, A. (1960), *The Golden House of Nero. Some Aspects of Roman Architecture*. Ann Arbor.

Boon, G.C. (1974), *Silchester: the Roman Town of Calleva*. Newton Abbot.

Brown, P. (1971), *The World of Late Antiquity*. London.

Crummy, P. (1982), 'The origins of some major Romano-British towns', *Britannia* 13, 125-34.

Crummy, P. (1984), *Excavations at Lion Walk, Balkerne Lane and Middleborough, Colchester, Essex*. Colchester Archaeological Report 3. Colchester.

D'Arms, J. (1981), *Commerce and Social Standing in Ancient Rome*. Cambridge, Mass.

Esmonde-Cleary, S.A. (1987), *Extra-Mural Areas of Romano-British Towns*, British Archaeological Reports 169. Oxford.

Frere, S.S. (1977), 'Town planning in the Western Provinces', in *Festschrift zum 75 jahrigen Bestehen der römisch-germanischen Komission*, 58, 87-103.

Frere, S.S. (1983), *Verulamium Excavations, vol. 2*. Oxford.

Fulford, M. (1982), 'Town and country in Roman Britain - A parasitical relationship?', in D. Miles (ed.), *The Romano-British Countryside: Studies in Rural Settlement and Economy*, British Archaeological Reports 103, 403-19. Oxford.

Garnsey, P. (1974), 'Aspects of the decline of the urban aristocracy in the Empire', in H. Temporini (ed.), *Aufstieg und Niedergang der römische Welt*, 2.1, 229-52. Berlin.

Gros, P. (1987), 'La Fonction symbolique des édifices théâtraux dans le paysage urbain de la Rome augustéenne', in *L'Urbs. Espace urbain et histoire. Ier siècle avant J.C. - IIIer siècle après J.C.*, Collection de l'Ecole Française de Rome, 98, 319-46. Rome.

Heers, J. (1977), *Family Clans in the Middle Ages*. Amsterdam, New York, Oxford.

Horne, P. (1981), 'Romano-Celtic temples in the third century', in
M.Henig and A.C. King (eds.), *The Roman West in the Third
Century*, British Archaeological Reports S.109, 21-6. Oxford.

Isaac, R. (1982), *The Transformation of Virginia 1740-1790*. Chapel
Hill.

Jashemski, W. (1979), *The Gardens of Pompeii*. New York.

Johnston, D. (1985), 'Munificence and municipia: bequests to towns
in classical Roman Law', *Journal of Roman Studies* 75, 105-25.

Jones, A.H.M. (1964), *The Later Roman Empire*. Cambridge.

Leone, M.P. (1984), 'Interpreting ideology in historical archaeology:
using the rules of perspective in the William Paca Gardens in
Annapolis, Maryland', in D. Miller and C. Tilley (eds.),
Ideology,   Power and Prehistory, 25-36. Cambridge.

Liebeschuetz, J.H.W.G. (1972), *Antioch, City and Imperial
Administration in the Later Roman Empire*. Oxford.

MacDonald, W.L. (1986), *The Architecture of the Roman Empire II:
An Urban Appraisal*. New Haven and London.

MacMullen, R. (1976), *Roman Governments' Response to Crisis
AD 235-337*. New Haven, London.

Meiggs, R. (1973), *Roman Ostia* (2nd edn). Oxford.

Millett, M. (1982), '"Town and country" - A review of some material
evidence', in D. Miles (ed.), *The Romano-British Countryside:
Studies in Rural Settlement and Economy*, British Archaeological
Reports 103, 421-32. Oxford.

Morel, J-P. (1987), 'La Topographie de l'artisan et du commerce dans
la Rome Antique', in *L'Urbs. Espace urbain et histoire. Ier siècle
avant J.C. - IIIer siècle après J.C.*, Collection de l'Ecole Française
de Rome, 98, 127-55. Rome.

Nicolet, C. (1980), *The World of the Citizen in Republican Rome*.
London.

Nippel, W. (1984), 'Policing Rome', *Journal of Roman Studies* 74,
20-9.

Palmer, R.E.A. (1980), 'Customs on market goods imported into the
city of Rome', in J. D'Arms and E. Kopff (eds.), *Roman Seaborne
Commerce*. Memoirs of the American Academy at Rome 36, 217-
33. Rome.

Perring, D. (1985), 'La Bretagne 2: Londres et les villes du Sud-Est',
in J. Lasfargues (ed.), *Architectures de terre et de bois*, Documents
d'Archéologie Française 2, 153-5.

Perring D. and Roskams, S.P. (forthcoming), *The Early Development of Roman London to the West of the Walbrook*, Council for British Archaeology Research Report. London.

Price, S.R.F. (1984), *Rituals and Power: The Roman Imperial Cult in Asia Minor*. Cambridge.

Raper, R.A. (1977), 'The analysis of the urban structure at Pompeii. A sociological examination of land use', in D.L. Clarke (ed.), *Spatial Archaeology*, 189-221. Cambridge.

Rawson, E. (1987), 'Discrimina Ordinum: The Lex Julia Theatralis', *Papers of the British School at Rome* 42, 83-114.

Reece, R. (1985), 'Roman towns and their plans', in F.O. Grew and B. Hobley (eds.), *Roman Urban Topography in Britain and the Western Empire*, Council for British Archaeology Research Report 59, 37-40. London.

Rickman, G. (1980), *The Corn Supply of Ancient Rome*. Oxford.

Ruggini, L.C. (1980), 'Nuclei immigrati e forze indigene in tre grandi centri commerciali dell' impero', in J. D'Arms and E. Kopff (eds.), *Roman Seaborne Commerce*. Memoirs of the American Academy at Rome 36, 55-76. Rome.

Rykwert, J. (1976), *The Idea of a Town: The Anthropology of Urban Form in Rome, Italy and the Ancient World*. London.

Saunders, P. (1986), *Social Theory and the Urban Question* (2nd edn). London.

Walthew, C.V. (1975), 'The town house and the villa house in Roman Britain', *Britannia* 6, 189-205.

Ward-Perkins, B. (1984), *From Classical Antiquity to the Middle Ages. Urban Public Building in Northern and Central Italy AD 300-850*. Oxford.

Ward-Perkins, J.B. (1974), *Cities of Ancient Greece and Italy: Planning in Classical Antiquity*. London.

Whittaker, C.R. (1983), 'Late Roman trade and traders', in P. Garnsey, K. Hopkins and C.R. Whittaker (eds.), *Trade in the Ancient Economy*, 163-80. London.

Wightman, E.M. (1981), 'The fate of Gallo-Roman villages in the third century', in M. Henig and A.C. King (eds.), *The Roman West in the Third Century*, British Archaeological Reports S.109, 235-43. Oxford.

Wightman, E.M. (1985), *Gallia Belgica*. London.

INDEX

Abdera 219
acropolis 6
    Athenian 17
    Narce 194
actio institoria 266
Aelius Aristides 211, 232, 234
Aesernia 149, 151
Ager
    Capenas 195
    Faliscus 192, 195, 197, 199,
    200, 202, 205
    Tarraconensis 176-80
    Veientanus 195
Agios Andreas 8
agora 6, 8, 10, 40, 241, 275
agriculture
    Athenian 120-40
    cash income 134
    development of 132
Aiantides 125
Aiskhines 139
Akharnai 72, 76, 122
Akraiphnion 71, 81, 86, 88
    Ptoion 82
Alba Fucens x
Aletrium 150
Alexandria Troas 159
alimenta 154-5
Alleius Nigidius Maius 266
amphitheatre 280, 281
Anagyrous 125
Andokides 133
Andros 8
angareia 215, 220, 222, 233
Anthedon 71
Antioch 159, 231, 232, 284, 288
Antium 150
Aosta 277, 278-9
Aphrodisias 221
aqueducts 150, 213, 215
    at Ephesus 159
    control of countryside x,
    150, 222
Aquincum 235

argentarius 263
Argos 10, 11, 19, 33, 71, 82, 87,
    108, 109
    cemeteries 29
    Heraion 69, 76-8, 82, 86
    industry 38
Aristomenes 125
Aristophanes 35
    Akharnians 122
Aristotle 139
    Constitution of Athens 37,
    44
    definition of polis x, 25, 98
    on polis 2, 5
    Politics 35, 37, 44, 49, 102,
    110
Arles 228
Arruntius Claudianus 162
artefact
    distribution 180-4
Asia
    koinon of 212
Asine 31-2, 78-9, 100, 107-8
Askra 14, 81, 82, 104
astu x, 5, 11, 12, 14, 18
astynomoi 141
Athens 33, 68, 76, 82-7
    Acropolis 17
    agora 11, 101
    burials 15
    cemeteries 29
    democracy xiii, 36, 122
    economy 122-42
    exceptional 121
    extreme case 35, 38
    food supply 34
    hoplite reform 19
    population 14-16, 28, 122
    potters' quarter 39
    silver mines 31, 122, 128,
    133
    tribute 136
atrium 254, 256, 257, 260, 262,
    263, 284

LIST OF CONTRIBUTORS

W.G. Cavanagh is Lecturer in Archaeology at the University of Nottingham.

Mireille Corbier is a Research Fellow at the C.N.R.S., Paris.

Martin Millett is Lecturer in Roman Archaeology at the University of Durham.

Ian Morris is Professor in Greek History at the University of Chicago.

Robin Osborne is Fellow and Tutor in Ancient History at Corpus Christi College, Oxford.

John R. Patterson is a Fellow of Magdalene College, Cambridge and University Assistant Lecturer in Ancient History.

Dominic Perring is former Research Assistant in Roman Archaeology at the University of Leicester.

T.W. Potter is Deputy Keeper in the Department of Prehistoric and Romano-British Antiquities at the British Museum.

John Rich is Lecturer in Classics at the University of Nottingham.

T.E. Rihll (formerly Research Fellow in the Schools of History and Geography at the University of Leeds) is Lecturer in Classics at St David's University College, Lampeter.

A.M. Snodgrass is Laurence Professor of Classical Archaeology in the University of Cambridge.

Andrew Wallace-Hadrill is Professor of Classics at the University of Reading

A.G. Wilson is Professor of Urban and Regional Geography at the University of Leeds.

.